To James.

Happy Cooking

Love, Elsie, Christmas 1999

x

classic
Italian
recipes

classic
Italian
recipes

Judy Bugg

Carole Handslip

Kathryn Hawkins

Wendy Lee

Penny Stephens

Rosemary Wadey

Pamela Westland

P

PARRAGON

This edition published by Parragon 1999
Parragon
Queen Street House
4 Queen Street
Bath BA1 1HE, UK

ISBN: 0-75253-349-5

Printed in Singapore

Edited, designed and produced by Haldane Mason, London

Acknowledgements
Editor: Linda A Doeser
Design: dap ltd
Photographers: Karl Adamson, Iain Bagwell, Amanda Heywood, Joff Lee, Patrick McLeavey
Home Economists: Judy Bugg, Carole Handslip, Kathryn Hawkins, Wendy Lee, Penny Stephens,
Rosemary Wadey, Pamela Westland

Note
Cup measurements in this book are for American cups.
Tablespoons are assumed to be 15 ml. Unless otherwise stated, milk is assumed to be
full-fat, eggs are medium and pepper is freshly ground black pepper.

Contents

Rice, Polenta & Gnocchi 170

Pizzas & Breads 188

Desserts 228

Index 252

Introduction

Italian cuisine is one of the best known outside its country of origin. Pasta, risotto and pizza are eaten worldwide and Italian cheeses, cold meats and salami are available in supermarkets everywhere. The keynote of classic Italian cooking is to use ingredients in peak condition, prepared in a way that enhances their particular flavour.

It is surely no coincidence that one of the first cookbooks ever written was by a Roman, Apicius, in the first century AD. Italian cuisine is one of the oldest in Europe, tracing its ancestry back to the gourmets of ancient Greece. While Apicius's recipes for flamingo and camel's heels no longer feature on Italian menus, polenta, on the other hand, has changed little since the days of ancient Rome.

The success of Italian cooking is largely to do with the fact that ingredients are used while they are in peak condition, and they are cooked in a way that enhances, rather than smothers, their particular flavour. Dishes are traditional, but always bear the individual cook's personal stamp. True to its venerable history, Italian cuisine is not innovatory and subject to the whims of fashion, but it is perfectly balanced and capable of infinite variation.

SEASONAL COOKING

Even today, Italians cook seasonally, using the freshest ingredients available. There is a special pleasure in waiting for the first delicate baby artichokes of the spring, the sun-ripened tomatoes and (bell) peppers of the summer or the succulent purple grapes and plums of the autumn (fall). Only in Italy is it traditional to make a wish when you eat the first fresh fruit of the year. No Italian cook would dream of preparing pumpkin soup before September or baked fennel after the winter has ended. Even in season, vegetables and fruit will be rejected if they are not in peak condition. This is because dishes depend on the fresh flavours of the individual ingredients, not on elaborate

sauces and flamboyant garnishes, so those ingredients must be at their very best.

REGIONAL COOKING

The cuisine of the north, characterized by its use of butter, cow's milk cheeses, meat and rice, was once completely separate from that of the south, known for its olive oil, pasta and ewe's or goat's milk cheeses. It was the people of Tuscany who made the first move, introducing steak and haricot (navy) beans to their southern neighbours, and they were soon followed by other regions. Pizza moved north and risotto and polenta moved south.

Nevertheless, regional cooking still dominates Italian cuisine. Italy has been a unified country for less than 150 years and, in many ways, Italians still think of themselves as Lombards, Tuscans, Calabrians, Sicilians and so on. Not only do they have extreme regional pride, but rivalry exists even between neighbouring towns and villages in the same region. This has resulted in a continuing culinary tradition of local excellence.

Piedmont in the north-west, bordering France and Switzerland, is a fertile, arable region, well-known for the wines Barolo and Asti Spumante. The food is substantial, including polenta, gnocchi and rice. Garlic features widely and the region is famous for its wonderfully fragrant white truffles. The Consorzio Gorgonzola, which protects the quality of Gorgonzola cheese, as well as the use of the name, is located in Novara in Piedmont.

Still in the north-west, **Lombardy** is the rice bowl of Italy and boasts of more than fifty variations of risotto. Veal features in many dishes and other regional specialities include hearty meat stews and pot roasts and superb vegetable soups. Lombardy is credited with the invention of butter and is the home of mascarpone cheese.

Liguria is said to produce the best basil in Italy and certainly put it to good use by inventing pesto sauce. The region is also known for its imaginative ways with vegetables and wonderfully varied fish and seafood dishes. The port of Genoa was one of the first cities to import spices from Asia and specialities of the region still include highly seasoned dishes.

The cuisine of **Trentino Alto-Adige**, in the mountainous north-east, betrays the powerful influence of nearby Austria. Dumplings, smoked pork, sausages and stuffed pasta are characteristic.

Veneto and **Friuli**, a vast area also in the north-east, is intensively farmed, producing cereals and almost 20 per cent of Italy's wine. Risotto, polenta and gnocchi are mainstays and the region is well known for its fish and seafood dishes. Polenta made with cornmeal, rather than the wheat flour previously used, was invented by Venetian cooks when cargoes of maize first arrived from the New World. Venetians also claim to have introduced the table fork to the civilized world.

Bologna, the capital of the extensive central Italian province of **Emilia-Romagna**, is known as la grassa, the fat city, and is home to the best restaurants outside Rome. Unusually for Italy, Emilia-Romagna includes large areas of flat land, ideal for agriculture and viticulture. Bologna is the home of mortadella, Parma produces both Parmesan cheese and Parma ham (prosciutto) and Modena is famous for balsamic vinegar. Food in Emilia-Romagna is rich and butter and cream are used unstintingly. Pasta dishes include tortellini and lasagne, as well as spaghetti alla Bolognese.

Tuscany is both the orchard and the vegetable garden of Italy and the main cattle-farming region. Its cuisine reflects this with its superb steak and veal dishes. Tripe is a speciality of the region and game also features. Panforte di Siena, a traditional Christmas cake made with honey and nuts, comes from Siena.

The people of **Umbria** pride themselves on the simplicity of their cuisine, which is especially noted for its pork, lamb, game and freshwater fish. This region is Italy's main producer of black truffles and the local olive oil is excellent. Umbria is also the home of Orvieto, one of Italy's most famous wines.

The cuisine of the **Marches** reflects the region's mixture of coastline and mountains. Fish, game, pork, pasta and olives all feature widely.

Rome is the capital of **Latium**, as well as of Italy and is at the heart of Italian cuisine. Specialities from all over the country have been drawn to the city, which is famous in its own right for its lamb and veal dishes, including saltimbocca. Vegetables and fruit are abundantly available and are characteristically prepared in simple, but delicious ways.

To the east of Rome, **Abruzzi** and **Molise**, now separate provinces, used to be a single region. They remain closely associated. The cuisine is traditional, making the most of local hams, cheeses, fish, lamb, seafood and herbs. A hot, red chilli called peperoncino is characteristic of Abruzzi.

To the south, Naples sets the tone for the cuisine of **Campania**. Pasta is so important that Neapolitans have been nicknamed 'macaroni eaters'. Other characteristic dishes include an infinite variety of tomato sauces, fried fish and seafood, robust stews strongly flavoured with herbs and garlic, and melt-in-the mouth pastries and fruit desserts. Naples is the home of pizza and while Sicilians are generally credited with the invention of pasta, it was the Neapolitans who perfected the technique of drying and preserving it.

Puglians, known by their westerly neighbours as 'leaf eaters', are renowned for their vegetable dishes. Although the region is very stony, it produces excellent olives, herbs, fruit, especially figs and melons, and vegetables. Wild mushrooms are frequently included in the local pizzas and there is an abundance of seafood, especially oysters and mussels. Calzone, a kind of pizza turnover, was invented in Apulia.

Basilicata is a rugged, windswept, mountainous, cold region, and therefore its cuisine is robust, warming and filling. Lamb, pork and game feature, and the salamis and other cured meats are excellent. Thick soups and freshwater fish are typical of the most mountainous parts of this area.

Calabria, in the 'toe' of Italy, is one of the most dramatic regions, with craggy mountains, abrupt cliffs and sun-soaked beaches. Oranges, lemons and olives are widely grown and there is a wide selection of vegetables. Calabria is famous for its aubergines (eggplants). Fish is abundant and particular favourites are tuna and swordfish. Chicken and game are both popular. Many desserts are based on local figs, honey or almonds.

The cuisine of **Sicily** is perhaps best known for its wonderfully self-indulgent cakes, desserts and ice cream. Fresh seafood, including tuna, swordfish and mussels, forms the basis of superb soups, stews and salads, and pasta, with many different sauces, is also very popular. Black olives, pistachios, almonds and citrus fruits, in particular, grow abundantly.

The national dish of **Sardinia** is suckling pig, spit-roasted over an open fire. Young lamb is also extremely popular for special occasions and celebrations. The fish is excellent and varied – sea bass, mullet, lobster, tuna, eels and mussels. Like other southern Italians, Sardinians love lavish desserts and cakes and fruit grows abundantly.

THE ITALIAN KITCHEN

Fish, vegetables, cereals and grains are the staples of Italian cooking. Meat is very much of secondary importance. Pork is the most frequently eaten meat because it provides such good value for money: meat for grilling (broiling), frying, roasting and braising, salami, ham, bacon, sausages and other cured meats.

The Italian refrigerator is likely to be stocked with some mozzarella and Parmesan cheeses, both of which keep quite well. Ricotta, on the other hand, is best eaten within 1 day of purchase. There is likely to be a supply of olives in oil, possibly flavoured with garlic and herbs. Pine nuts keep well in the refrigerator and capers are useful. Pancetta, a bacon streaked with fat, is essential for providing a depth of flavour in casseroles. Anchovy paste and tomato paste are also important. Butter is always unsalted (sweet) in Italy.

The Italian store cupboard is likely to contain a large bottle of extra virgin olive oil, red wine vinegar and, possibly, balsamic vinegar. Standard items include risotto rice, cornmeal for making polenta, several different pasta shapes, including tiny ones for adding to soups, and a supply of various dried pulses, such as lentils, chick peas (garbanzo beans) and haricot (navy) and other beans. Useful canned items are tuna, anchovies, tomatoes, cannellini beans and borlotti beans. Salami,

hanging from a hook overhead, completes the picture.

Bread, vegetables, fruit, herbs, fish and meat are bought as fresh as possible.

THE ITALIAN MEAL

A traditional family meal usually consists of two courses of equal size and importance. Lunch usually starts with pasta or risotto, while soup is usually served at dinner. The second course is usually a fish or meat dish, often served with one vegetable accompaniment. The two courses should always be complementary. For example, if the second course is to be Beef in Barolo, then the first course should be equally robust, such as Tuscan Bean Soup, or if the second course is to be Sole in Marsala and Cream, then a first course such as Genoese Seafood Risotto would be appropriate.

Dessert is usually fresh fruit, possibly served with cheese. Elaborate desserts are served only on special occasions. A basket of bread is always available for mopping up the cooking juices in which most Italian dishes are served. In fact, Italians are thought to eat more bread than any other nation. Wine or water are drunk during the meal and a cup of espresso is served at the end. On special occasions, a digestivo, liqueur or a glass of grappa, a kind of brandy, may also be served.

Italians strive to make all meals a special occasion and celebrations are feasts. They enjoy their food, especially if they are sharing it with family and friends. 'Mangiare in compagnia' – to eat together – is an art that the Italians have successfully perfected. Sharing a meal and discussing ideas and news is virtually a rite.

Basic Ingredients

Anchovies are widely available canned in oil. The fillets have been salted beforehand, but soaking them in milk before using will remove some of the saltiness. Whole anchovies preserved in salt are sometimes available and have a fresher flavour.

Artichokes are native to Italy and come in two varieties. The thornless variety come from Liguria and are often eaten raw dressed with oil. The other type, from Rome, are purple and usually cooked.

Aubergines (Eggplants), unlike their close relation the tomato, are native to Italy, but for many years were thought to be poisonous. They grow best in the south, the source also of the best recipes. They range in colour from purple to creamy white and in size from small and round to large and bulbous. Large aubergines (eggplants) should be sprinkled with salt and set aside to allow the bitter juices to drain off. This makes them sweeter, quicker to fry and means they absorb less oil.

Basil is the most frequently used herb in Italian cooking. Always use fresh basil, as dried is disappointingly inferior. If fresh basil is not available, use ready-made pesto sauce as a substitute.

Bay Leaves, both fresh and dried, are useful for flavouring meat dishes and creamy sauces.

Bouquet Garni is a combination of fresh or dried herbs, such as thyme, parsley and bay leaves, used in soups, stews and sauces.

Capers are small green flower buds, preserved in brine or vinegar. They are often sprinkled on pizzas and add sharpness to other dishes.

Clams are small shellfish used to make sauces for pasta and soups. They are best bought fresh, but they are also available canned or bottled in brine. Fresh clams should be well scrubbed

before cooking and any that remain open should be discarded. Their shells open during cooking and any that remain closed should also be discarded.

Cornmeal, called polenta in Italy, is used for making polenta, the dish. Finely ground cornmeal makes soft, thin polenta, while coarser cornmeal makes a harder and more flavourful polenta. The latter takes rather longer to cook. Pre-cooked instant polenta is available, but it does not taste as good as traditional home-made polenta.

Dolcelatte is a blue-veined, very creamy cheese with a delicate piquant flavour.

Dried Fruit, such as currants, raisins, sultanas (golden raisins), dates, apricots, figs and prunes, are used in lots of different recipes.

Fennel is a sweet, aniseed-like vegetable. The crisp, rounded white bulbs should have no discoloration. Italians used to serve wedges of raw fennel with a little salt at the end of a meal as an aid to digestion and this custom still

1 sundried tomatoes, 2 pancetta; 3 white onion;
4 pesto; 5 plum tomatoes; 6 dried pasta shapes; 7 pumpkin;
8 bouquet garni; 9 garlic; 10 porcini mushrooms

continues in some parts of Tuscany. Fennel is available all year, but it is at its best in the autumn (fall) and winter.

Garlic is essential. Depending on how finely it is sliced or chopped, it can have a milder or stronger flavour. The flavour also becomes milder with prolonged cooking. Chopped garlic in jars is available and is a useful time-saver.

Gorgonzola is a blue-veined semi-soft cheese with a piquant flavour. It should not smell unpleasant or feel dry. It is made from hot and cold curd from cow's milk taken from two different milkings. It may be used in sauces for pasta or gnocchi or eaten on its own. The little town of Gorgonzola, once a stopping place for cattle on the way home after a summer in the pastures, has been absorbed by Milan.

Italian Sausages are highly seasoned, fresh sausages that require cooking. They vary considerably in size. The filling can be squeezed out and used to make a sauce for pasta.

Mascarpone is a creamy soft cheese made from cow's milk. It is used in many desserts.

Mozzarella is a spongy white cheese with a slightly sour flavour. It was originally made from buffalo's milk in Campania, but is now made all over Italy, usually from cow's milk. Some mozzarella from the south is made from a mixture of milks. It becomes very elastic when cooked and is a standard ingredient for many dishes and the classic cheese for pizza.

Mushrooms are an essential flavouring in Italian cooking. Wild mushrooms, particularly porcini, also known as ceps or boletus, and chanterelles, are gathered almost as a matter of course. Do not wash mushrooms, but wipe them with damp kitchen paper (paper towels) to remove any dirt. Cook briskly to begin with and then lower the heat to allow the aroma to be released. Wild mushrooms tend to give off more liquid than cultivated ones. Dried porcini are available, although expensive. Rehydrate according to the packet instructions. A small quantity will add a strong flavour to any dish.

Mussels, like clams, are best used fresh and should be scrubbed and cooked in the same way. Cooked frozen mussels are available.

Olive Oil has a unique flavour and, although it is expensive, it is essential for an authentic Italian taste. Extra virgin olive oil is the best quality and is made from the first cold pressing. Always use this for salad dressings. Virgin olive oil, also made by cold pressing, is quite fine with a pleasant aroma. It is slightly less expensive than extra virgin oil and is suitable for cooking. Other oils, labelled 'pure olive oil', are refined by heat treatment and/or solvents and lack the distinctive taste of the virgin oils.

Olives are indispensable for adding richness to sauces and stews and for topping pizza. Black olives are more rounded in flavour than green and are full of oil.

Onions play a central role in Italian cooking. White onions are especially popular, as they have a mild, sweet taste, but they may be difficult to obtain. Red and purple onions are also mild and add colour to salads and other dishes.

Oregano is among the most popular of Italian herbs. It is closely related to marjoram, which has a slightly sweeter flavour. When in flower, both herbs make an attractive garnish.

Pancetta is bacon streaked with fat that adds a surprising depth of flavour to a wide variety of dishes. It may be smoked or unsmoked, sliced or in a single piece and is usually available from Italian delicatessens.

Parma Ham (Prosciutto) is taken from the hind thigh of the pig, salted and then air-cured for 12–18 months. It is an extremely skilled process and the risk of failure is high,

1 Parma ham (prosciutto); 2 Italian sausages; 3 bay leaves; 4 black peppercorns; 5 salami

which explains its high cost. Another excellent raw ham – prosciutto crudi – is made in San Daniele.

Parmesan Cheese is a hard cheese made from semi-skimmed, unpasteurized cow's milk. It has a grainy texture and a fragrant flavour. It is used grated or shaved as a garnish with many pasta sauces and other dishes. It is best to buy it in a piece and grate or shave it freshly when required, rather than using ready-grated Parmesan, which quickly loses its flavour. Parmesan cheese comes from a small specified area and the brown rind is always stamped with the words Parmigiano Reggiano as a guarantee of origin. You can store Parmesan wrapped in foil in the freezer – it keeps its flavour quite well, but the texture becomes a little more crumbly. Parmesan cheese for regular use can be wrapped in muslin (cheesecloth) and stored in the vegetable drawer of the refrigerator.

Parsley is an all-purpose herb, adding a fresh taste to almost any dish. Flat leaf parsley is most often used in Italy.

Pasta is available dried and fresh and there are many types to choose from. Good basics are lasagne sheets, tagliatelle or fettucine and spaghetti. You could also try making your own pasta at home.

Passata (sieved tomatoes) is made from pulped and strained tomatoes.

Pecorino Cheese is hard cheese, made from ewe's milk, that is often used grated or shaved to garnish dishes. It has a sharp flavour, a little like Parmesan, and is only used in small quantities.

Peppercorns, are available in three colours – white, black and green. They have a warm, aromatic flavour.

(Bell) Peppers are used raw and cooked. They may be green, red, orange, yellow and even purple, but red ones are most frequently used in Italy. They are usually skinned by being grilled (broiled) until they begin to char.

Pesto is available in jars, but brands vary considerably in quality. Some supermarkets sell fresh pesto in tubs from the chill cabinet. This usually has a better flavour than the bottled varieties, but nothing is as good as home-made pesto.

Pine Nuts are small and cream-coloured. They are essential for making pesto.

Pistachios are Middle Eastern nuts widely used in both savoury and sweet dishes.

Pumpkins can be used as a fruit and a vegetable. In Italy, mashed pumpkin is often used as a filling for sweet ravioli.

Rice is a staple in the north of Italy. Italian rice has rounder, smaller grains than other rices and a capacity to absorb a great deal of cooking liquid without becoming soggy. Arborio is probably the best risotto rice, but Carnaroli, Baldo and Roma are also good. Rice is also used for thickening soups and in stuffings, but it is never served as an accompaniment to either meat or fish dishes.

Ricotta is a soft, creamy whey cheese used for both savoury and sweet dishes. Strictly speaking it is a by-product of the cheese-making process. Whey is separated from the curd and when the whey is reheated, ricotta forms on the surface. Ricotta means reheated. Ricotta piemontese is made from cow's milk, while ricotta romana is made from ewe's milk. It does not keep for more than 2 days and cannot be frozen.

Rosemary leaves contain oil of camphor, and are widely used for flavouring meat dishes, most notably lamb.

Sage, together with basil, oregano and marjoram, is one of the four classic Italian herbs, especially in northern Italy. It has a strong flavour and is good with meat and cheese dishes.

Salad Leaves can now be bought ready-prepared in bags from most supermarkets. Choose from a wide selection,

1 Parma ham; 2 salad leaves; 3 Pecorino cheese; 4 fennel;
5 sultanas; 6 sage leaves; 7 rosemary; 8 potatoes; 9 pine nuts;
10 onions; 11 tomatoes

including chicory (endive), radiccio, oakleaf, curly endive, sorrel and lamb's lettuce.

Salami is made from minced (ground) meat and pork fat, stuffed into a casing. Most salami are made from pork, but a few, such as salame Milano, are made from beef or other meat. Those from the south are often flavoured with garlic and chillies and those from the north with white wine. The proportion of fat to lean meat varies and they may be coarsely or finely minced (ground). Salami are cured for at least 2 months and the best ones may be cured for as long as 1 year.

Sun-dried Tomatoes have a concentrated, almost roasted flavour. Drain or soak and chop before adding to the dish. Sun-dried tomatoes are an important export from Calabria. After harvesting, they are split open, sprinkled with salt and laid on bamboo racks to dry in the sun. When all the water has evaporated, they shrivel up and may be packaged without further treatment or bottled in oil.

Tomato Purée (Paste) intensifies the flavour of tomatoes and is especially useful if you are using canned tomatoes. Sun-dried tomato paste is also available.

Tomatoes are best when fully ripe and sun-ripened tomatoes in season have a much sweeter and stronger flavour than out of season tomatoes ripened under glass. Plum tomatoes are typically Italian and small cherry tomatoes are useful for salads. Canned tomatoes are an essential store cupboard ingredient.

Truffles are underground fungi that grow only in the wild. Many species grow all over Italy and white truffles grow only there. Black truffles, also known as truffles du Périgord, grow in the north. They are a luxurious and expensive ingredient with a unique flavour and aroma. White truffles are usually served raw, while black ones are cooked. Fresh truffles do not keep for very long, but they are available bottled in jars.

Vinegar is used mainly in salad dressings, but is also frequently used as a flavouring in place of wine in meat and game stews and casseroles, especially in Umbria. Red wine vinegar is more commonly used than white.

Walnuts are used in both sweet and savoury dishes and can be used to make walnut pesto.

Pasta

Making pasta, which simply means paste or dough, is one of the earliest culinary inventions. Records dating back to the second century BC show that pasta was a staple in the diets of numerous peoples. Countries with a long history of pasta making include China, Mongolia, Greece, Spain, Israel, Russia and, of course, Italy. The popular story that Marco Polo brought the art of pasta making back to Italy when he returned from his travels in China in 1295 is entirely false. Pasta was being made by the Etruscans in central Italy in 500 BC. So venerable is the pasta making tradition that in Liguria there is a museum dedicated entirely to it, the Museo Storico degli Spaghetti.

Italian pasta is usually made from durum wheat, a hard wheat, mixed with water. Fresh pasta and pasta all'uovo includes eggs. It is also sometimes made from ground buckwheat or whole-wheat. Pasta made without any additional colouring is a clear yellow colour, sometimes flecked with ground wheat germ. Pasta may also be coloured by adding a variety of different ingredients to the dough: spinach produces green pasta, tomato produces red pasta, saffron pasta is yellow-orange, beetroot makes deep pink pasta and squid ink creates black pasta – sure to create an eye-catching dinner party dish.

Unless you have access to a good Italian delicatessen it is hardly worth buying fresh unfilled pasta. Fresh filled pasta is increasingly available from supermarkets, as well as delicatessens. Home-made fresh pasta is delicious and worth the time it takes to make.

Pasta Shapes

There are thought to be at least 200 different shapes of pasta with over 600 different names. New varieties are being designed constantly and also the same shape may have different names in different regions of Italy. Basically, pasta falls into four categories: long round, long ribbons, tubes and small shapes. Pasta may also be stuffed with a variety of fillings. The following is a list of some of the most frequently used types of unfilled pasta.

Anelli, Anellini, Anelletti small rings used for soup

Bavette, Bavettini thin, oval tubes

Bigoli whole-wheat pasta from the Veneto

Bozzoli deeply-ridged, cocoon-like shapes

Brichetti 'small bricks'

Bucatini long, medium-thick tubes

Cappelletti wide-brimmed hat shapes

Capelli hair, fine tubes

Cappelli D'Angelo angel's hair pasta, thinner than cappellini

Cappellini fine strands of ribbon pasta

Casareccia short, curled lengths of pasta twisted at one end from Sicily

Cavatappi short, thick corkscrew shapes

Chifferi, Chifferini, Chifferotti small, curved tubes

Conchiglie ridged shells

Conchigliette little shells used for soup

Corallini small rings

Cornetti ridged shells

Cravatte, Cravattini bows

Cresti Di Gallo 'cock's comb', curved shapes

Dischi Volante 'flying saucers'

Ditali, Ditalini 'little thimbles', short tubes

Eliche loose, spiral shapes

Elicoidali short, ridge tubes

Farfalle bows

Fedeli, Fedelini fine tubes twisted into skeins

Festonati short lengths, like festoons

Fettuccine narrow ribbon pasta

Fiochette, Fiochelli small bows

Frezine broad, flat ribbons

Fusilli spindles or short spirals

Fusilli Bucati thin spirals, like springs

Gemelli, 'twins', two pieces wrapped together

Gramigna meaning 'grass' or 'weed', look like sprouting seeds from Emilia Romagna

Lasagne flat, rectangular sheets

Linguine long, flat ribbons

Lumache smooth, snail-like shells

Lumachine U-shaped flat pasta

Macaroni, Maccheroni long or short-cut tubes, may be ridged or elbow-shaped

Maltagliati triangular

Orecchiette ear-shaped

Orzi tiny, rice-like grains

Pappardelle widest ribbons, straight with sawtooth edges

Pearlini tiny discs

Penne quills, short, thick tubes with diagonally cut ends

Pipe Rigate ridged, curved pipe shapes

Rigatoni thick, ridged tubes

Rotelle wheels

Ruote wheels

Semini seed shapes

Spaghetti fine, medium and thick rods

Spirale two rods twisted into spirals

Strozzapreti 'priest strangler', double twisted strands

Tagliarini flat ribbons, thinner than tagliatelle

Tagliatelle broad, flat ribbons

Tortiglione thin, twisted tubes

Vermicelli fine, slender strands usually twisted into skeins

Ziti Tagliati short, thick tubes

Basic Pasta Dough

Making your own pasta is time consuming, but immensely satisfying. You will need plenty of space for the rolled-out dough and somewhere to hang it to dry.

Serves 4
115 g/4 oz/1 cup strong white flour, plus extra for dusting
115 g/4 oz/²/₃ cup fine semolina
1 tsp salt
2 tbsp olive oil
2 eggs
2-3 tbsp hot water

1 Sift the flour, semolina and salt into a bowl and make a well in the centre. Pour in the oil and add the eggs and 1 tablespoon of the water. Using your fingertips, draw in the dry ingredients and mix to a smooth dough. Add more water, a little at a time, if necessary to make the dough pliable.

2 Lightly dust a surface with flour, turn out the dough and knead for 10–15 minutes, until it is elastic and silky. Dust the dough with flour if your hands become sticky.

3 Divide the dough into two pieces. Cover a surface with a clean tea towel (dish cloth) and dust it generously with flour. Place one portion of dough on the cloth and roll out as thinly and evenly as possible, stretching the dough gently until the pattern of the weave shows through. Cover it with a cloth and roll out the second piece of dough in the same way.

4 Cut the pasta into the required shapes, cover with a clean cloth and set aside in a cool place (not the refrigerator) for 30–45 minutes, until partly dry. To dry pasta ribbons, place a tea towel (dish cloth) over the back of a chair and hang the ribbons over it.

Making Pasta Dough in a Food Processor

1 Put the olive oil, eggs and 1 tablespoon of hot water in a food processor and process for a few seconds to mix thoroughly.

2 Add the flour, semolina and salt and process until smooth, adding a little more hot water if necessary to make the dough pliable.

3 Fit the dough hooks or transfer to a mixer with dough hooks and knead for 2–3 minutes, until elastic and silky. Alternatively, turn out on to a floured surface and knead by hand for 10–15 minutes. Continue from step 3 (Basic Pasta Dough, left).

COLOURING BASIC PASTA DOUGH

Red Pasta
Add 2 tbsp tomato purée (paste) in step 1 (Basic Pasta Dough, left) and reduce the amount of egg by about one quarter

Pink Pasta
Add 2 tbsp grated cooked beetroot in step 1 (Basic Pasta Dough, left) and reduce the amount of egg by about one quarter.

Orange Pasta
Soak a sachet of powdered saffron in 2 tbsp hot water for 15 minutes. Add in step 1 (Basic Pasta Dough, left) and reduce the quantity of water by 2 tbsp.

Green Pasta
Cook 150 g/5 oz frozen leaf spinach, drain and squeeze out the moisture. Process in a food processor until a smooth purée is formed. Add in step 1 (Basic Pasta Dough, left).

CUTTING SHAPES

Macaroni
Cut squares of pasta dough using a sharp knife. Lay a pencil or chopstick on one square from one corner to another and wrap the pasta around it to form a tube. Slip the pencil or chopstick out and set the macaroni aside to dry slightly.

Pasta Ribbons
Roll up a square of pasta like a Swiss (jelly) roll and cut the roll into thin slices. Unravel the slices immediately. Alternatively, use a rule and a sharp knife or serrated pastry wheel to cut thin ribbons.

Other Shapes
Use small confectionery cutters to cut rounds, stars and other decorative shapes.

PASTA MACHINES

A pasta machine saves some time and effort and is worth having if you make your own pasta fairly frequently. The method is to feed the pasta through the rollers several times, one notch thinner each time.

Divide the Basic Pasta Dough (see page 15) into two pieces. Roll until both pieces have gone through the machine at each setting. if the strips become too long, cut them into manageable lengths.

Lay the pasta out on tea towels (dish cloths) to dry until it feels leathery. It is now ready for cutting. The machine will cut the pasta into ribbons, other shapes will have to be cut by hand. Dry as in step 4 (Basic Pasta Dough, page 15).

COOKING PASTA

Perfect pasta depends upon cooking it for exactly the right amount of time. If it is undercooked, it will be unyielding and taste of flour. If it is overcooked, it will be sticky and soggy. It should be cooked until it is tender, but still firm to the bite, known to the Italians as al dente (to the tooth).

It can be difficult to calculate how much dried pasta to allow for each serving. As a general rule, allow about 40–50 g/1$\frac{1}{2}$–2 oz per serving for a first course or salad, and 75–115 g/3–4 oz per serving for a main course.

Bring a large saucepan of lightly salted water to the boil and add 1 tablespoon of olive oil. Then add the pasta and bring back to the boil. Start timing from when it comes back to the boil. Do not cover the pan and keep an eye on the pasta because the length of cooking time varies depending on the type and how much you are using. As a general guide, dried unfilled pasta takes 8–12 minutes; fresh unfilled pasta takes 2–3 minutes; dried filled pasta takes 15–20 minutes; fresh filled pasta takes 8–10 minutes.

As soon as the pasta is al dente, drain it in a colander. If you are not going to mix a sauce with it immediately, return it to the pan and toss lightly in a little olive oil or butter.

PASTA SAUCES

Creative cooks will enjoy partnering their favourite sauces with a variety of pastas. Although there are classic combinations, such as Spaghetti Bolognese and Spaghetti Carbonara, there are no rules, just guidelines, which are largely a matter of practicality, appearance and taste. For example long ribbons or round pasta give tomato- or oil-based sauces something to cling to, while shapes and hollow tubes are ideal for trapping chunkier sauces in their crevices. Béchamel and cheese sauces add creamy richness and moisture to baked dishes.

Béchamel Sauce

300 ml/^{1}/$_2$ pint/1^1/$_4$ cups milk
2 bay leaves
3 cloves
1 small onion
50 g/2 oz/^{1}/$_4$ cup butter
40 g/1^1/$_2$ oz/6 tbsp plain (all-purpose) flour
300 ml/^{1}/$_2$ pint/1^1/$_4$ cups single (light) cream
pinch of freshly grated nutmeg
salt and pepper

1 Pour the milk into a small pan and add the bay leaves. Press the cloves into the onion, add to the pan and bring the milk to the boil. Remove the pan from the heat and set aside to cool.

2 Strain the milk into a jug (pitcher) and rinse the pan. Melt the butter in the pan over a medium heat and stir in the flour. Stir for 1 minute, then gradually add the milk, stirring constantly. Cook the sauce, stirring constantly, for 3 minutes then add the cream and bring to the boil.

3 Remove the pan from the heat and season the sauce to taste with nutmeg, salt and pepper.

Lamb Sauce

2 tbsp olive oil
1 large onion, sliced
2 celery sticks, thinly sliced
450 g/1 lb lean minced (ground) lamb
3 tbsp tomato purée (paste)
150 g/5 oz bottled sun-dried tomatoes, drained and chopped
1 tbsp chopped fresh oregano
1 tbsp red wine vinegar
150 ml/^{1}/$_4$ pint/^{2}/$_3$ cup chicken stock
salt and pepper

1 Heat the oil in a frying pan (skillet) over a medium heat. Add the onion and celery and sauté until the onion is translucent. Add the lamb and cook, stirring frequently, until browned.

2 Stir in the tomato purée (paste), sun-dried tomatoes, oregano, vinegar and stock and season to taste with salt and pepper. Bring to the boil and cook, uncovered, for 20 minutes, or until the meat has absorbed the stock. Adjust the seasoning if necessary.

Basic Tomato Sauce

2 tbsp olive oil
1 small onion, chopped
1 garlic clove, chopped
400 g/14 oz can chopped tomatoes
2 tbsp chopped fresh parsley
1 tbsp chopped fresh oregano
2 bay leaves
2 tbsp tomato purée (paste)
1 tsp sugar
salt and pepper

1 Heat the oil in a pan over a medium heat and sauté the onion until translucent. Add the garlic and sauté for 1 minute.

2 Stir in the tomatoes, parsley, oregano, bay leaves, tomato purée (paste) and sugar and season to taste with salt and pepper.

3 Bring the sauce to the boil, lower the heat and simmer for 15-20 minutes, or until reduced by half. Adjust the seasoning if necessary and remove and discard the bay leaves.

Cheese Sauce

25 g/1 oz/2 tbsp butter
1 tbsp plain (all-purpose) flour
250 ml/8 fl oz/1 cup milk
2 tbsp single (light) cream
pinch of freshly grated nutmeg
50 g/2 oz/^{1}/$_2$ cup grated mature (sharp) Cheddar cheese
1 tbsp grated Parmesan cheese
salt and pepper

1 Melt the butter in a pan over a medium heat. Stir in the flour and cook, stirring constantly, for about 1 minute. Gradually add the milk, stirring constantly. Stir in the cream and season to taste with nutmeg, salt and pepper.

2 Lower the heat and simmer for 5 minutes to reduce slightly, then remove the pan from the heat and stir in the cheeses. Stir until the cheeses have melted and blended into the sauce.

Pizza

Although there is speculation about where pizza in its simplest form was first invented, it is usually associated with the old Italian city of Naples. It was then a simple street food, richly flavoured and quickly made. it was not always round and flat as we know it today, but was originally folded up like a book, with the filling inside, and eaten by hand. Pizzas were usually sold by street criers who carried them around in cylindrical copper drums kept hot with coals from the pizza ovens.

The word pizza actually means any kind of pie. The classic Napoletana pizza is probably the best known of the many varieties. It consists of a thin dough crust topped with a fresh tomato sauce, mozzarella cheese, anchovies, olives and a sprinkling of oregano. When baked, the flavours blend perfectly together to produce the distinctive, aromatic pizza. Another classic is the Margherita, named after the Italian queen. Bored with the usual cuisine when she was on a visit to Naples, she asked to sample a local speciality. The local Pizzaiolo created a pizza in the colours of the Italian flag – red tomatoes, green basil and white mozzarella. The queen was delighted and it became widely celebrated.

As well as being economical and popular, the pizza is more versatile than most other dishes, thanks to the countless possible permutations of bases and toppings that can be served to suit every taste and every occasion.

Fortunately for the busy cook, pizzas are an easy to food to chill or freeze, ready to be cooked on demand. There is a wide range of ready-made pizza bases, as well as dry mixes that only need the addition of water before they are ready for kneading and baking.

Pizzas are also sold complete with a variety of toppings. which you can bake as they are, or add more toppings yourself. Although they never seem to taste as good as a real home-made pizza, these can be very useful to keep on hand. Jars of (bell) peppers, sun-dried tomatoes and artichokes in olive oil make very good toppings, and will keep for quite a while in your store cupboard.

THE DOUGH BASE

Although making your own pizza base can be a little time consuming, the method is very straightforward (see pages 192–194) and you end up with a delicious home-baked dish as well as a sense of achievement. The ingredients are very basic. There are three types of yeast available: fresh, dried and easy-blend (active dry). Fresh yeast is usually found in healthfood shops and is inexpensive. Buy it in bulk and freeze in 15 g/^{1}/2 oz quantities ready to use whenever it is needed. Mix 15 g/^{1}/2 oz fresh yeast in 90 ml/3^1/2 fl oz tepid water with ^{1}/2 teaspoon of sugar and let dissolve before adding to the flour. This takes about 5 minutes. The frothiness indicates that the yeast is working. Fresh yeast will keep for 4–5 days in the refrigerator. Make sure that it is well covered as it will dry out very quickly.

Dried yeast is sold in sachets (envelopes) or small tubs. It has a shelf life of about 6 months, so buy only a small amount if you are not going to make bread dough on a regular basis. Like fresh yeast, add it to the tepid water with a little sugar and stir to dissolve. Let stand for 10–15 minutes until froth develops on the surface.

Easy-blend (active dry) yeast is the simplest to use as it is stirred dry into the flour before the water is added. It is sold in sachets (envelopes) by most supermarkets.

Traditional pizza bases are usually made from bread dough, which is usually made from strong flour. You can also use one of the many types of wholemeal (whole-wheat) flours available, such as stoneground, wheatmeal and granary. Try adding a handful of wheat germ or bran to white flour for extra flavour, fibre and interest. You could also mix equal quantities of white and wholemeal (whole-wheat) flour. Always sift the flour first as this will remove any lumps and help to incorporate air into the flour which will in turn help to produce a light dough. If you sift wholemeal (whole-wheat) flours, there will be some bran and other bits left in the strainer which are normally then tipped on to the mixing bowl so that their goodness and fibre are added to the sifted flour.

Yeast thrives in warm surroundings, so all the ingredients and equipment for the dough should be warm. If tepid yeast liquid is added to a cold bowl of cold flour, it will quickly cool down. This will retard the growth of the yeast and the dough will take much longer to rise. If the flour is kept in a cool cupboard, remember to remove it in enough time to warm to room temperature before you use it. Sift the flour into a large mixing bowl and place it somewhere warm, such as in the oven on its lowest setting. Do not allow it to overheat, as this will kill the yeast.

Italian Wines

Grape vines grow virtually everywhere in Italy and Italians have been making wine for 3,500 years. Italy produces more wine than any other country and exports nearly 40 per cent of total world-wide wine exports. Yet people rarely think of Italian wines as great wines in the way they think of Grand Cru and Auslese wines from France or Germany. Much of the Italian wine that is exported is of a very basic quality and is often used by other wine-producing nations for blending with their own. Otherwise, cheapness seems to be the deciding factor and uninspiring Lambrusco, Frascati and Valpolicella line the shelves of supermarkets. In fact, Italy produces some extremely good wines but, wisely perhaps, keeps them for Italians to drink.

Although there are several laws concerning the style and production of wine in Italy, they are often flouted because wine production is very much a local concern. Viticulturists show the same fierce regional pride as cooks and each is convinced that his methods and vintages are the best throughout the whole of Italy.

Burton Anderson, the world's greatest authority on Italian wine, says that if there are 1,605, 785 registered vineyards in Italy, then there are 1,605, 785 individual wines. There are, however, a large number of co-operatives, some of which are responsible for churning out the unmemorable wine that is exported in such large quantities.

The following list of wines is by no means exhaustive. Most of the wines are DOC, Denominazione di Origine Controllata, the appellation of origin. A few are DOCG, which are subject to stricter controls and may, therefore, be of higher quality.

PIEDMONT
Asti Spumante – white, sweet, sparkling and severely underrated
Babararesco – red and very fine
Barolo – red and very fine
Freisa d'Asti – red and still

LOMBARDY
Franciacorta – red, white and rosé, still and sparkling
Lugana – white
Oltrepò Pavese – red, white and rosé

LIGURIA
Rossese di Dolceacqua – red

TRENTINO-ALTO ADIGE
Moscato Giallo – white
Rosenmuskateller – rosé and fine
Santa Maddalena – red

VENETO
Bardolino – red and rosé, look for 'Classico'
Bianca di Custoza – white
Raboso – red
Recioto della Valpolicella Amarone – red and white
Soave – white, look for 'Classico'
Valpolicella – red, look for 'Classico'

EMILIA ROMAGNA
Albana di Romagna – white and sweet sparkling white
Lambrusco – red, white and rosé, sparkling and still

TUSCANY
Bianco Vergine della Valdichiana – white
Carmignano – red and rosé
Chianti – red, look for 'Classico'
Montecarlo – white
Rosso di Montalcino – red
Vino Nobile di Montepulciano – red
Vernaccia di san Gimignano – white

UMBRIA
Grechetto – white
Orvieto – white
Torgiano – white

THE MARCHES
Rosso Cònero – red
Rosso Piceno – red
Verdicchio di Castelli di Jesu – white and sparkling white
Verdicchio di Matelica – white

LATIUM
Frascati – white
Marino – white
Velletri – red and white

ABRUZZI AND MOLISE
Montepulciano d'Abruzzo – red
Trebbiano d'Abruzzo – white

CAMPANIA
Greco di Tufo – white
Taurasi – red

APULIA
Castel del monte – red, white and rosé

BASILICATA
Aglianico del Vulture – red

CALABRIA
Cirò – red, white and rosé
Greco di Bianco – sweet white

SICILY
Malvasia delle Lipari – amber-coloured dessert wine (fortified)
Marsala – amber-coloured dessert wine (fortified)

SARDINIA
Nuragus di Cagliaru – white
Vermentino – white
Vernaccia di Oristano – white

Antipasti & Accompaniments

Antipasti are hors d'oeuvres served before the meal and may be as simple as a platter of cured meats and salami. The keynote is variety and on special occasions a selection might include half a dozen different dishes. Vegetables often feature, cooked until just tender, but still crisp and colourful.

Antipasti are not usually elaborate or rich; they are designed to stimulate not to satisfy the appetite. The flavours of the individual ingredients are unadorned and intended to set the taste buds tingling.

What could be simpler or more delicious than Fresh Figs with Parma Ham or Roast (Bell) Pepper Salad?

Many of the recipes in this chapter, such as Black Olive Pâté, spread on rounds of fried bread, and Crostini alla Fiorentina, can be served as cocktail nibbles or as appetizers. Other dishes are substantial enough to make delicious snacks – try Mozzarella in Carozza, a melt-in-the-mouth deep-fried sandwich.

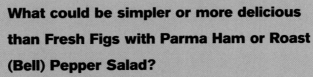

Pickled (Bell) Peppers

Pickled (bell) peppers are widely used throughout Italy and make
a delicious antipasto or pizza topping. They are excellent in a pasta sauce or, in fact,
anywhere you would otherwise use (bell) peppers.

Serves 4

1 kg/2¹/₄ lb mixed red and yellow (bell) peppers
4 basil leaves
2 bay leaves
5 black peppercorns
2 cloves garlic, peeled
600 ml/1 pint/2¹/₂ cups white wine vinegar

1 Preheat the grill (broiler) to hot. Halve and seed the (bell) peppers. Place them skin side up and grill (broil) for 15 minutes until charred.

2 Place the (bell) peppers in a plastic bag to sweat for 10 minutes. Peel the skin off and slice the flesh into thick strips. Set aside to cool.

3 Gently bruise the basil leaves between your fingers and put in a sterilized jar with the (bell) peppers, herbs, peppercorns and garlic. Add the vinegar, seal and use within 6 months.

COOK'S TIP

When peeling the charred skin from the (bell) peppers, hold them over a bowl to catch the juices, which can then be added to the jar in step 3.

Green Salsa Salad Dressing

This is a Sicilian sauce which is great for all
kinds of salads and also makes an interesting alternative
to pesto for pasta.

Serves 4
1 bunch basil
1 bunch mint
1 bunch flat leaf parsley
virgin olive oil

1 Strip the leaves from the stems of all the herbs.

2 If making by hand, use a pestle and mortar to pound the leaves to a paste.

3 Gradually add enough olive oil to make a thick dressing.

4 Alternatively, put all the herb leaves into a food processor or blender. Process for 1–2 minutes and, with the motor still running, add enough olive oil to make the dressing.

COOK'S VARIATION

For a change, try adding 3 anchovy fillets or 1 tablespoon capers and blend to a smooth paste with the herbs. The dressing will keep in the refrigerator for 1 month.

Mediterranean (Bell) Pepper Salad

Colourful marinated Mediterranean vegetables make a tasty appetizer.
Serve with fresh bread or Tomato Toasts.

Serves 4
1 onion
2 red (bell) peppers
2 yellow (bell) peppers
3 tbsp olive oil
2 large courgettes (zucchini), sliced
2 garlic cloves, sliced
1 tbsp balsamic vinegar
50 g/2 oz anchovy fillets, chopped
25 g/1 oz/$^1/_4$ cup black olives, halved and stoned (pitted)
1 tbsp chopped fresh basil
salt and pepper

TOMATO TOASTS

small French loaf
1 garlic clove, crushed
1 tomato, peeled and chopped
2 tbsp olive oil
salt and pepper

1 Cut the onion into wedges. Core and seed the (bell) peppers and cut the flesh into thick slices.

2 Heat the oil in a frying pan (skillet). Add the onion, (bell) peppers, courgettes (zucchini) and garlic, and sauté gently, stirring, for 20 minutes.

3 Add the vinegar, anchovies and olives and season to taste. Mix thoroughly and set aside to cool.

4 Spoon on to individual plates and sprinkle with the basil.

5 To make the tomato toasts, cut the French bread diagonally into 1-cm/ ½-inch slices.

6 Mix the garlic, tomato, oil, and seasoning together, and spread thinly over each slice of bread.

7 Place on a baking tray (cookie sheet), drizzle with the olive oil and bake in a preheated oven at 220°C/ 425°F/Gas Mark 7, for 5–10 minutes, or until crisp.

COOK'S TIP

Extra virgin olive oil is more expensive than other kinds, but it has the best flavour and is worth buying for dishes, such as this, where it plays an integral role.

Yellow (Bell) Pepper Salad

A colourful combination of yellow (bell) peppers, red radishes and celery combine to give a wonderfully crunchy texture and fresh taste.

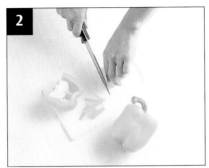

Serves 4
4 slices pancetta or bacon, chopped
2 yellow (bell) peppers
8 radishes, washed and trimmed
1 celery stick, finely chopped
3 plum tomatoes, cut into wedges
3 tbsp olive oil
1 tbsp fresh thyme
salt and pepper

1 Dry fry the chopped bacon in a frying pan (skillet) for 4–5 minutes, or until crispy. Remove the bacon from the frying pan (skillet) and set aside to cool until required.

2 Using a sharp knife, halve and seed the (bell) peppers and cut the flesh into long strips.

3 Using a sharp knife, halve the radishes and cut them into wedges.

4 Mix together the (bell) peppers, radishes, celery and tomatoes and toss the mixture in the olive oil and fresh thyme. Season to taste with a little salt and pepper.

5 Transfer the salad to serving plates and garnish with the reserved crispy bacon.

COOK'S TIP

Packaged diced bacon can be purchased from most supermarkets, which helps to save on preparation time.

Green Salad

This is a green salad with a difference – herb-flavoured croûtons are topped with peppery rocket (arugula), red chard, green olives and pistachios to make an elegant combination.

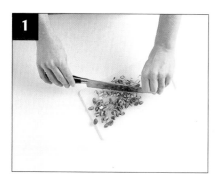

Serves 4
25 g/1 oz/¼ cup pistachio nuts
5 tbsp extra virgin olive oil
1 tbsp rosemary, chopped
2 garlic cloves, chopped
4 slices rustic bread
1 tbsp red wine vinegar
1 tsp wholegrain mustard
1 tsp sugar
25 g/1 oz rocket (arugula)
25 g/1 oz red chard
50 g/2 oz/½ cup green olives, (stoned) pitted
2 tbsp fresh basil, shredded

1 Shell the pistachios and roughly chop them, using a sharp knife.

2 Place 2 tablespoons of the extra virgin olive oil in a frying pan (skillet). Add the rosemary and garlic and cook for 2 minutes.

3 Add the slices of bread to the pan and fry for 2–3 minutes on both sides until golden. Remove the bread from the pan and drain on absorbent kitchen paper (paper towels).

4 To make the dressing, mix together the remaining olive oil with the red wine vinegar, mustard and sugar.

5 Place a slice of bread on each of 4 individual serving plates and top with the rocket (arugula) and red chard. Sprinkle the green olives over the top.

6 Drizzle the dressing over the top of the salad leaves. Sprinkle with the chopped pistachios and shredded basil leaves and serve the salad immediately.

COOK'S TIP

If you cannot find red chard, try slicing a tomato into very thin wedges to add a splash of vibrant red colour to the salad.

Roast (Bell) Pepper Salad

Serve chilled as an antipasto with cold meats, such as salame or mortadella, or warm as a side dish. Garlic bread makes a delicious accompaniment.

Serves 4
4 large mixed red, green and yellow (bell) peppers
4 tbsp olive oil
1 large red onion, sliced
2 garlic cloves, crushed
4 tomatoes, peeled and chopped
pinch of sugar
1 tsp lemon juice
salt and pepper

1 Trim and halve the (bell) peppers and remove the seeds.

2 Place the (bell) peppers skin side up under a preheated hot grill (broiler) and cook until the skins char. Rinse under cold water and remove the skins. Alternatively, place them in a plastic bag and sweat for 10 minutes before peeling.

3 Trim off any thick membranes and slice the flesh thinly.

4 Heat the oil and sauté the onion and garlic until softened. Then add the (bell) peppers and tomatoes and sauté over a low heat for 10 minutes.

5 Remove from the heat, add the sugar and lemon juice, and season to taste. Serve immediately or let cool. The flavours will continue to develop as the salad cools.

Seafood Salad

Fish and seafood are plentiful in Italy and seafood salads of all kinds are found almost everywhere. Each region has its own speciality.

Serves 4
175 g/6 oz squid rings, thawed if frozen
600 ml/1 pint/2½ cups water
150 ml/¼ pint/⅔ cup dry white wine
250 g/8 oz hake or monkfish fillets, cut into cubes
16–20 mussels, scrubbed and debearded
20 clams, scrubbed, if available (otherwise use extra mussels)
125–175 g/4–6 oz peeled cooked prawns (shrimp)
3–4 spring onions (scallions), trimmed and sliced
lemon wedges, to garnish
radicchio and curly endive leaves, to serve

DRESSING

6 tbsp olive oil
1 tbsp white wine vinegar
2 tbsp chopped fresh parsley
1–2 garlic cloves, crushed
salt and pepper

GARLIC MAYONNAISE

5 tbsp thick mayonnaise
2–3 tbsp fromage frais or plain (unsweetened) yogurt
2 garlic cloves, crushed
1 tbsp capers
2 tbsp chopped fresh parsley

1 Poach the squid in the water and wine for 20 minutes, or until nearly tender. Add the fish and continue to cook gently for 7–8 minutes, or until tender. Remove the fish and set aside. Strain the stock into a clean pan.

2 Bring the fish stock to the boil and add the mussels and clams. Cover the pan and simmer gently for about 5 minutes or until the shells open. Discard any that remain closed.

3 Drain the shellfish and remove them from their shells. Put them into a bowl with the cooked fish, prawns (shrimp) and spring onions (scallions).

4 For the dressing, beat together the oil, vinegar, parsley, garlic, salt and plenty of black pepper. Pour over the fish, mixing well, but without breaking it up. Cover and chill for several hours.

5 Arrange small leaves of radicchio and curly endive on 4 plates and spoon the fish salad into the centre. Garnish with lemon wedges. Combine all the ingredients for the garlic mayonnaise and serve with the salad.

Capri Salad

This tomato, olive and mozzarella salad, dressed
with balsamic vinegar and olive oil, makes a delicious starter on its own.
Increase the quantity by half to make for a full salad for four people.

Serves 4
2 beefsteak tomatoes
130 g/4¹/₂ oz mozzarella cheese
12 black olives
1 tbsp balsamic vinegar
1 tbsp olive oil
salt and pepper
basil leaves, to garnish

COOK'S TIP

Balsamic vinegar, which has
grown in popularity over the past
decade, is produced in the Emilia-
Romagna region of Italy. It is made
from wine which is distilled until it
is dark brown and extremely
strongly flavoured.

COOK'S TIP

Buffalo mozzarella cheese, although
it is usually more expensive because
of the comparative rarity of buffalo,
does have a better flavour than the
cow's milk variety. It is popular in
salads, but also provides a tangy
layer in baked dishes.

1 Using a sharp knife, cut the
tomatoes into thin slices.

2 Using a sharp knife, cut the
mozzarella into slices.

3 Stone (pit) the olives and slice
them into rings.

4 Layer the tomatoes, mozzarella
cheese and olives in a stack, finishing
with a layer of cheese on top.

5 Place each stack under a preheated
grill (broiler) for 2–3 minutes, or just
long enough to melt the mozzarella.

6 Drizzle over the vinegar and olive
oil, and season to taste with salt
and pepper.

7 Transfer to individual serving
plates and garnish with basil leaves.
Serve immediately.

Artichoke & Parma Ham (Prosciutto) Salad

Use bottled artichokes rather than canned ones
if possible, as they have a better flavour.

Serves 4
250 ml/9 fl oz bottle artichokes in oil
4 small tomatoes
25 g/1 oz/¼ cup sun-dried tomatoes, cut into strips
25 g/1 oz/¼ cup black olives, halved and pitted
25 g/1 oz/¼ cup Parma ham (prosciutto), cut into strips
1 tbsp torn fresh basil leaves
fresh basil sprigs, to garnish

FRENCH DRESSING

3 tbsp olive oil
1 tbsp white wine vinegar
1 small garlic clove, crushed
½ tsp Dijon or Meaux mustard
1 tsp clear honey
salt and pepper

1 Drain the artichokes, then cut them into quarters and place in a bowl.

2 Cut each tomato into six wedges and place in the bowl, together with the sun-dried tomatoes, olives and Parma ham (prosciutto).

3 To make the dressing, put all the ingredients into a screw-top jar and shake vigorously until the ingredients are thoroughly blended.

4 Pour the dressing over the salad and toss well together.

5 Transfer to individual plates, sprinkle the torn basil on top, garnish with the basil sprigs and serve.

Tuna, Bean & Anchovy Salad

Serve as part of a selection of antipasti, or for a
summer lunch with hot garlic bread and, perhaps, a bottle
of red wine.

Serves 4
500 g/1¼ lb tomatoes
200 g/7 oz can tuna fish, drained
2 tbsp chopped fresh parsley
½ cucumber
1 small red onion, sliced
225 g/8 oz/1½ cups cooked French (green) beans
1 small red (bell) pepper, cored and seeded
1 small crisp lettuce
6 tbsp French dressing (see page 30)
3 hard-boiled (hard-cooked) eggs
50 g/2 oz can anchovies, drained
12 black olives, stoned (pitted)

1 Cut the tomatoes into wedges, flake the tuna fish and put both into a bowl, together with the parsley.

2 Cut the cucumber in half lengthways, then cut into slices. Slice the onion. Add the cucumber and onion to the bowl.

3 Cut the French (green) beans in half, chop the red (bell) pepper and add both to the bowl, together with the lettuce leaves.

4 Pour over the French dressing and toss thoroughly, then transfer to a salad bowl to serve.

5 Cut the eggs into quarters, arrange over the top of the salad, together with the anchovies. Finally, scatter the olives over the salad.

COOK'S TIP

If you find canned anchovies too salty, after draining them, soak them in a saucer of milk for 5–10 minutes, drain and pat dry with kitchen paper (paper towels).

COOK'S VARIATION

For an extra touch, use 12 hard-boiled (hard-cooked) quails' eggs. Shell them under cold running water to prevent them from breaking up.

Baked Fennel Gratinati

Fennel is often used in Italian cooking. In this dish its
distinctive, sweet, aniseed-like flavour is offset by the smooth,
creamy besciamella.

Serves 4
4 fennel bulbs
25 g/1 oz/2 tbsp butter
Béchamel Sauce (see page 17), enriched with 2 egg yolks
150 ml/¼ pint/⅔ cup dry white wine
25 g/1 oz/½ cup fresh white breadcrumbs
3 tbsp freshly grated Parmesan cheese
salt and pepper
fennel fronds, to garnish

1 Remove any bruised or tough outer layers from the fennel and cut each bulb in half.

2 Put the fennel into a saucepan of boiling salted water and simmer for 20 minutes, until tender. Drain well.

3 Butter an ovenproof dish liberally and arrange the drained fennel in it.

4 Mix the wine into the Béchamel sauce and season to taste. Pour the sauce over the fennel.

5 Sprinkle the breadcrumbs and then the Parmesan evenly over the top.

6 Bake in a preheated oven at 200°C/ 400°F/Gas Mark 6 for 20 minutes, until the top is golden. Garnish with fennel fronds and serve immediately.

Tuscan Bean Salad with Tuna

The combination of beans and tuna is a favourite
with the people of Tuscany. The hint of honey and lemon in the
dressing makes this salad refreshing as well as hearty.

Serves 4
1 small white onion or 2 spring onions (scallions), finely chopped
2 x 400g/14 oz cans butter (lima) beans, drained
2 medium tomatoes
200 g/7 oz can tuna, drained
2 tbsp flat leaf parsley, chopped
2 tbsp olive oil
1 tbsp lemon juice
2 tsp clear honey
1 garlic clove, crushed

COOK'S TIP

This salad will keep for several days in a covered container in the refrigerator. Make the dressing just before serving and toss the ingredients together to mix well.

COOK'S VARIATION

You could substitute fresh salmon for the canned tuna if you wish to create a more luxurious version of this recipe for a special occasion.

1 Place the chopped onions or spring onions (scallions) and the beans in a bowl and mix well to combine.

2 Cut the tomatoes into wedges. Add the tomatoes to the onion and bean mixture.

3 Flake the tuna with a fork and add it to the onion and bean mixture, together with the parsley.

4 In a screw-top jar, mix together the olive oil, lemon juice, honey and garlic. Shake the jar until the dressing emulsifies and thickens.

5 Pour the dressing over the bean salad. Toss the ingredients together using 2 spoons and serve.

Aubergine (Eggplant) Salad

A starter with a difference from Sicily. It has a real bite,
both from the sweet-sour sauce and from the texture of the celery.

Serves 4
2 large aubergines (eggplant), about 1 kg/2 lb
6 tbsp olive oil
1 small onion, finely chopped
2 garlic cloves, crushed
6–8 celery sticks, cut into 1-cm/^{1}/$_2$-inch slices
2 tbsp capers
12–16 green olives, stoned (pitted) and sliced
2 tbsp pine nuts
25 g/1 oz bitter or plain (dark) chocolate, grated
4 tbsp white wine vinegar
1 tbsp brown sugar
salt and pepper
2 hard-boiled (hard-cooked) eggs, sliced, to serve
celery leaves or curly endive, to garnish

1 Cut the aubergines (eggplant) into 2.5-cm/1-inch cubes and sprinkle liberally with 2–3 tablespoons salt. Let stand for 30 minutes to extract the bitter juices. Rinse off the salt thoroughly under cold running water, drain and pat dry with kitchen paper (paper towels).

2 Heat 5 tablespoons of the oil in a frying pan (skillet) and fry the aubergine (eggplant) cubes until golden brown all over. Drain on kitchen paper (paper towels), then put in a large bowl.

3 Add the onion and garlic to the pan with the remaining oil and sauté until

just soft. Add the celery and sauté for a few minutes, stirring frequently, until lightly coloured but still crisp.

4 Add the celery mixture to the aubergines (eggplant). Add the capers, olives and pine nuts and mix lightly.

5 Add the chocolate, vinegar and sugar to the residue in the pan

(skillet). Heat gently until melted, then bring to the boil. Season with a little salt and plenty of freshly ground black pepper. Pour the mixture over the salad and mix lightly. Cover, cool and then chill thoroughly.

6 Serve with sliced hard-boiled (hard-cooked) eggs and garnish with celery leaves or curly endive.

Minted Fennel Salad

This is a very refreshing salad. The subtle liquorice flavour of fennel combines well with the cucumber and mint.

Serves 4
1 bulb fennel
2 small oranges
1 small or $^1/_2$ large cucumber
1 tbsp chopped mint
1 tbsp virgin olive oil
2 eggs, hard-boiled (hard-cooked)

1 Using a sharp knife, trim the outer leaves from the fennel. Slice the fennel bulb thinly into a bowl of water and sprinkle with lemon juice (see Cook's Tip).

2 Grate the rind of the oranges over a bowl. Using a sharp knife, pare away the orange peel, then segment the orange by carefully slicing between each line of pith. Do this over the bowl in order to retain the juice.

3 Using a sharp knife, cut the cucumber into 1-cm/$^1/_2$-inch thick rounds and then cut each round into quarters. Add the cucumber to the fennel and orange mixture, together with the mint.

4 Pour the olive oil over the fennel and cucumber salad and toss well.

5 Shell and quarter the eggs and use them to garnish the top of the salad. Serve at once.

COOK'S TIP

Fennel will discolour if it is left for any length of time without a dressing. To prevent any discolouration, place it in a bowl of water and sprinkle with lemon juice.

COOK'S TIP

Virgin olive oil, which has a fine aroma and flavour, is made by the cold pressing of olives. However, it usually has a slightly higher acidity level than extra virgin oil.

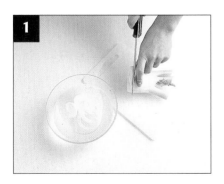

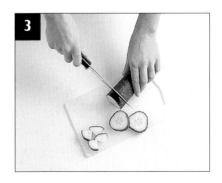

Mushroom Salad

Raw mushrooms are a great favourite in Italian dishes –
they have a fresh, almost creamy flavour.

Serves 4
150 g/5 oz firm white mushrooms
4 tbsp virgin olive oil
1 tbsp lemon juice
5 canned anchovy fillets, drained and chopped
1 tbsp fresh marjoram
salt and pepper

1 Gently wipe each mushroom with a damp cloth to remove any excess dirt. Slice the mushrooms thinly, using a sharp knife.

2 Beat together the olive oil and lemon juice and pour the mixture over the mushrooms. Toss together so that the mushrooms are completely coated with the mixture.

3 Stir the chopped anchovy fillets into the mushrooms. Season the mushroom mixture with black pepper and garnish with the fresh marjoram.

4 Let the mushroom salad stand for 5 minutes before serving in order for all the flavours to be absorbed. Season with a little salt and then serve.

COOK'S TIP

If you use dried herbs rather than fresh, remember that you need only about one third of dried to fresh.

Baked Aubergine (Eggplant) Parma-Style

Simmer the tomato sauce gently to reduce it slightly before using.

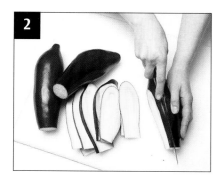

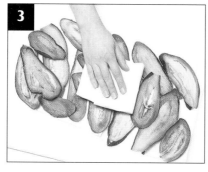

Serves 4
4 aubergines (eggplants), trimmed
3 tbsp olive oil
300 g/10¹/₂ oz mozzarella cheese, thinly sliced
4 slices Parma ham (prosciutto), shredded
1 tbsp chopped fresh marjoram
1 tbsp chopped fresh basil
¹/₂ quantity Béchamel Sauce (see page 17)
25 g/1 oz/¹/₃ cup grated Parmesan cheese
salt and pepper

TOMATO SAUCE

4 tbsp olive oil
1 large onion, sliced
4 garlic cloves, crushed
400 g/14 oz can chopped tomatoes
500 g/1¹/₄ lb fresh tomatoes, peeled and chopped
4 tbsp chopped fresh parsley
600 ml/1 pint/2¹/₂ cups hot vegetable stock
1 tbsp sugar
2 tbsp lemon juice
150 ml/¹/₄ pint/²/₃ cup dry white wine
salt and pepper

1 To make the sauce, heat the oil in a large saucepan. Fry the onion and garlic until beginning to soften. Add the canned and fresh tomatoes, parsley, stock, sugar and lemon juice. Cover and simmer for 15 minutes. Stir in the wine and season to taste.

2 Thinly slice the aubergines (eggplant) lengthways. Bring a large saucepan of water to the boil and cook the aubergine (eggplant) slices for 5 minutes.

3 Drain the aubergine (eggplant) slices on kitchen paper (paper towels) and pat dry.

4 Pour half the tomato sauce into a greased ovenproof dish. Cover with half the cooked aubergines (eggplants) and drizzle with a little oil. Cover with half the mozzarella, Parma ham

(prosciutto), marjoram and basil. Season to taste with salt and pepper.

5 Repeat the layers and cover with the Béchamel Sauce. Sprinkle the top evenly with the Parmesan cheese. Bake in a preheated oven at 190°C/375°F/Gas Mark 5, for 35–40 minutes, until golden on top. Serve hot.

Spinach Salad

Fresh baby spinach is tasty and light, and it makes an excellent
salad to go with the chicken and creamy dressing.

Serves 4
115 g/4 oz baby spinach, washed
75 g/3 oz radicchio leaves, shredded
50 g/2 oz mushrooms
115 g/4 oz cooked chicken, preferably breast
50 g/2 oz Parma ham (prosciutto)
2 tbsp olive oil
finely grated rind of $1/2$ orange and juice of 1 orange
1 tbsp plain (unsweetened) yogurt

COOK'S VARIATION

Try raw spinach in a salad garnished
with bacon or garlicky croûtons. The
young leaves have a sharp flavour.

COOK'S TIP

Radicchio is a variety of chicory
(endive) originating in Italy.
It has a slightly bitter flavour.

1 Wipe the mushrooms with a damp
cloth to remove any excess dirt.

2 Gently mix together the spinach
and radicchio in a large salad bowl.

3 Thinly slice the wiped mushrooms
and add them to the bowl.

4 Tear the cooked chicken breast and
Parma ham (prosciutto) into strips
and mix them into the salad.

5 To make the dressing, place the
olive oil, orange rind, orange juice and
yogurt in a screw-top jar. Shake the
jar vigorously until the mixture is
thoroughly combined. Season to taste
with salt and pepper.

6 Drizzle the dressing over the
spinach salad and toss to mix well.
Serve immediately.

Italian Potato Salad

Potato salad is always a favourite, but it is even more delicious
with the addition of sun-dried tomatoes and fresh parsley.

Serves 4
450 g/1 lb baby potatoes, unpeeled, or larger potatoes, halved
4 tbsp plain (unsweetened) yogurt
4 tbsp mayonnaise
8 sun-dried tomatoes
2 tbsp chopped fresh flat leaf parsley
salt and pepper

1 Rinse and clean the potatoes and place them in a large pan of water. Bring to the boil and cook for 8–12 minutes, or until just tender. (The cooking time will vary according to the size of the potatoes.)

2 Using a sharp knife, cut the sun-dried tomatoes into thin slices.

3 To make the dressing, mix together the yogurt and mayonnaise in a bowl and season to taste with a little salt and pepper. Stir in the sun-dried tomato slices and the chopped flat leaf parsley.

4 Remove the potatoes with a slotted spoon, drain them thoroughly and then set aside to cool. If you are using larger potatoes, cut them into 5-cm/2-inch chunks.

5 Pour the dressing over the potatoes and toss to mix.

6 Chill the potato salad in the refrigerator for about 20 minutes, then serve either as a starter or as an accompaniment.

Potatoes with Olives & Anchovies

This side dish makes a delicious accompaniment for grilled (broiled) fish
or lamb chops. The fennel adds a subtle aniseed flavour.

Serves 4
450 g/1 lb baby new potatoes, scrubbed
75 g/3 oz mixed olives
8 canned anchovy fillets, drained and chopped
2 tbsp olive oil
2 fennel bulbs, trimmed and sliced
2 sprigs rosemary, stalks removed
salt and pepper

1 Bring a large saucepan of water to the boil and cook the potatoes for 8–10 minutes, or until tender. Remove the potatoes from the saucepan using a slotted spoon and set aside to cool slightly.

2 Once the potatoes are cool enough to handle, cut them into wedges, using a sharp knife.

3 Stone (pit) the mixed olives and cut them in half, using a sharp knife.

4 Using a sharp knife, chop the anchovy fillets into smaller strips.

5 Heat the oil in a large frying pan (skillet). Add the potato wedges, sliced fennel and rosemary. Cook for 7–8 minutes, or until the potatoes are golden.

6 Stir in the olives and anchovies and cook over a low heat for 1 minute, or until warmed through.

7 Transfer to individual serving plates and serve immediately.

COOK'S TIP

Fresh rosemary is particularly popular with Italians, but you can experiment with your favourite herbs in this recipe, if you prefer.

COOK'S TIP

Baby new potatoes taste better when they have been cooked in the skins and this also helps to preserve essential nutrients.

Preserved Meats (Salumi)

Mix an attractive selection of these preserved meats (Salumi)
with olives and marinated vegetables for extra colour and variety.

Serves 4
3 ripe tomatoes
3 ripe figs
1 small melon
20 g/2 oz Italian salami, thinly sliced
4 thin slices mortadella
6 slices Parma ham (prosciutto)
6 slices bresaola
4 fresh basil leaves, chopped
olive oil
75 g/3 oz/$^3/_4$ cup marinated stoned (pitted) olives
freshly ground black pepper, to serve

1 Slice the tomatoes thinly.

2 Cut the figs into quarters.

3 Cut the melon in half. Scoop out
and discard the seeds and cut the
flesh into wedges.

4 Arrange the meats on one half of a
serving platter. Arrange the tomato
slices in the centre and sprinkle with
the basil leaves and oil.

5 Cover the rest of the platter with
the fruit and scatter the olives over
the meats.

6 Serve with a little extra olive oil to
drizzle over the bresaola, and coarsely
ground black pepper.

Lentil & Tuna Salad

In this recipe, lentils, combined with spices, lemon juice and
tuna, make a wonderfully tasty and filling salad.

Serves 4
3 tbsp virgin olive oil
1 tbsp lemon juice
1 tsp wholegrain mustard
1 garlic clove, crushed
1/2 tsp cumin powder
1/2 tsp ground coriander
1 small red onion
2 ripe tomatoes
400 g/14 oz can lentils, drained
200 g/7 oz can tuna, drained
2 tbsp chopped fresh coriander (cilantro)
pepper

1 Using a sharp knife, seed the
tomatoes and finely dice the flesh.

2 Using a sharp knife, finely chop the
red onion.

3 To make the dressing, beat together
the virgin olive oil, lemon juice,
mustard, garlic, cumin powder and
ground coriander in a small bowl. Set
aside until required.

4 Mix together the chopped onion,
diced tomatoes and drained lentils in
a large bowl.

5 Flake the tuna with a fork and
stir it into the onion, tomato and
lentil mixture.

6 Gently stir in the chopped fresh
coriander (cilantro).

7 Pour the dressing over the lentil
and tuna salad and season with
freshly ground black pepper. Serve
at once.

COOK'S TIP

Lentils are an excellent source of
protein and contain important
vitamins and minerals. Buy them
dried for soaking and cooking
yourself, or buy canned varieties for
speed and convenience.

Baked Fennel

Fennel is used a lot in northern Italy. It is a very versatile vegetable, which is good cooked or raw in salads.

Serves 4
2 fennel bulbs
2 celery sticks cut into 7.5-cm/3-inch sticks
6 sun-dried tomatoes, halved
200 g/7 oz passata (sieved tomatoes)
2 tsp dried oregano
50 g/2 oz/$^2/_3$ cup freshly grated Parmesan cheese

1 Using a sharp knife, trim the fennel, discarding any tough outer leaves, and cut the bulb into quarters.

2 Bring a large pan of water to the boil, add the fennel and celery and cook for 8–10 minutes or until just tender. Remove with a slotted spoon and drain.

3 Arrange the fennel pieces, celery and sun-dried tomatoes in an ovenproof dish.

4 Mix together the passata (sieved tomatoes) and oregano and pour the mixture over the fennel.

5 Sprinkle with the Parmesan cheese and bake in a preheated oven at 190°C/375°F/Gas Mark 5 for 20 minutes, or until hot.

6 Serve as a starter with crusty bread or as a vegetable side dish.

COOK'S VARIATION

If you cannot find any fennel in the shops, leeks make a delicious alternative. Use about 750 g/1 lb 10 oz, chopped, making sure that they are washed thoroughly to remove all traces of soil.

COOK'S VARIATION

If you wish, you could add a drained 400 g/14 oz can of beans, such as cannellini, borlotti or haricot (navy) beans, in step 3 for a substantial vegetarian supper dish.

Black Olive Pâté

This pâté is delicious served as a starter on crisp tomato bread.
It can also be served as a cocktail snack on small rounds of fried bread.

Serves 4
250 g/8 oz/1½ cups stoned (pitted) juicy black olives
1 garlic clove, crushed
finely grated rind of 1 lemon
4 tbsp lemon juice
25 g/1 oz/½ cup fresh breadcrumbs
50 g/2 oz/¼ cup full-fat soft cheese
salt and pepper
lemon wedges, to garnish

1 Roughly chop the olives and mix with the garlic, lemon rind and juice, breadcrumbs and soft cheese. Pound until smooth, or place in a food processor and process until fully blended. Season to taste with salt and freshly ground black pepper.

2 Store in a screw-top jar and chill for several hours before using – this allows the flavours to develop.

3 For a delicious cocktail snack, use a pastry (cookie) cutter to cut out small rounds from a thickly sliced loaf.

4 Fry the bread rounds in a mixture of olive oil and butter until they are a light golden brown. Drain on kitchen paper (paper towels).

5 Top each round with a little of the pâté, garnish with lemon wedges and serve immediately. This pâté will keep in an airtight jar in the refrigerator for up to 2 weeks.

Tomatoes Stuffed with Tuna Mayonnaise

Deliciously sweet roasted tomatoes are filled with
home-made lemon mayonnaise and tuna.

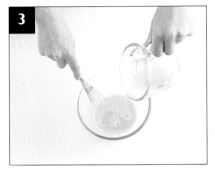

Serves 4
4 plum tomatoes
2 tbsp sun-dried tomato paste
2 egg yolks
2 tsp lemon juice
finely grated rind of 1 lemon
4 tbsp olive oil
115g/4 oz can tuna, drained
2 tbsp capers, rinsed
salt and pepper

GARNISH
2 sun-dried tomatoes, cut into strips
fresh basil leaves

1 Halve the tomatoes and scoop out
the seeds with a teaspoon. Divide the
sun-dried tomato paste among the
tomato halves and spread it around
the inside of the skins.

2 Place the tomato halves on a baking
tray (cookie sheet) and roast in a
preheated oven at 200°C/400°F/Gas
Mark 6 for 12–15 minutes, until just
tender, but still firm. Set aside until
they are cool enough to handle.

COOK'S TIP

For a picnic, do not roast the
tomatoes, just scoop out the seeds,
drain, cut side down, on absorbent
kitchen paper (paper towels) for 1
hour, and fill with the mayonnaise
mixture. They are easier to eat with
the fingers this way. Shop-bought
mayonnaise may be used instead –
just stir in the lemon rind.

3 Meanwhile, make the mayonnaise.
In a food processor, blend the egg
yolks and lemon juice with the lemon
rind until smooth. With the motor
still running, gradually add the olive
oil. Stop as soon as the mayonnaise
has thickened. Alternatively, use a
hand whisk, beating the mixture
continuously until it thickens.

4 Add the tuna and capers to the
mayonnaise and season.

5 Spoon the tuna mayonnaise
mixture into the tomato shells and
garnish with sun-dried tomato strips
and basil leaves. Return to the oven
for a few minutes and serve warm or
chill before serving.

Fresh Figs with Parma Ham (Prosciutto)

Traditionally made with Kadota figs, this colourful fresh salad is delicious at any time of the year.

Serves 4
40 g/1½ oz rocket (arugula)
4 fresh figs
4 slices Parma ham (prosciutto)
4 tbsp olive oil
1 tbsp fresh orange juice
1 tbsp clear honey
1 small red chilli

COOK'S TIP

Parma, in the Emilia–Romagna region of Italy, is famous for its ham, prosciutto di Parma, thought to be the best in the world.

COOK'S TIP

Chillies can burn the skin for several hours after chopping, so it is advisable to wear gloves when you are handling the very hot varieties.

1 Separate the rocket (arugula) leaves and tear into manageable pieces. Arrange them on 4 serving plates.

2 Using a sharp knife, cut each of the figs into quarters and place them on top of the rocket (arugula) leaves.

3 Using a sharp knife, cut the Parma ham (prosciutto) into strips and scatter them over the rocket (arugula) and figs.

4 Place the oil, orange juice and honey in a screw-top jar. Shake the jar vigorously until the mixture emulsifies and forms a thick dressing. Transfer to a bowl.

5 Using a sharp knife, dice the chilli, remembering not to touch your face before you have washed your hands (see Cook's Tip, right). Add the chopped chilli to the dressing and mix well.

6 Drizzle the dressing over the Parma ham (prosciutto), rocket (arugula) and figs, tossing gently to mix well. Serve at once.

Sweet & Sour Baby Onions

This is a typical Sicilian dish, combining honey and vinegar
to give a delicate sweet and sour flavour. Serve hot as
an accompaniment or cold with cured meats.

Serves 4
350 g/12 oz baby or pickling onions
2 tbsp olive oil
2 fresh bay leaves, torn into strips
thinly pared rind of 1 lemon
1 tbsp light brown sugar
1 tbsp clear honey
4 tbsp red wine vinegar

1 Soak the onions in a bowl of boiling water – this will make them easier to peel. Using a sharp knife, peel and halve the onions.

2 Heat the oil in a large frying pan (skillet). Add the bay leaves and onions to the pan and cook over a medium-high heat for 5–6 minutes, or until browned all over.

3 Cut the lemon rind into thin matchsticks. Add to the frying pan (skillet) with the sugar and honey. Cook for 2–3 minutes, stirring occasionally, until the onions are lightly caramelized.

4 Add the red wine vinegar to the frying pan (skillet), being careful because it will spit. Cook, stirring, for about 5 minutes, or until the onions are tender and most of the liquid has disappeared.

5 Transfer the onions to a serving dish and serve at once.

COOK'S TIP

To make the onions easier to peel, place them in a large saucepan, pour over boiling water and leave for 10 minutes. Drain the onions thoroughly, and when they are cold enough to handle, peel them.

COOK'S TIP

Adjust the piquancy of this dish to your liking by adding more light brown sugar for a sweeter, more caramelized taste, or extra red wine vinegar for a sharper, more savoury flavour.

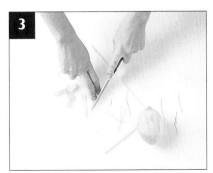

Stewed Artichokes

This is a traditional Roman dish. The artichokes
are stewed in olive oil with fresh herbs.

Serves 4
4 small globe artichokes
4 garlic cloves, peeled
2 bay leaves
finely grated rind and juice of 1 lemon
extra virgin olive oil
2 tbsp fresh marjoram
lemon wedges, to garnish

1 Using a sharp knife, carefully peel away the tough outer leaves surrounding the artichokes. Trim the stems to about 2.5 cm/1 inch.

2 Using a knife, cut each artichoke in half and scoop out the choke (heart).

3 Place the artichokes in a large heavy based saucepan. Pour over enough olive oil to half cover the artichokes in the pan.

4 Add the garlic cloves, bay leaves and half the grated lemon rind.

5 Heat the artichokes gently, cover the pan and continue to cook over a low heat for about 40 minutes. The artichokes should be stewed in the oil, not fried.

6 Once the artichokes are tender, remove them with a slotted spoon and drain thoroughly. Remove and discard the bay leaves.

7 Transfer the artichokes to warm individual serving plates. Sprinkle the artichokes with the remaining grated lemon rind, the fresh marjoram and a little lemon juice. Garnish with the lemon wedges and serve.

COOK'S TIP

To prevent the artichokes from oxidizing and turning brown before cooking, brush them with a little lemon juice. In addition, use the oil used for cooking the artichokes for salad dressings – it will impart a lovely lemon and herb flavour.

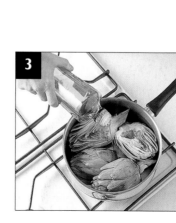

Chickpeas (Garbanzo Beans) with Parma Ham (Prosciutto)

Prosciutto is a cured ham, which is air- and salt-dried for up to 1 year. There are many different varieties available, and the one used here is *crudo*, which is slightly coarser than other types.

Serves 4
1 tbsp olive oil
1 medium onion, thinly sliced
1 garlic clove, chopped
1 small red (bell) pepper, seeded and cut into thin strips
200 g/7 oz Parma ham (prosciutto), cut into chunks
400g/14 oz can chickpeas (garbanzo beans), drained and rinsed
1 tbsp chopped parsley, to garnish
crusty bread, to serve

1 Heat the oil in a large frying pan (skillet). Add the sliced onion, chopped garlic and sliced (bell) pepper and cook for 3–4 minutes, or until the vegetables have softened.

2 Add the Parma ham (prosciutto) to the frying pan (skillet) and sauté gently over a low heat for 5 minutes, or until the ham (prosciutto) is just beginning to brown.

3 Add the chickpeas (garbanzo beans) to the frying pan (skillet) and cook,

stirring, for 2–3 minutes, until they are thoroughly warmed through.

4 Sprinkle with chopped parsley and transfer to warm serving plates. Serve with lots of fresh crusty bread.

COOK'S VARIATION

Try adding a small finely diced chilli in step 1 for a spicier taste, if you prefer.

COOK'S TIP

Whenever possible, use fresh herbs when cooking. They are becoming more readily available, especially since the introduction of 'growing' herbs, small pots of herbs which you can buy from the supermarket or greengrocer and grow at home. This ensures the herbs are fresh and also provides a continuous supply.

Deep-fried Seafood

Deep-fried seafood is popular all around the Mediterranean,
where fish of all kinds is fresh and abundant.
Serve with garlic mayonnaise and lemon wedges.

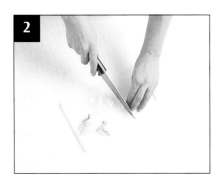

Serves 4
200 g/7 oz prepared squid
200 g/7 oz peeled raw tiger prawns (jumbo shrimp)
150 g/5 oz whitebait
oil, for deep-frying
50 g/2 oz plain (all-purpose) flour
1 tsp dried basil
salt and pepper

TO SERVE

garlic mayonnaise (see Cook's Tip)
lemon wedges

1 Carefully rinse the squid, prawns (shrimp) and whitebait under cold running water, completely removing any dirt or grit.

2 Using a sharp knife, slice the squid bodies into rings, leaving the tentacles whole.

3 Heat the oil in a large saucepan to 180°–190°C/350°–375°F or until a cube of bread browns in 30 seconds.

4 Place the flour in a bowl and season with the salt, pepper and basil.

5 Roll the squid, prawns (shrimp) and whitebait in the seasoned flour until coated all over. Carefully shake off any excess flour.

6 Cook the seafood in the hot oil in batches for 2–3 minutes, or until crispy and golden all over. Remove all the seafood with a slotted spoon and drain thoroughly on kitchen paper (paper towels).

7 Transfer the deep-fried seafood to individual serving plates and serve with garlic mayonnaise (see Cook's Tip) and lemon wedges.

COOK'S TIP

To make garlic mayonnaise for serving with the deep-fried seafood, crush 2 garlic cloves, stir into 8 tablespoons mayonnaise and season with salt and pepper and a little chopped parsley.

Bruschetta with Tomatoes

Using sun-ripened cherry tomatoes and the
best-quality olive oil will make this simple
Tuscan dish absolutely delicious.

Serves 4
300 g/10¹/₂ oz cherry tomatoes
4 sun-dried tomatoes
4 tbsp extra virgin olive oil
16 fresh basil leaves, shredded
8 slices ciabatta or other Italian bread
2 garlic cloves, peeled
salt and pepper

1 Using a sharp knife, cut the cherry tomatoes in half.

2 Using a sharp knife, slice the sun-dried tomatoes into strips.

3 Place the cherry tomatoes and sun-dried tomatoes in a bowl. Add the olive oil and the shredded basil leaves and toss to mix well. Season to taste with a little salt and pepper.

4 Using a sharp knife, cut the garlic cloves in half. Lightly toast the ciabatta or Italian bread.

5 Rub the garlic, cut-side down, over both sides of the toasted Italian bread.

6 Top the toasted bread with the tomato mixture, transfer to individual serving plates and serve immediately.

COOK'S TIP

Ciabatta is an Italian rustic bread which is slightly chewy. It is very good in this recipe, as it absorbs the full flavour of the garlic and extra virgin olive oil.

COOK'S VARIATION

Plum tomatoes also work very well in this recipe. Halve them, then cut them into wedges. Mix the plum tomatoes with the sun-dried tomatoes in step 3.

Italian Omelette

This baked omelette is of substantial proportions with
potatoes, onions, artichokes and sun-dried tomatoes.

Serves 4
900 g/2 lb potatoes
1 tbsp oil
1 large onion, sliced
2 garlic cloves, chopped
6 sun-dried tomatoes, cut into strips
400 g/14 oz can artichoke hearts, drained and halved
250 g/9 oz/1 cup ricotta cheese
4 large eggs, beaten
2 tbsp milk
50 g/2 oz/²/₃ cup grated Parmesan cheese
3 tbsp chopped thyme

1 Peel the potatoes and place them in a bowl of cold water (see Cook's Tip). Cut the potatoes into thin slices.

2 Bring a large pan of water to the boil and add the potato slices. Simmer for 5–6 minutes, or until just tender.

3 Heat the oil in a large frying pan (skillet). Add the onions and garlic to the pan and cook, stirring occasionally, for about 3–4 minutes.

4 Add the sun-dried tomatoes and continue cooking over a low heat for 2 minutes.

5 Arrange a layer of potatoes on the base of an ovenproof dish. Cover with a layer of the onion mixture, then artichoke hearts, then ricotta cheese. Repeat the layers in the same order, finishing with a layer of potatoes.

6 Beat together the eggs, milk, half the grated Parmesan cheese, the

thyme and salt and pepper to taste and carefully pour the mixture over the potatoes.

7 Top with the remaining grated Parmesan cheese and bake in a preheated oven, at 190°C/375°F/Gas 5, for 20–25 minutes, or until golden brown. Cut into slices and serve.

COOK'S TIP

Placing the potatoes in a bowl of cold water as each one is peeled will prevent them from turning brown while you peel and cut the rest into slices.

Casserole of Beans in Tomato Sauce

This quick and easy casserole can be eaten as a healthy
supper dish or as a side dish to accompany sausages or grilled (broiled) fish.

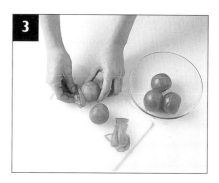

Serves 4
400 g/14 oz can cannellini beans
400 g/14 oz can borlotti beans
2 tbsp olive oil
1 celery stick
2 garlic cloves, chopped
175 g/6 oz baby onions, halved
450 g/1 lb tomatoes
75 g/3 oz rocket (arugula)

1 Drain both cans of beans and
reserve 6 tablespoons of the liquid.

2 Heat the oil in a large saucepan.
Add the celery, garlic and onions and
sauté for 5 minutes, or until the
onions are golden.

3 Cut a cross in the base of each
tomato and plunge them into a bowl
of boiling water for 30 seconds, until
the skins split. Remove them with a
slotted spoon and leave until they are
cool enough to handle. Peel off the
skin and chop the flesh. Add the
tomato flesh and the reserved bean
liquid to the pan and cook over a low
heat for 5 minutes.

4 Add the beans to the pan and cook
for a further 3–4 minutes, or until the
beans are hot.

5 Stir in the rocket (arugula) and
allow to wilt slightly before serving.

COOK'S VARIATION

For a spicier tasting dish, add
1–2 teaspoons hot pepper sauce
with the beans in step 4.

COOK'S TIP

Another way to peel a tomato is
once you have cut a cross in the
base, push it on to a fork and hold
it over a gas flame, turning it
slowly so that the skin heats evenly
all over. The skin will start to
bubble and split, and should then
slide off easily.

Omelette Strips in Tomato Sauce

These cheese-and-onion-flavoured omelette strips smothered in a rich tomato sauce are easy to make and taste absolutely delicious.

Serves 4
25 g/1 oz/2 tbsp butter
1 onion, finely chopped
2 garlic cloves, chopped
4 eggs, beaten
150 ml/¼ pint/⅔ cup milk
75 g/3 oz Gruyère (Swiss) cheese, diced
400g/14 oz can tomatoes, chopped
1 tbsp rosemary, stalks removed
150 ml/¼ pint/⅔ cup vegetable stock
freshly grated Parmesan cheese, for sprinkling
crusty bread, to serve

1 Melt the butter in a large frying pan (skillet). Add the onion and garlic and cook for 4–5 minutes, until softened.

2 Beat together the eggs and milk until thoroughly combined and add the mixture to the frying pan (skillet).

3 Using a spatula, gently raise the cooked edges of the omelette and tip any uncooked egg around the edge of the pan.

4 Scatter the Gruyère (Swiss) cheese on top. Cook for 5 minutes, turning once, until golden on both sides. Remove from the pan and roll up.

5 Add the tomatoes, rosemary and vegetable stock to the frying pan (skillet) and bring to the boil, stirring.

6 Simmer the tomato sauce over a low heat for about 10 minutes, until reduced and thickened.

7 Slice the omelette into strips and add to the tomato sauce in the frying pan (skillet). Cook for 3–4 minutes, until piping hot.

8 Sprinkle the freshly grated Parmesan cheese over the omelette strips in tomato sauce and serve with fresh crusty bread.

Courgette (Zucchini) & Thyme Fritters

These tasty little fritters are great with roasted (bell) peppers
(see page 27) as a relish for a drinks party.

Makes 16 medium-sized fritters
100 g/3¹/₂ oz self–raising flour
2 eggs, beaten
50 ml/2 fl oz/¹/₄ cup milk
300 g/10¹/₂ oz courgettes (zucchini)
2 tbsp fresh thyme
1 tbsp oil
salt and pepper

1 Sift the self-raising flour into a large bowl and make a well in the centre. Add the eggs to the well, and using a wooden spoon, gradually draw in the flour.

2 Gradually add the milk to the mixture, stirring constantly to form a thick batter.

3 Meanwhile, wash the courgettes (zucchini). Grate the courgettes (zucchini) over a sheet of kitchen paper (paper towel) placed in a bowl to absorb some of the juices.

4 Add the courgettes (zucchini) and thyme and salt and pepper to taste to the batter and mix thoroughly.

5 Heat the oil in a large, heavy-based frying pan (skillet). Taking a tablespoon of the batter for a medium-sized fritter or half a tablespoon of batter if you prefer a smaller-sized fritter, spoon the mixture into the hot oil and cook, in batches, for 3–4 minutes on each side.

6 Remove the fritters with a slotted spoon and drain thoroughly on absorbent kitchen paper (paper towels). Keep each batch of fritters warm in the oven while you are making the rest. Transfer the fritters to warm serving plates and serve immediately.

COOK'S VARIATION

Try adding ¹/₂ teaspoon of dried, crushed chillies in step 4 for spicier tasting fritters.

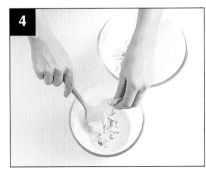

Mozzarella in Carozza

A delicious way of serving mozzarella – the cheese stretches out
into melted strings as you cut into the carozza.

Serves 4
200 g/7 oz mozzarella cheese
4 slices Parma ham (prosciutto)
8 two-day old slices white bread, crusts removed
butter for spreading
2–3 eggs
3 tbsp milk
vegetable oil, for deep-frying
salt and pepper

TOMATO AND (BELL) PEPPER SAUCE

1 onion, chopped
2 garlic cloves, crushed
3 tbsp olive oil
1 red (bell) pepper, seeded and chopped
400 g/14 oz can peeled tomatoes
2 tbsp tomato purée (paste)
3 tbsp water
1 tbsp lemon juice
salt and pepper
flat leaf parsley, to garnish (optional)

1 First make the sauce: sauté the onion and garlic in the oil until soft. Add the (bell) pepper and cook for a few minutes. Add the tomatoes, tomato purée (paste), water, lemon juice and seasoning. Bring to the boil, cover and simmer for 10–15 minutes, or until tender. Cool the sauce a little, then purée in a food processor or rub through a strainer until smooth.

2 Cut the mozzarella into 4 slices as large as possible; if the cheese is a square piece, cut into 8 slices. Trim the Parma ham (prosciutto) slices to the same size as the cheese.

3 Lightly butter the bread and use the cheese and ham to make four sandwiches, pressing the edges firmly together. If liked, they may be cut in half at this stage. Cover with cling film (plastic wrap) and chill.

4 Lightly beat the eggs with the milk and salt and pepper to taste in a shallow dish.

5 Carefully dip the sandwiches in the egg and milk mixture until they are

thoroughly coated. Set aside to soak for a few minutes if possible.

6 Heat the oil in a large pan or deep-fryer until it just begins to smoke, or until a cube of bread browns in about 30 seconds. Fry the sandwiches in batches until golden brown on both sides. Drain well on kitchen paper (paper towels) and keep warm. Serve the sandwiches hot, with the reheated tomato and (bell) pepper sauce, and garnished with parsley.

Spinach & Ricotta Patties

'Nudo' or naked is the word used to describe this mixture, which can also be made into thin pancakes or used as a filling for tortelloni.

Serves 4
450 g/1 lb fresh spinach
250 g/9 oz/1 cup ricotta cheese
1 egg, beaten
2 tsp fennel seeds, lightly crushed
50 g/2 oz/$^2/_3$ cup finely grated pecorino or Parmesan cheese
25 g/1 oz/$^1/_4$ cup plain (all-purpose) flour, mixed with 1 tsp dried thyme
75 g/3 oz/6 tbsp butter
2 garlic cloves, crushed
salt and pepper

1 Wash the spinach and trim off any long stalks. Place in a pan, cover and cook for 4–5 minutes, until wilted. This will probably have to be done in batches as the volume of spinach is quite large. Place in a colander and set aside to drain and cool.

2 Mash the ricotta and beat in the egg and the fennel seeds. Season with plenty of salt and pepper, then stir in the pecorino or Parmesan cheese.

3 Squeeze as much excess water as possible from the spinach and finely chop the leaves. Stir the spinach into the cheese mixture.

4 Take about 1 tablespoon of the mixture, shape it into a ball and flatten it slightly to form a patty. Gently roll in the seasoned flour. Continue this process until all of the mixture has been used up.

5 Half fill a large frying pan (skillet) with water and bring to the boil.

Carefully add the patties, in batches if necessary, and cook for 3–4 minutes, or until they rise to the surface. Remove with a slotted spoon and drain thoroughly.

6 Melt the butter in a pan. Add the garlic and cook for 2–3 minutes. Pour the garlic butter over the patties, season with freshly ground black pepper and serve at once.

Deep-fried Risotto Balls

The Italian name for this dish translates as 'telephone wires' which refers to the strings of melted mozzarella cheese, the surprise contained within the risotto balls.

Serves 4
2 tbsp olive oil
1 medium onion, finely chopped
1 garlic clove, chopped
1/2 red (bell) pepper, seeded and diced
150 g/5 oz/3/4 cup arborio (risotto) rice, washed
1 tsp dried oregano
400 ml/14 fl oz/1 2/3 cups hot vegetable or chicken stock
100 ml/3 1/2 fl oz/1/2 cup dry white wine
75 g/3 oz mozzarella cheese
oil, for deep-frying
fresh basil sprig, to garnish

1 Heat the oil in a frying pan (skillet). Add the onion and garlic and sauté for 3–4 minutes, or until just softened.

2 Add the (bell) pepper, rice and oregano to the pan. Sauté over a low heat, stirring to coat the rice in the oil, for 2–3 minutes.

3 Mix the stock together with the wine and add to the pan a ladleful at a time, waiting for the liquid to be absorbed by the rice before you add the next ladleful of liquid.

4 Once all of the liquid has been absorbed and the rice is tender (it should take about 15 minutes in total), remove the pan from the heat and set aside until the mixture is cool enough to handle.

5 Cut the cheese into 12 pieces. Taking about a tablespoon of risotto,

shape the mixture around the cheese pieces to make 12 balls.

6 Heat the oil until a piece of bread browns in 30 seconds. Cook the risotto balls, in batches of 4, for 2 minutes until golden all over.

7 Remove the risotto balls with a slotted spoon and drain thoroughly on absorbent kitchen paper (paper towels). Transfer to a warm serving dish, garnish with a sprig of basil and serve hot.

Crostini alla Fiorentina

Serve as a starter, or simply spread on small pieces of
crusty fried bread (crostini) as an appetizer with drinks.

Serves 4
3 tbsp olive oil
1 onion, chopped
1 celery stalk, chopped
1 carrot, chopped
1–2 garlic cloves, crushed
115 g/4 oz chicken livers
115 g/4 oz calf's, lamb's or pig's liver
150 ml/^{1}/$_2$ pint/^{2}/$_3$ cup red wine
1 tbsp tomato purée (paste)
2 tbsp chopped fresh parsley
3–4 canned anchovy fillets, chopped finely
2 tbsp stock or water
25–45 g/1–1^1/$_2$ oz/2–3 tbsp butter
1 tbsp capers
salt and pepper
chopped fresh parsley, to garnish
small pieces of fried crusty bread, to serve

1 Heat the oil in a pan, add the onion, celery, carrot and garlic, and sauté gently for 4–5 minutes, or until the onion is soft, but not coloured.

2 Meanwhile, rinse and dry the chicken livers. Dry the calf's or other liver, and slice into thin strips. Add both types of liver to the pan and fry gently for a few minutes until the strips are well sealed on all sides.

3 Add half the wine and cook over a medium heat until most of it has evaporated. Then add the remaining wine, the tomato purée (paste), half the parsley, the anchovy fillets, stock or water, a little salt and plenty of black pepper.

4 Cover the pan and simmer for 15–20 minutes, or until tender and most of the liquid has been absorbed.

5 Cool the mixture a little, then either coarsely mince (grind) or transfer to a food processor and process briefly to a chunky purée.

6 Return the mixture to the pan and add the butter, capers and remaining parsley. Heat through gently until the butter melts. Adjust the seasoning and turn into a bowl. Serve either just warm or cold spread on the slices of crusty bread and sprinkled with chopped parsley.

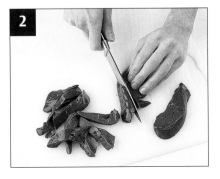

Garlic & Pine Nut Tarts

A crisp lining of bread is filled with garlic butter
and pine nuts to make a delightful starter.

Serves 4
4 slices wholemeal (whole-wheat) or granary bread
50 g/2 oz/¹/₂ cup pine nuts
150 g/5 oz/10 tbsp butter
5 garlic cloves, peeled and halved
2 tbsp fresh oregano, chopped, plus extra for garnish
4 black olives, halved
oregano leaves, to garnish

1 Using a rolling pin, flatten the bread slightly. Using a pastry (cookie) cutter, cut out 4 rounds to fit your individual tart tins (muffin pans) – they should measure about 10 cm/ 4 inches across. Reserve the offcuts of bread and leave them in the refrigerator for 10 minutes, or until required.

2 Meanwhile, place the pine nuts on a baking tray (cookie sheet). Toast the pine nuts under a preheated grill (broiler) for 2–3 minutes, or until golden brown.

3 Put the bread offcuts, pine nuts, butter, garlic and oregano into a food processor and process for about 20 seconds. Alternatively, pound the ingredients by hand in a mortar with a pestle. The mixture should have a rough texture.

4 Spoon the pine nut butter mixture into the lined tart tins (muffin pans) and top with the olive halves. Bake in a preheated oven at 200°C/400°F/Gas Mark 6 for 10–15 minutes, until golden.

5 Transfer the garlic and pine nut tarts to warm individual serving plates and serve immediately, garnished with the fresh oregano leaves.

COOK'S VARIATION

Phyllo pastry can be used instead of the bread for the tart cases (shells).

Onion & Mozarella Tarts

These melt-in-the-mouth individual tarts are delicious served hot or cold
and are great for picnics.

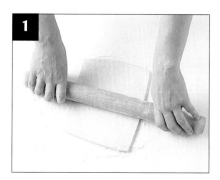

Serves 4
250g/9 oz ready-made puff pastry dough, thawed if frozen
2 medium red onions
1 red (bell) pepper
8 cherry tomatoes, halved
115g/4 oz Mozzarella cheese, cut into chunks
8 sprigs thyme

1 Roll out the dough to make 4 × 7.5-cm/3-inch squares. Using a sharp knife, trim the edges of the squares, reserving the trimmings. Chill the dough squares and trimmings in the refrigerator for 30 minutes.

2 Place the dough squares on a large baking tray (cookie sheet). Brush a little water along each edge of the squares and use the reserved dough trimmings to make a rim around each tart.

3 Cut the red onions into thin wedges and halve and seed the red (bell) pepper.

4 Place the onions and (bell) pepper in a roasting tin (pan). Cook under a preheated grill (broiler) for about 15 minutes, or until charred.

5 Place the roasted (bell) pepper halves in a plastic bag and set aside to sweat for 10 minutes. Peel off the skin from the (bell) peppers and cut the flesh into strips.

6 Line the dough squares with squares of foil. Bake in a preheated oven at 200°C/400°F/Gas Mark 6 for 10 minutes. Remove from the oven and discard the foil squares. Return the tarts to the oven and bake for a further 5 minutes.

7 Divide the onions, (bell) pepper strips, tomatoes and mozzarella cheese between the tarts and sprinkle them with the fresh thyme.

8 Return to the oven for 15 minutes, or until the pastry is golden.

Soups

Soup is normally served as the *primo* – first course – at dinner in Italy. Vegetable soups have pride of place, with minestrone as the first among equals. Italians rarely make smooth, creamy soups; they prefer to be aware of both the flavour and texture of the individual ingredients.

Rice and pasta are often features of soups from the north, while bean soups are a Tuscan speciality. Tomatoes and garlic flavour the soups of the south, and all coastal regions have their own particular recipes using fish and seafood. Some of the soups in this chapter are delicate and light, while others are hearty enough to serve for lunch.

Ingredients in season play an important role in Italian cooking. Dried pulses are widely used in the winter, because many vegetables are unavailable. In the summer, tomatoes, artichokes and green beans abound, while autumn (fall) is the time to gather wild mushrooms.

Minestrone with Pesto

One of the many versions of minestrone, which always contains
a variety of vegetables, pasta and rice and often includes beans.

Serves 6
175 g/6 oz/1 cup dried cannellini beans, soaked overnight
2.5 litres/4 pints/10 cups water or stock
1 large onion, chopped
1 leek, trimmed and thinly sliced
2 celery sticks, very thinly sliced
2 carrots, chopped
3 tbsp olive oil
2 tomatoes, peeled and chopped roughly
1 courgette (zucchini), trimmed and thinly sliced
2 potatoes, diced
90 g/3½ oz elbow macaroni (or other small macaroni)
salt and pepper
4–6 tbsp freshly grated Parmesan cheese, to serve

PESTO
2 tbsp pine nuts
5 tbsp olive oil
2 bunches basil, stems removed
4–6 garlic cloves, crushed
75 g/3 oz/1 cup pecorino or Parmesan cheese, grated
salt and pepper

1 Drain the beans, rinse and put in a
pan with the water or stock. Bring to
the boil, cover and simmer for 1 hour.

2 Add the onion, leek, celery, carrots
and oil. Cover and simmer for
4–5 minutes.

3 Add the tomatoes, courgette
(zucchini), potatoes and macaroni and

salt and pepper to taste. Cover again
and continue to simmer for about
30 minutes, or until the ingredients
are very tender.

4 Meanwhile, make the pesto. Fry the
pine nuts in 1 tablespoon of the oil
until pale brown, then drain. Put the
basil into a food processor or blender
with the pine nuts and garlic. Process
until well chopped. Alternatively, chop

finely by hand and pound with a
pestle in a mortar. Gradually add the
remaining oil until smooth. Turn into
a bowl, add the cheese and seasoning,
and mix thoroughly.

5 Stir 1½ tablespoons of the pesto
into the soup until well blended.
Simmer for a further 5 minutes and
adjust the seasoning. Serve very hot,
sprinkled with the cheese.

Minestrone

Minestrone translates as 'big soup' in Italian. It is made all over Italy, but this version comes from Livorno, a port on the western coast.

Serves 4
1 tbsp olive oil
115 g/4 oz pancetta ham, diced
2 medium onions, chopped
2 cloves garlic, crushed
1 potato, peeled and cut into 1-cm/^{1}/$_2$-inch cubes
1 carrot, cut into chunks
1 leek, sliced into rings
^{1}/$_2$ green cabbage, shredded
1 celery stick, chopped
450 g/1 lb can chopped tomatoes
200 g/7 oz can flageolet (small navy) beans, drained and rinsed
600 ml/1 pint/2^1/$_2$ cups hot ham or chicken stock diluted with 600 ml/ 1 pint/2^1/$_2$ cups boiling water
bouquet garni (2 bay leaves, 2 sprigs rosemary and 2 sprigs thyme, tied together)
salt and pepper
freshly grated Parmesan cheese, to serve

1 Heat the oil in a large saucepan. Add the diced pancetta, chopped onions and garlic and fry for about 5 minutes, or until the onions are soft and golden.

2 Add the prepared potato, carrot, leek, cabbage and celery to the saucepan. Cook for 2 minutes, stirring frequently to coat all of the vegetables in the oil.

3 Add the tomatoes, flageolet (small navy) beans, hot ham or chicken stock and bouquet garni to the pan, stirring to mix. Cover and simmer over a low heat for 15–20 minutes, or until all the vegetables are just tender.

4 Remove the bouquet garni and season to taste with salt and pepper. Transfer to warm soup bowls and serve with plenty of freshly grated Parmesan cheese.

COOK'S VARIATION

Any combination of vegetables will work equally well in this soup. For a special minestrone, try adding 115 g/4 oz/^{3}/$_4$ cup shredded Parma ham (prosciutto) in step 1.

Green Soup

This fresh-tasting soup with green (dwarf) beans, cucumber and watercress can be served warm or chilled on a hot summer day.

Serves 4
1 tbsp olive oil
1 onion, chopped
1 garlic clove, chopped
200 g/7 oz potato, cut into 2.5-cm/ 1-inch cubes
750 ml/1¼ pint/scant 3 cups vegetable or chicken stock
1 small cucumber or ½ large cucumber, cut into chunks
75 g/3 oz bunch watercress
115 g/4 oz green (dwarf) beans, trimmed and halved in length
salt and pepper

1 Heat the oil in a large pan and sauté the onion and garlic for 3–4 minutes, or until softened. Add the cubed potato and sauté for a further 2–3 minutes.

2 Stir in the stock, bring to the boil and simmer for 5 minutes.

3 Add the cucumber chunks to the pan and cook for a further 3 minutes, or until the potatoes are tender. Test by inserting the tip of a knife into the potato cubes – it should pass through easily.

4 Add the watercress and cook briefly until it wilts. Then transfer the soup to a food processor and process until completely smooth. Alternatively, before adding the watercress, mash the vegetables with a potato masher and rub through a strainer, then finely chop the watercress and stir into the soup.

5 Bring a small pan of water to the boil and steam the beans for about 3–4 minutes, or until tender.

6 Add the beans to the soup, season and warm through. Serve hot or cold.

COOK'S VARIATION

Try using 115 g/4 oz mangetout (snow peas) instead of the beans, if you prefer.

Red Bean Soup

Beans feature widely in Italian soups, making them hearty and tasty.
You can use other varieties of beans in this soup, if wished.

Serves 4–6
175 g/6 oz/1 cup dried red kidney beans, soaked overnight
1.75 litres/3 pints/7½ cups water
1 large ham bone or bacon knuckle
2 carrots, chopped
1 large onion, chopped
2 celery stalks, thinly sliced
1 leek, trimmed and sliced
1–2 bay leaves
2 tbsp olive oil
2–3 tomatoes, peeled and chopped
1 garlic clove, crushed
1 tbsp tomato purée (paste)
50 g/2 oz/⅓ cup arborio (risotto) rice
115–175 g/4–6 oz green cabbage, finely shredded
salt and pepper

1 Drain the beans and put them into a saucepan with enough water to cover. Bring to the boil and boil vigorously for 15 minutes to remove any harmful toxins. Reduce the heat and simmer for 45 minutes.

2 Drain the beans and put them into a large clean saucepan with the water, ham bone or knuckle, carrots, onion, celery, leek, bay leaves and olive oil. Bring to the boil, then cover and simmer for 1 hour, or until the beans are very tender.

3 Remove and discard the bay leaves. Remove and reserve any pieces of ham and discard the bone. Remove a cupful of the beans and reserve. Put the soup in a food processor or blender and process until smooth, or

rub through a coarse strainer. Transfer to a clean pan.

4 Add the tomatoes, garlic, tomato purée (paste), rice and plenty of seasoning. Bring back to the boil and simmer for about 15 minutes, or until the rice is tender.

5 Add the cabbage and reserved beans and ham and continue to simmer for 5 minutes. Adjust the seasoning and serve very hot. If liked, a piece of toasted crusty bread may be put in the base of each soup bowl before ladling in the soup. If the soup is too thick, add a little boiling water or stock.

Tuscan Bean Soup

A thick and creamy soup that is based on a traditional Tuscan recipe.
It is delicious served with fresh, warm bread and butter.

Serves 4

225 g/8 oz dried butter (lima) beans,
soaked overnight or 2 x 420 g/14½ oz
cans butter (lima) beans

1 tbsp olive oil

2 garlic cloves, crushed

1 vegetable or chicken stock (bouillon)
cube, crumbled

150 ml/¼ pint/⅔ cup milk

2 tbsp chopped fresh oregano

salt and pepper

1 If you are using dried beans that
have been soaked overnight, drain
them thoroughly. Bring a large pan of
water to the boil, add the beans and
boil for 10 minutes. Cover the pan
and simmer for a further 30 minutes,
or until tender. Drain the beans,
reserving the cooking liquid. If you
are using canned beans, drain them
thoroughly and reserve the liquid.

2 Heat the oil in a large frying pan
(skillet) and sauté the garlic for
2–3 minutes or until just beginning
to brown.

3 Add the beans and 400 ml/
14 fl oz/1⅔ cups of the reserved
liquid to the pan (skillet), stirring. You
may need to add a little water if there
is insufficient liquid. Stir in the
crumbled stock (bouillon) cube. Bring
the mixture to the boil and then
remove the pan from the heat.

4 Place the bean mixture in a food
processor and process to form a
smooth purée. Alternatively, mash the

bean mixture by hand to form a
smooth consistency. Season to taste
with salt and pepper and stir in
the milk.

5 Pour the soup back into the pan and
gently heat to just below boiling point.
Stir in the chopped oregano, transfer
to warm soup bowls and serve.

COOK'S VARIATION

If you prefer, use 2 teaspoons of
dried oregano instead of fresh, but
add with the beans in step 3. This
soup can also be made with
cannellini or borlotti beans
following the same method.

Haricot (Navy) Bean & Pasta Soup

A dish with proud Mediterranean origins, this soup
is a winter warmer, to be served with warm, crusty bread and,
if you like, a slice of cheese.

Serves 4
225 g/8 ounces/1¼ cups dried haricot (navy) beans, soaked, drained and rinsed
4 tbsp olive oil
2 large onions, sliced
3 garlic cloves, chopped
400 g/14 oz can chopped tomatoes
1 tsp dried oregano
1 tsp tomato purée (paste)
900 ml/1½ pints/3½ cups water
75 g/3 oz/¾ cup small pasta shapes, such as fusilli or conchigliette
115 g/4 oz sun-dried tomatoes, drained and thinly sliced
1 tbsp chopped fresh coriander (cilantro), or flat leaf parsley
2 tbsp freshly grated Parmesan cheese
salt and pepper

1 Put the soaked beans into a large pan, cover with cold water and bring them to the boil. Boil rapidly for 15 minutes to remove any harmful toxins. Drain the beans in a colander.

2 Heat the oil in a pan over a medium heat and sauté the onions until they are just beginning to change colour. Stir in the garlic and cook for 1 minute. Stir in the chopped tomatoes, oregano and the tomato purée (paste) and add the water. Add the beans, bring to the boil and cover the pan. Simmer for about 45 minutes, or until the beans are almost tender.

3 Add the pasta, season with salt and pepper to taste and stir in the sun-dried tomatoes. Bring the soup back to the boil, partly cover the pan, lower the heat and cook for 10 minutes, or until the pasta is tender, but still firm to the bite.

4 Stir in the coriander (cilantro) or parsley. Adjust the seasoning if necessary. Transfer to a warmed soup tureen, sprinkle with the grated Parmesan cheese and serve hot.

Brown Lentil Soup with Pasta

In Italy, this soup is called Minestrade Lentiche. A minestra is a soup cooked with pasta; in this case farfalline, a small bow-shaped variety, is used.

Serves 4
115 g/4 oz/³⁄₄ cup diced pancetta or bacon
1 onion, chopped
2 garlic cloves, crushed
2 celery sticks, chopped
50 g/2 oz/¹⁄₂ cup farfalline or spaghetti broken into small pieces
420 g/14¹⁄₂ oz can brown lentils, drained
1.2 litres/2 pints/5 cups hot ham or vegetable stock
2 tbsp chopped, fresh mint

1 Place the pancetta or bacon in a large frying pan (skillet), together with the onions, garlic and celery. Dry-fry for 4–5 minutes, stirring, until the onion is soft and the pancetta or bacon is just beginning to brown.

2 Add the farfalline or spaghetti pieces to the pan (skillet) and cook, for about 1 minute, stirring to coat the pasta in the fat.

3 Add the lentils and the stock and bring to the boil. Reduce the heat and simmer for 12–15 minutes, or until the pasta is tender, but still firm to the bite.

4 Remove the pan (skillet) from the heat and stir in the chopped mint.

5 Transfer the soup to warm soup bowls and serve immediately.

COOK'S TIP

If you prefer to use dried lentils, add the stock before the pasta and cook for 1–1¼ hours, until the lentils are tender. Add the pasta and cook for a further 12–15 minutes.

COOK'S VARIATION

Any small variety of pasta can be used in this recipe, try fusilli, conchiglie or rigatoni, if you prefer. For serving children, you could add alphabet and numerals pasta.

Cream of Artichoke Soup

A creamy soup with the unique, subtle flavouring of Jerusalem artichokes
and a garnish of grated carrots for extra crunch.

Serves 4–6

675 g/1¹/₂ lb Jerusalem artichokes
1 lemon, sliced thickly
50 g/2 oz/4 tbsp butter or margarine
2 onions, chopped
1 garlic clove, crushed
1.25 litres/2¹/₄ pints/5¹/₂ cups chicken or vegetable stock
2 bay leaves
¹/₄ tsp ground mace or ground nutmeg
1 tbsp lemon juice
150 ml/¹/₄ pint/²/₃ cup single (light) cream or natural fromage frais
salt and pepper

GARNISH

coarsely grated carrot

chopped fresh parsley or coriander (cilantro)

1 Peel and slice the artichokes. Put them into a bowl of water with the lemon slices to prevent them from discolouring.

2 Melt the butter or margarine in a large pan. Add the onions and garlic and sauté over a low heat for 3–4 minutes, until soft.

3 Drain the artichokes and add to the pan. Mix well and sauté gently for 2–3 minutes without allowing them to colour.

4 Add the stock, bay leaves, mace or nutmeg and lemon juice and season to taste with salt and pepper. Bring to the boil, then cover and simmer gently for about 30 minutes until the vegetables are very tender.

5 Discard the bay leaves. Cool the soup slightly, then rub through a strainer or process in a food processor until smooth.

6 Pour into a clean pan and bring to the boil. Adjust the seasoning if necessary and stir in the cream or fromage frais. Reheat gently without boiling. Transfer to a warm tureen, garnish with grated carrot and parsley or coriander (cilantro).

Creamy Tomato Soup

This quick and easy creamy soup has a lovely fresh tomato flavour and a delicious aroma. Served on winter evenings, it will evoke the warm Italian sunshine.

Serves 4
50 g/2 oz/4 tbsp butter
700 g/1 lb 9 oz ripe tomatoes, preferably plum, roughly chopped
900 ml/1$\frac{1}{2}$ pints/ 3$\frac{3}{4}$ cups hot vegetable stock
150 ml/ $\frac{1}{4}$ pint/$\frac{2}{3}$ cup milk or single (light) cream
50 g/2 oz/$\frac{1}{2}$ cup ground almonds
1 tsp sugar
2 tbsp shredded basil leaves
salt and pepper

1 Melt the butter in a large saucepan. Add the tomatoes and cook over a medium heat for 5 minutes, until the skins start to wrinkle. Season to taste with salt and pepper.

2 Add the stock to the pan, bring to the boil, cover and simmer for 10 minutes.

3 Meanwhile, under a preheated grill (broiler), lightly toast the ground almonds until they are golden brown. This will take only 1–2 minutes, so watch them closely.

4 Remove the pan from the heat. Transfer the soup to a food processor and process the mixture to a smooth consistency. Alternatively, thoroughly mash the tomato mixture with a potato masher.

5 Rub the soup through a fine strainer to remove any pieces of tomato skin or seeds.

6 Return the soup to the pan and return it to the heat. Stir in the milk or single (light) cream, ground almonds and sugar. Warm the soup through, but do not boil. Add the shredded basil, transfer the soup to a warm soup tureen or individual bowls and serve hot.

COOK'S VARIATION

Very fine breadcrumbs can be used instead of the ground almonds, if you prefer. Toast them in the same way as the almonds and add with the milk or cream in step 6.

Tuscan Onion Soup

This soup is best made with white onions, which have a milder flavour.
If you cannot get hold of them, try using large Spanish onions instead.

Serves 4
50 g/2 oz/²/₃ cup diced pancetta
1 tbsp olive oil
4 large white onions, thinly sliced and pushed out into rings
3 garlic cloves, chopped
1 litre/1³/₄ pints/3³/₄ cups hot chicken or ham stock
4 slices ciabatta or other Italian bread
50 g/2 oz/4 tbsp butter
75 g/3 oz/³/₄ cup grated Gruyère (Swiss) or Cheddar cheese
salt and pepper

1 Dry-fry the pancetta in a large saucepan for 3–4 minutes, until it begins to brown and the fat runs. Remove the pancetta from the pan and set aside until it is required.

2 Add the olive oil to the pan and cook the onions and garlic over a high heat, stirring frequently, for about 4 minutes. Reduce the heat, cover and cook for 15 minutes, until they are lightly caramelized.

3 Add the chicken or ham stock to the saucepan and bring to the boil. Reduce the heat, cover and simmer for about 10 minutes.

4 Meanwhile, toast the slices of ciabatta or other bread on both sides, under a preheated grill (broiler), for 2–3 minutes, or until golden and crisp. Spread the toasted bread with butter and top with the Gruyère (Swiss) or Cheddar cheese. Cut the bread into bite-size pieces.

5 Add the reserved pancetta to the soup and season to taste with salt and pepper. Pour into 4 warm individual soup bowls, top with the toasted bread and serve immediately.

COOK'S TIP

Pancetta is similar to bacon, but it is air- and salt-cured for about 6 months. Pancetta is available from most delicatessens and some large supermarkets. If you cannot obtain pancetta, use unsmoked bacon instead.

Mussels in White Wine

This soup of mussels cooked in white wine with onions and cream
can be served as an appetizer or a main dish, with plenty of crusty bread.

Serves 4
675 g/1¹/₂ lb fresh mussels
50 g/2 oz/¹/₄ cup butter
1 large onion, very finely chopped
2–3 garlic cloves, crushed
350 ml/12 fl oz/1¹/₂ cups dry white wine
150 ml/¹/₄ pint/²/₃ cup water
2 tbsp lemon juice
pinch of finely grated lemon rind
1 bouquet garni sachet
1 tbsp plain (all-purpose) flour
4 tbsp single (light) or double (heavy) cream
2–3 tbsp chopped fresh parsley
salt and pepper
warm crusty bread, to serve

1 Scrub the mussels in several changes of cold water to remove all mud, sand, grit and barnacles. Pull off all the 'beards'. Discard any that have damaged shells or that do not shut immediately when sharply tapped with the back of a knife.

2 Melt half the butter in a large saucepan. Add the onion and garlic, and sauté over a medium heat until soft, but not coloured.

3 Add the wine, water, lemon juice and rind, bouquet garni and plenty of seasoning. Bring to the boil, then cover and simmer for 4–5 minutes.

4 Add the mussels to the pan, cover tightly and simmer, shaking the pan frequently, for 5–6 minutes, or until all the mussels have opened. Discard any mussels that remain closed. Remove and discard the bouquet garni.

5 Remove and discard the empty half shell from each mussel. Blend the remaining butter with the flour and beat it into the soup, a little at a time. Simmer gently for 2–3 minutes until slightly thickened.

6 Add the cream and half the parsley to the soup and reheat gently, without boiling. Adjust the seasoning, if necessary. Ladle the mussels and soup into warm, large individual soup bowls, sprinkle with the remaining parsley and serve with plenty of warm crusty bread.

Fish Soup

There are many varieties of fish soup in Italy, some including shellfish.
This one, from Tuscany, is more like a chowder.

Serves 4–6
1 kg/2 lb assorted prepared fish (including mixed fish fillets, squid, etc)
2 onions, thinly sliced
2 celery sticks, thinly sliced
a few sprigs of parsley
2 bay leaves
150 ml/$^1/_4$ pint/$^2/_3$ cup white wine
1 litre/1$^3/_4$ pints/4 cups water
2 tbsp olive oil
1 garlic clove, crushed
1 carrot, finely chopped
400 g/14 oz can peeled tomatoes, puréed
2 potatoes, chopped
1 tbsp tomato purée (paste)
1 tsp chopped fresh oregano or $^1/_2$ tsp dried oregano
350 g/12 oz fresh mussels
175 g/6 oz peeled prawns (shrimp)
2 tbsp chopped fresh parsley
salt and pepper
crusty bread, to serve

1 Cut the cleaned and prepared fish into slices or cubes and put into a large saucepan with half the onion and celery, the parsley sprigs, bay leaves, wine and water. Bring to the boil, then cover and simmer for about 25 minutes.

2 Strain the fish stock and discard the vegetables. Skin the fish, remove any bones and set aside.

3 Heat the oil in a pan. Finely chop the remaining onion and sauté with the garlic, carrot and remaining celery until soft, but not coloured. Add the

puréed canned tomatoes, potatoes, tomato purée (paste), oregano and reserved stock and season to taste with salt and pepper. Bring to the boil, lower the heat and and simmer for about 15 minutes, or until the potatoes are almost tender.

4 Scrub and debeard the mussels. Add to the pan with the prawns (shrimp) and simmer for about 5 minutes, or until the mussels have opened (discard any that stay closed).

5 Add the reserved fish to the soup, together with the chopped parsley. Bring back to the boil and simmer for 5 minutes. Adjust the seasoning if necessary.

6 Serve the soup in warm individual bowls with chunks of fresh crusty bread, or put a toasted slice of crusty bread in the bottom of each bowl before adding the soup. If possible, remove a few half shells from the mussels before serving.

Orange, Thyme & Pumpkin Soup

This thick, creamy soup has a wonderful, warming
golden colour. It is flavoured with orange and thyme.

Serves 4
2 tbsp olive oil
2 medium onions, chopped
2 cloves garlic, chopped
900 g/2 lb pumpkin, peeled and cut into 2.5-cm/1-inch chunks
1.5 litres /2³/₄ pints/6¹/₄ cups boiling vegetable or chicken stock
finely grated rind and juice of 1 orange
3 tbsp fresh thyme, stalks removed
150 ml/¹/₄ pint/²/₃ cup milk
salt and pepper
crusty bread, to serve

1 Heat the olive oil in a large
saucepan. Add the onions to the pan
and sauté for 3–4 minutes, or until
softened. Add the garlic and pumpkin
and cook, stirring constantly, for a
further 2 minutes.

2 Add the boiling vegetable or
chicken stock, orange rind and juice
and 2 tablespoons of the thyme to the
pan. Lower the heat, cover and
simmer for 20 minutes, or until the
pumpkin is tender.

3 Place the mixture in a food
processor and process until smooth.
Alternatively, mash the mixture with
a potato masher until smooth. Season
to taste with salt and pepper.

4 Return the soup to the saucepan
and add the milk. Reheat the soup for
3–4 minutes, or until it is piping hot
but not boiling. Sprinkle with the

remaining fresh thyme just before
serving.

5 Ladle the soup into 4 warm
individual soup bowls and serve with
lots of fresh crusty bread.

COOK'S TIP

Pumpkins are usually large
vegetables. To make things a little
easier, ask the greengrocer to cut a
chunk off for you. Alternatively,
make double the quantity and
freeze the soup for up to 3 months.

Calabrian Mushroom Soup

The Calabrian Mountains in southern Italy provide masses of wild mushrooms.
They are rich in flavour and colour and make a wonderful soup.

Serves 4
2 tbsp olive oil
1 onion, chopped
450g/1 lb mixed mushrooms, such as porcini, oyster and button
300 ml/$^1/_2$ pint/1$^1/_4$ cups milk
850 ml/1$^1/_2$ pints/3$^3/_4$ cups hot vegetable stock
8 slices of rustic bread or French bread
50 g/2 oz/4 tbsp butter, melted
2 garlic cloves, crushed
75 g/3 oz/$^3/_4$ cup finely grated Gruyère (Swiss) cheese,
salt and pepper

1 Heat the oil in a large frying pan (skillet) and cook the onion for 3–4 minutes, or until soft and golden.

2 Wipe the mushrooms with a damp cloth and cut any large mushrooms into smaller, bite-size pieces.

3 Add the mushrooms to the frying pan (skillet), stirring quickly to coat them in the oil.

4 Add the milk to the pan, bring to the boil, cover and simmer for about 5 minutes. Gradually stir in the hot vegetable stock.

5 Under a preheated grill (broiler), toast the bread on both sides until golden and crisp.

6 Mix together the garlic and butter and spoon generously over the toast.

7 Place the toast in the bottom of a large tureen or divide it among 4 warm individual serving bowls and pour in the hot soup. Top with the grated Gruyère (Swiss) cheese and serve at once.

COOK'S TIP

Mushrooms absorb liquid, which can lessen the flavour and affect cooking properties. Wipe them with a damp cloth rather than rinsing them in water.

Pasta Dishes

Pasta is economical, nourishing and versatile, as it goes with virtually everything from fish and seafood to meat and poultry, and from vegetables and mushrooms to cheese and cream. There is a pasta sauce to suit all tastes, most of them very quick and easy to prepare. Dishes may be as simple and inexpensive as Spaghetti Carbonara or Spaghetti with Tuna & Parsley

Sauce, or they may be special enough for a celebration, such as home-made Tortellini or Pasta Shells with Mussels. Serve

pasta as a first course as the Italians do, or in a larger quantity for a main course.

The recipes in this chapter suggest a type of pasta for each dish, but you can substitute your own favourites. It is best to use long ribbons, such as fettucine or tagliatelle, for oil- and tomato-based sauces and chunkier pasta, such as penne or fusilli, for meat sauces.

Spicy Tomato Tagliatelle

A deliciously fresh and slightly spicy tomato sauce which is excellent for lunch or a light supper. You could top any long pasta, such as spaghetti, tagliarini or fettuccine, with this sauce.

Serves 4
50 g/2 oz/4 tbsp butter
1 onion, finely chopped
1 garlic clove, crushed
2 small red chillies, seeded and diced
450 g/1 lb fresh tomatoes, peeled, seeded and diced
200 ml/7 fl oz/$^3/_4$ cup vegetable stock
2 tbsp tomato purée (paste)
1 tsp sugar
salt and pepper
675 g/1$^1/_2$ lb fresh green and white tagliatelle, or 350 g/12 oz dried

1 Melt the butter in a large saucepan. Add the onion and garlic and sauté for 3–4 minutes, or until softened.

2 Add the chillies to the pan and continue cooking for about 2 minutes.

3 Add the tomatoes and stock, reduce the heat and simmer, stirring frequently, for 10 minutes.

4 Pour the sauce into a food processor and process for 1 minute, until smooth. Alternatively, rub the sauce through a strainer.

5 Return the sauce to the pan and add the tomato purée (paste) and sugar and season to taste with salt and pepper. Gently reheat over a low heat, until piping hot.

6 Cook the tagliatelle in a pan of lightly salted boiling water for about 2–3 minutes if fresh or for about

8–12 minutes if dried, until it is tender, but still firm to the bite. Drain the tagliatelle thoroughly,

7 Transfer to serving plates, top with the tomato sauce and serve immediately.

COOK'S VARIATION

Try topping your pasta dish with 50 g/2 oz/$^1/_3$ cup diced pancetta or unsmoked bacon, dry-fried for 5 minutes until crispy.

Spaghetti Carbonara

Ensure all the cooked ingredients are as hot as possible,
so that the beaten eggs are cooked on contact.
Serve this classic dish with a flourish.

Serves 4
400 g/14 oz dried spaghetti
2 tbsp olive oil
1 large onion, thinly sliced
2 garlic cloves, chopped
175 g/6 oz bacon slices, rind removed, cut into thin strips
25 g/1 oz/2 tbsp butter
175 g/6 oz mushrooms, thinly sliced
300 ml/½ pint/1¼ cups double (heavy) cream
3 eggs, beaten
75 g/3 oz/1 cup grated Parmesan cheese, plus extra to serve (optional)
freshly ground black pepper
sprigs of sage, to garnish

1 Heat a large serving dish. Cook the spaghetti in a large pan of boiling salted water, adding 1 tablespoon of the oil. When the pasta is tender, but still firm to the bite, drain it. Return it to the pan, cover and keep warm.

2 While the spaghetti is cooking, heat the remaining oil in a frying pan (skillet) over a medium heat. Fry the onion until it is translucent, then add the garlic and bacon and fry until the bacon is crisp.

3 Remove the onion, garlic and bacon with a slotted spoon, set aside and keep warm. Melt the butter in the pan and sauté the mushrooms for 3–4 minutes, stirring occasionally. Return the bacon mixture to the pan and mix with the mushrooms. Cover and keep warm.

4 Stir together the cream, the beaten eggs and Parmesan cheese, and season to taste with salt and pepper.

5 Working very quickly to avoid cooling the cooked ingredients, tip the spaghetti into the bacon and mushroom mixture and pour the egg mixture on top. Toss the spaghetti quickly, using two forks. Transfer to the heated dish and serve at once with extra grated Parmesan if desired.

Basil & Tomato Pasta

Roasting the tomatoes produces a sweeter and smoother flavour
to this sauce. Try to buy Italian tomatoes, such as plum or flavia,
as these have a better flavour and colour.

Serves 4
1 tbsp olive oil
2 sprigs rosemary
2 garlic cloves, unpeeled
450 g/1 lb tomatoes, halved
1 tbsp sun-dried tomato paste
12 fresh basil leaves, plus extra to garnish
salt and pepper
675 g/1½ lb fresh farfalle or 350 g/12 oz dried farfalle

1 Place the oil, rosemary, garlic and
tomatoes, skin side up, in a shallow
roasting tin (pan).

2 Drizzle with a little oil and cook
under a preheated grill (broiler) for
20 minutes, or until the tomato skins
are slightly charred.

3 Peel the tomatoes. Roughly chop
the tomato flesh and place in a pan.

4 Squeeze the pulp from the garlic
cloves and mix with the tomato flesh
and sun-dried tomato paste.

5 Roughly tear the fresh basil leaves
into smaller pieces and then stir them
into the sauce. Season with a little
salt and pepper to taste.

6 Cook the farfalle in a saucepan of
boiling salted water until it is tender,
but still firm to the bite. Drain.

7 Place the pan of tomato and basil
sauce over a low heat until it is
warmed through.

8 Transfer the farfalle to warm
serving plates and serve immediately
with the basil and tomato sauce.

COOK'S TIP

This sauce tastes just as good when
served cold in a pasta salad.

Tagliatelle with Chicken Sauce

Spinach ribbon noodles covered with a rich tomato sauce
and topped with creamy chicken makes a very appetizing dish,
which is also quick and easy to prepare.

Serves 4
Basic Tomato Sauce (see page 17)
250 g/8 oz fresh green ribbon noodles
1 tbsp olive oil
salt
basil leaves, to garnish

CHICKEN SAUCE

50 g/2 oz/$^{1}/_{4}$ cup unsalted (sweet) butter
400 g/14 oz boneless, skinless chicken breasts, cut into thin strips
75 g/3 oz/$^{3}/_{4}$ cup blanched almonds
300 ml/$^{1}/_{2}$ pint/1$^{1}/_{4}$ cups double (heavy) cream
salt and pepper
basil leaves, to garnish

1 First make the tomato sauce, set aside and keep warm.

2 To make the chicken sauce, melt the butter in a pan over a medium heat and fry the chicken strips and almonds, stirring frequently, for 5–6 minutes, until the chicken is cooked through.

3 Meanwhile, pour the cream into a small pan set over a low heat, bring to the boil and boil for about 10 minutes, until reduced by almost half. Pour the cream over the chicken and almonds, stir well, and season. Set aside and keep warm.

4 Cook the pasta in a large pan of boiling salted water, first adding the oil. When the pasta is tender, but still firm to the bite, drain, then return it to the pan, cover and keep warm.

5 Turn the pasta into a warmed serving dish and spoon the tomato sauce over it.

6 Spoon the chicken and cream sauce over the centre, scatter the basil leaves on top and serve at once.

COOK'S VARIATION

This dish would work equally
well with a turkey breast,
pork tenderloin or veal
cream sauce.

Spaghetti Bolognese

This familiar meat sauce, known as ragù, may also be used in lasagne,
and in other baked dishes. It can be made in large quantities and frozen.

Serves 4
400 g/14 oz dried spaghetti
1 tbsp olive oil
salt
15 g/½ oz/1 tbsp butter
2 tbsp chopped fresh parsley, to garnish
RAGÙ
3 tbsp olive oil
40 g/1½ oz/3 tbsp butter
2 large onions, chopped
4 celery sticks, thinly sliced
175 g/6 oz/1 cup finely diced bacon
2 garlic cloves, chopped
500 g/1¼ lb minced (ground) lean beef
2 tbsp tomato purée (paste)
1 tbsp plain (all-purpose) flour
400 g/14 oz can chopped tomatoes
150 ml/¼ pint/⅔ cup beef stock
150 ml/¼ pint/⅔ cup red wine
2 tsp dried oregano
½ tsp freshly grated nutmeg
salt and pepper

1 To make the ragù: heat the oil and the butter in a large frying pan (skillet) over a medium heat. Add the onions, celery and bacon and fry for 5 minutes, stirring once or twice.

2 Stir in the garlic and minced (ground) beef and cook, stirring, until the meat has broken up and lost its redness. Lower the heat and continue cooking for a further 10 minutes, stirring once or twice.

3 Increase the heat to medium, stir in the tomato purée (paste) and the flour and cook for 1–2 minutes, stirring constantly. Stir in the chopped tomatoes, beef stock and wine and bring to the boil, stirring constantly. Season with salt and pepper to taste and stir in the oregano and nutmeg. Cover the pan and simmer for 45 minutes, stirring occasionally.

4 Cook the spaghetti in a large pan of boiling salted water, adding the olive oil. When it is tender, but still firm to the bite, drain in a colander, then return to the pan. Dot the spaghetti with the butter and toss thoroughly, using 2 forks.

5 Taste the sauce and adjust the seasoning if necessary. Pour the sauce over the spaghetti and toss well. Sprinkle with the parsley, transfer to a serving dish and serve immediately.

Tortellini

According to legend, the shape of the tortellini resembles
Venus's navel. When you make tortellini you will know what they should look like!

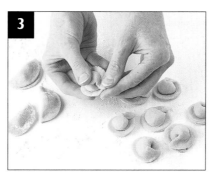

Serves 4
Basic Pasta Dough (see page 15)

FILLING

115 g/4 oz boneless skinless chicken breast
50 g/2 oz Parma ham (prosciutto)
40 g/1 1/2 oz cooked spinach, well drained
1 tbsp finely chopped onion
2 tbsp freshly grated Parmesan cheese
pinch of ground allspice
1 egg, beaten
salt and pepper

SAUCE

300 ml/1/2 pint/1 1/4 cups single (light) cream
1–2 garlic cloves, crushed
115 g/4 oz button mushrooms, thinly sliced
4 tbsp freshly grated Parmesan cheese
1–2 tbsp chopped fresh parsley

1 Poach the chicken in well-seasoned water for about 10 minutes, until tender. Drain and chop roughly. When cool put it into a food processor with the Parma ham (prosciutto), spinach and onion and process until finely chopped. Stir in the Parmesan cheese, allspice, seasonings and egg.

2 Roll out the pasta dough, half at a time, on a lightly floured surface. Cut into 4–5 cm/1 1/2–2 inch rounds using a plain cutter.

3 Place 1/2 teaspoon of the filling in the centre of each dough round, fold the pieces in half to make a semi-

circle and press the edges firmly together. Wrap one semi-circle around your index finger and cross over the two ends, pressing firmly together, curling the rest of the dough backwards to make a 'tummy button' shape. Slip the tortellini off your finger and lay on a lightly floured tray. Repeat with the remaining dough semi-circles. Re-roll the trimmings and use to make more tortellini until the filling is used up.

4 Heat a large pan of salted boiling water and add a few tortellini. Bring back to the boil and once they rise to

the surface, cook for about 5 minutes, giving an occasional stir. Remove with a slotted spoon and drain on kitchen paper (paper towels). Keep warm in a dish while cooking the remainder.

5 To make the sauce, heat the cream with the garlic in a pan and bring to the boil. Simmer for a few minutes. Add the mushrooms and half the Parmesan and season to taste. Simmer for 2–3 minutes. Stir in the parsley and pour the sauce over the warm tortellini. Sprinkle the tortellini with the remaining Parmesan cheese and serve immediately.

Tortelloni

These tasty little squares of pasta stuffed with mushrooms
and cheese are surprisingly filling. Serve about 3 pieces
for a starter and up to 9 for a main course.

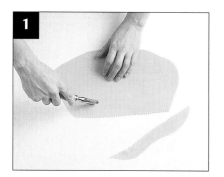

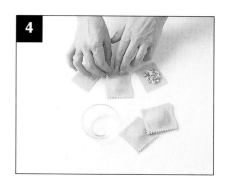

Makes 36 Pieces
about 300 g/11 oz Basic Pasta Dough (see page 15), rolled out to thin sheets
75 g/3 oz/6 tbsp butter
50 g/2 oz shallots, finely chopped
3 garlic cloves, crushed
50 g/2 oz mushrooms, wiped and finely chopped
1/2 celery stick, finely chopped
25 g/1 oz/1/3 cup finely grated pecorino cheese, plus extra, to garnish
1 tbsp oil
salt and pepper

1 Using a serrated pasta cutter, cut
5-cm/2-inch squares from the sheets
of fresh pasta. To make 36 tortelloni
you will need 72 squares. Once the
pasta is cut, cover the squares with
cling film (plastic wrap) to stop them
from drying out.

2 Heat 25 g/1 oz/2 tbsp of the butter
in a frying pan (skillet). Add the
shallots, 1 crushed garlic clove, the
mushrooms and celery and cook for
4–5 minutes.

3 Remove the pan from the heat, stir
in the cheese and season to taste with
salt and pepper.

4 Spoon 1/2 teaspoon of the mixture
on to the middle of each of 36 pasta
squares. Brush the edges of the
squares with water and top with the
remaining 36 squares. Press the edges
together to seal. Set aside to rest for
5 minutes.

5 Bring a large pan of lightly salted
water to the boil, add the oil and cook
the tortelloni, in batches, for
2–3 minutes. The tortelloni will rise to
the surface when cooked and the
pasta should be tender but still firm to
the bite. Remove from the pan with a
slotted spoon, drain thoroughly and
keep warm.

6 Meanwhile, melt the remaining
butter in a pan. Add the remaining
garlic and plenty of pepper and cook
for 1–2 minutes.

7 Transfer the tortelloni to serving
plates and pour the garlic butter over
them. Garnish with grated pecorino
cheese and serve immediately.

Tagliatelle with Meatballs

There is an appetizing contrast of textures and flavours
in this satisfying family dish, which must be one of the most
famous of Italian recipes.

Serves 4
500 g/1¼ lb minced (ground) lean beef
50 g/2 oz/1 cup soft white breadcrumbs
1 garlic clove, crushed
2 tbsp chopped fresh parsley
1 tsp dried oregano
pinch of freshly grated nutmeg
¼ tsp ground coriander
50 g/2 oz/⅔ cup grated Parmesan cheese
2–3 tbsp milk
flour, for dusting
4 tbsp olive oil
400 g/14 oz tagliatelli
25 g/1 oz/2 tbsp butter, diced
salt
2 tbsp chopped fresh parsley, to garnish
green salad, to serve
SAUCE
3 tbsp olive oil
2 large onions, sliced
2 celery stalks, thinly sliced
2 garlic cloves, chopped
400 g/14 oz can chopped tomatoes
125 g/4 oz bottled sun-dried tomatoes, drained and chopped
2 tbsp tomato purée (paste)
1 tbsp dark muscovado sugar
150 ml/¼ pint/⅔ cup white wine, or water
salt and pepper

1 To make the sauce, heat the oil in a frying pan (skillet), add the onion and celery and sauté until translucent. Add the garlic and cook for 1 minute. Stir in the tomatoes, tomato purée (paste), sugar and wine, and season to taste with salt and pepper. Bring to the boil and simmer for 10 minutes.

2 Break up the meat in a bowl with a wooden spoon until it becomes a sticky paste. Stir in the breadcrumbs, garlic, herbs and spices. Stir in the cheese and enough milk to make a firm paste. Dust your hands with flour, take large spoonfuls of the mixture and shape it into 12 balls. Heat the oil in a frying pan (skillet), add the meatballs and fry for 5–6 minutes, until browned all over.

3 Pour the tomato sauce over the meatballs. Lower the heat, cover the pan and simmer for 30 minutes, turning once or twice. Add a little extra water if the sauce begins to dry.

4 Cook the pasta in a saucepan of boiling salted water, with the remaining oil. When tender, but still firm to the bite, drain, turn into a warm serving dish, dot with the butter and toss. Spoon the meatballs and sauce over the pasta and sprinkle on the parsley. Serve with a green salad.

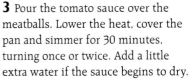

Warm Pasta with Basil Vinaigrette

Sun-dried tomatoes and olives enhance this delicious
pesto-inspired salad, which is just as tasty served cold.

Serves 4–6

250 g/8 oz dried pasta spirals
4 tomatoes, peeled
50 g/2 oz/⅓ cup black olives
25 g/1 oz/¼ cup sun-dried tomatoes
2 tbsp pine nuts, toasted
2 tbsp Parmesan shavings
sprig fresh basil, to garnish

BASIL VINAIGRETTE

4 tbsp chopped fresh basil
1 garlic clove, crushed
2 tbsp freshly grated Parmesan cheese
4 tbsp olive oil
2 tbsp lemon juice
pepper

1 Cook the pasta in boiling salted
water for 10–12 minutes, until tender,
but still firm to the bite. Drain and
rinse in hot water, then drain again.

2 To make the vinaigrette, beat
together the basil, garlic, Parmesan
cheese, olive oil, lemon juice and
pepper to taste until well blended.

3 Put the pasta into a bowl, pour the
basil vinaigrette over it and toss well.

4 Cut the tomatoes into wedges.
Halve and pit the olives and slice the
sun-dried tomatoes.

5 Add the tomatoes, olives and sun-
dried tomatoes to the pasta and mix
thoroughly. Transfer to a salad bowl
and scatter the nuts and Parmesan
shavings over the top. Serve warm,
garnished with a sprig of basil.

Lasagne Verde

The sauce in this delicious baked pasta dish is the same sauce
that is served with Spaghetti Bolognese (page 84).

Serves 6
Ragù (see page 84)
1 tbsp olive oil
250 g/9 oz lasagne verde
50 g/2 oz/¹/₃ cup grated Parmesan cheese
Béchamel Sauce (see page 17)
salt and pepper
green salad, tomato salad or black olives, to serve

1 Begin by making the ragù as
described on page 84. Cook, in an
uncovered pan, for 10–12 minutes
longer than the time given to allow
the excess liquid to evaporate. To
layer the sauce with lasagne, it needs
to be reduced to the consistency of a
thick paste.

2 Have ready a large pan of boiling,
salted water and add the olive oil.
Drop the pasta sheets into the boiling
water a few at a time, and return the
water to the boil before adding
further pasta sheets. If you are using
fresh lasagne, cook the sheets for a
total of 8 minutes. If you are using
dried or partly precooked pasta, cook
it according to the instructions given
on the packet.

3 Remove the pasta sheets from the
pan with a slotted spoon. Spread
them in a single layer on damp tea
towels (dish cloths).

4 Grease a rectangular ovenproof
dish, about 25–28 cm/10–11 inches
long. Spoon a little of the meat sauce
into the base of the prepared dish,

cover with a layer of lasagne, then
spoon a little Béchamel Sauce on top
and sprinkle some of the cheese over
it. Continue making layers in this way
until all the ingredients are used up,
ending with a layer of lasagne covered
with the Béchamel Sauce.

5 Sprinkle the remaining cheese on
top and bake in a preheated oven at
190°C/375°F/Gas Mark 5, for 40 minutes,
until the sauce is golden brown and
bubbling. Serve immediately, straight
from the dish with a green salad, a
tomato salad, or a bowl of black olives.

Courgette (Zucchini) & Aubergine (Eggplant) Lasagne

This rich, baked pasta dish is packed full of vegetables, tomatoes and Italian mozzarella cheese.

Serves 6
1 kg/2¼ lb aubergines (eggplants)
4 tbsp salt
8 tbsp olive oil
25 g/1 oz/2 tbsp garlic and herb butter or margarine
500 g/1¼ lb courgettes (zucchini), sliced
250 g/8 oz/2 cups grated mozzarella cheese
600 ml/1 pint/2½ cups passata (sieved tomatoes)
6 sheets pre-cooked green lasagne
600 ml/1 pint/2½ cups Béchamel Sauce (see page 17)
50 g/2 oz/⅔ cup grated Parmesan cheese
1 tsp dried oregano
black pepper

1 Thinly slice the aubergines (eggplants). Layer the slices in a bowl, sprinkling with the salt as you go. Set aside for 30 minutes. Rinse well in cold water and pat dry with kitchen paper (paper towels).

2 Heat 4 tablespoons of the oil in a large frying pan (skillet) until very hot and gently fry half the aubergine (eggplant) slices for 6–7 minutes until lightly golden all over. Drain on kitchen paper (paper towels). Repeat with the remaining aubergine (eggplant) slices and remaining oil.

3 Melt the garlic and herb butter or margarine in the frying pan (skillet) and fry the courgettes (zucchini) for 5–6 minutes until golden. Drain on kitchen paper (paper towels).

4 Place half the aubergine (eggplant) and half the courgette (zucchini) slices in a large ovenproof dish. Season with pepper and sprinkle in half of the mozzarella cheese. Spoon half of the passata (sieved tomatoes) on top and cover with three sheets of lasagne.

5 Arrange the remaining aubergine (eggplant) and courgette (zucchini) slices on top. Season with pepper and top with the remaining mozzarella cheese, passata (sieved tomatoes) and another layer of lasagne.

6 Spoon the Béchamel sauce on top to cover the lasagne. Sprinkle it with Parmesan and oregano. Put on a baking tray (cookie sheet) and bake in a preheated oven at 220°C/425°F/ Gas Mark 7, for 30–35 minutes, until golden. Serve immediately.

Stuffed Cannelloni

Cannelloni, the thick round pasta tubes, make perfect containers
for close-textured sauces of all kinds. Fillings vary from one region of Italy to another
and from season to season.

Serves 4
8 cannelloni tubes
1 tbsp olive oil
fresh herb sprigs, to garnish

FILLING
25 g/1 oz/2 tbsp butter
300 g/10 oz frozen spinach, thawed and chopped
115 g/4 oz/$^1\!/_2$ cup ricotta
25 g/1 oz/$^1\!/_3$ cup grated Parmesan cheese
50 g/2 oz/$^1\!/_3$ cup chopped ham
$^1\!/_4$ tsp freshly grated nutmeg
2 tbsp double (heavy) cream
2 eggs, lightly beaten
salt and pepper

SAUCE
25 g/1 oz/2 tbsp butter
25 g/1 oz/$^1\!/_4$ cup plain (all-purpose) flour
300 ml/$^1\!/_2$ pint/1$^1\!/_4$ cups milk
2 bay leaves
pinch of grated nutmeg
25 g/1 oz /$^1\!/_3$ cup grated Parmesan cheese

1 To prepare the filling, melt the butter in a pan and stir in the spinach. Stir for 2–3 minutes to allow the moisture to evaporate, then remove the pan from the heat. Stir in the ricotta, Parmesan and the ham. Season with nutmeg, and salt and pepper. Beat in the cream and eggs to make a thick paste. Set aside to cool.

2 Cook the cannelloni in a large pan of boiling salted water, adding the olive oil, for 10–12 minutes, until tender, but still firm to the bite. Drain in a colander and set aside to cool.

3 To make the sauce, melt the butter in a pan, stir in the flour and cook, stirring, for 2 minutes. Gradually stir in the milk. Add the bay leaves, bring to simmering point and cook for 5 minutes. Season with nutmeg, salt and pepper. Remove the pan from the heat. Discard the bay leaves.

4 Spoon the filling into a piping (pastry) bag and pipe it into each of the cannelloni tubes.

5 Spoon a little of the sauce into the base of a large shallow ovenproof dish. Arrange the cannelloni in a single layer, then pour the remaining sauce on top. Sprinkle it with the remaining Parmesan cheese and bake in a preheated oven at 190°C/375°F/Gas Mark 5, for 40–45 minutes, until the sauce is golden brown and bubbling. Divide the cannelloni between 4 individual warm serving plates, garnish with fresh herb sprigs and serve.

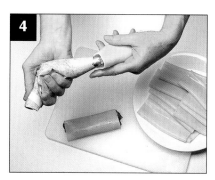

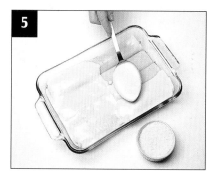

Layered Meat Loaf

The cheese-flavoured pasta layer comes as a pleasant surprise inside
this lightly spiced meat loaf.

Serves 6
25 g/1 oz/2 tbsp butter, plus extra for greasing
1 onion, finely chopped
1 small red (bell) pepper, seeded and chopped
1 garlic clove, chopped
500 g/1¼ lb minced (ground) lean beef
25 g/1 oz/½ cup soft white breadcrumbs
½ tsp cayenne pepper
1 tbsp lemon juice
½ tsp grated lemon rind
2 tbsp chopped fresh parsley
75 g/3 oz/1 cup dried short pasta, such as fusilli
4 bay leaves
1 tbsp olive oil
Cheese Sauce (see page 17)
175 g/6 oz bacon slices, rind removed
salt and pepper
salad leaves, to garnish

1 Melt the butter in a frying pan (skillet) over a medium heat, add the onion and (bell) pepper and sauté for about 3 minutes, until the onion is translucent. Stir in the garlic and sauté for 1 minute.

2 Put the minced (ground) beef into a large bowl and mash it with a wooden spoon until it becomes a sticky paste. Tip the sautéed vegetables into the bowl and stir in the breadcrumbs, cayenne pepper, lemon juice, lemon rind and chopped parsley. Season the mixture with salt and pepper to taste and set aside.

3 Cook the pasta in a large pan of boiling water to which you have added salt and the olive oil. When it is tender, but still firm to the bite, drain in a colander. Stir the pasta into the cheese sauce.

4 Grease a 1-kg/2-lb loaf tin (pan) with butter and arrange the bay leaves in the base. Stretch the bacon slices with the back of a knife blade and arrange them to line the base and the sides of the tin (pan).

5 Spoon in half the meat mixture, level the surface and cover with the pasta. Add the remaining meat mixture, level and cover with foil.

6 Cook the meat loaf in a preheated oven at 180°C/350°F/Gas Mark 4, for 1 hour, or until the juices run clear and the loaf has shrunk away from the sides of the tin (pan). Pour off any excess fat and turn the loaf out on to a warm serving dish. Garnish with the salad leaves and serve hot.

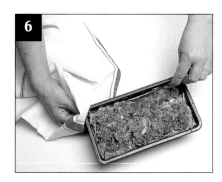

Aubergine (Eggplant) Cake

Layers of toasty-brown aubergine (eggplant), meat sauce and cheese-flavoured pasta make this a popular family supper dish.

Serves 4
1 aubergine (eggplant), thinly sliced
5 tbsp olive oil
250 g/9 oz/3 cups dried short pasta shapes, such as fusilli
50 g/2 oz/¹/₄ cup butter, plus extra for greasing
40 g/1¹/₂ oz/6 tbsp plain (all-purpose) flour
300 ml/¹/₂ pint/1¹/₄ cups milk
150 ml/¹/₄ pint/²/₃ cup single (light) cream
150 ml/¹/₄ pint/²/₃ cup chicken stock
large pinch of freshly grated nutmeg
75 g/3 oz/³/₄ cup grated mature (sharp) Cheddar
25 g/1 oz/¹/₃ cup grated Parmesan cheese
Lamb Sauce (see page 17)
salt and pepper
artichoke heart and tomato salad, to serve

4 Melt the butter in a small pan, stir in the flour and cook, stirring constantly, for 1 minute. Gradually pour in the milk, stirring all the time, then stir in the cream and chicken stock. Season with nutmeg, salt and pepper, bring to the boil and simmer for 5 minutes, stirring constantly. Stir in the Cheddar cheese and remove the pan from the heat. Pour half the sauce over the pasta and mix well. Reserve the remaining sauce.

5 Grease a shallow ovenproof dish. Spoon in half the pasta, cover it with half of the lamb sauce and then with the aubergine (eggplant) in a single layer. Repeat the layers of pasta and lamb sauce and spread the remaining cheese sauce over the top. Sprinkle the Parmesan over it. Bake in a preheated oven at 190°C/375°F/Gas Mark 5 for 25 minutes, until golden brown. Serve hot or cold, with artichoke heart and tomato salad.

1 Put the aubergine (eggplant) slices in a colander, sprinkle with salt and set aside for about 45 minutes. Rinse in cold, running water and drain. Pat dry with kitchen paper (paper towels).

2 Heat 4 tablespoons of the oil in a frying pan (skillet) over a medium heat. Fry the aubergine (eggplant) slices for about 4 minutes each side, until golden. Remove with a slotted spoon and drain on paper towels.

3 Meanwhile, cook the pasta in a large pan of boiling salted water, adding 1 tablespoon of olive oil. When the pasta is tender, but still firm to the bite, drain it and return to the pan. Cover and keep warm.

Basil & Pine Nut Pesto

Delicious stirred into pasta, soups and salad dressings, pesto is available in
most supermarkets, but making your own produces a much fresher, fuller flavour.

1
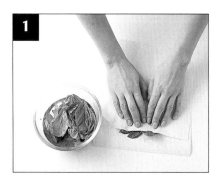

2

3

Serves 4
about 40 fresh basil leaves, washed and dried
3 garlic cloves, crushed
25 g/1 oz/$^1\!/_4$ cup pine nuts
50 g/2 oz/$^2\!/_3$ cup finely grated Parmesan cheese
2–3 tbsp extra virgin olive oil
salt and pepper
675 g/1$^1\!/_2$ lb fresh pasta or 350 g/12 oz dried pasta

COOK'S TIP

You can store pesto in the
refrigerator for about 4 weeks.
Cover the surface of the pesto
with olive oil before sealing the
container or bottle, to prevent
the basil from oxidizing and
turning black.

COOK'S VARIATION

You could try making a walnut
pesto instead of this basil and pine
nut pesto, if you like. Substitute
25 g/1 oz/$^1\!/_4$ cup walnuts
for the pine nuts and add 1
tablespoon of walnut
oil in step 2.

1 Rinse the basil leaves and pat them
dry with kitchen paper (paper towels).

2 Put the basil leaves, garlic, pine
nuts and grated Parmesan into a food
processor and process for about
30 seconds, or until smooth.
Alternatively, pound the ingredients
by hand, using a mortar and pestle.

3 If you are using a food processor,
keep the motor running and slowly
add the olive oil. Alternatively, add
the oil drop by drop while stirring
briskly. Season with salt and pepper.

4 Meanwhile, cook the pasta in a
saucepan of boiling lightly salted
water according to the instructions on
the packet, until it is tender, but still
firm to the bite. Drain thoroughly.

5 Transfer the pasta to a warm
serving plate and serve with the
pesto. Toss to mix well and serve hot.

Pasticcio

A recipe that has both Italian and Greek origins,
this dish may be served hot or cold, cut into thick, satisfying squares.

Serves 6
250 g/9 oz/3 cups dried fusilli, or other short pasta shapes
1 tbsp olive oil
4 tbsp double (heavy) cream
salt
rosemary sprigs, to garnish
raw vegetable crudités, to serve

SAUCE

2 tbsp olive oil, plus extra for brushing
1 onion, thinly sliced
1 red (bell) pepper, seeded and chopped
2 garlic cloves, chopped
500 g/1¼ lb minced (ground) lean beef
400 g/14 oz can chopped tomatoes
125 ml/4 fl oz/½ cup dry white wine
2 tbsp chopped fresh parsley
50 g/2 oz can anchovies, drained and chopped
salt and pepper

TOPPING

300 ml/½ pint/1¼ cups natural (unsweetened) yogurt
3 eggs
pinch of freshly grated nutmeg
50 g/2 oz/⅓ cup grated Parmesan cheese

1 To make the sauce, heat the oil in a large frying pan (skillet) and sauté the onion and red (bell) pepper for 3 minutes. Stir in the garlic and cook for 1 minute. Stir in the beef and cook, stirring frequently, until it is broken up and no longer pink.

2 Stir in the tomatoes and wine and bring to the boil. Simmer, uncovered, for 20 minutes, until the sauce is fairly thick. Stir in the parsley and anchovies, and season to taste.

3 Cook the pasta in a large pan of boiling salted water, adding the oil. When tender, but still firm to the bite, drain in a colander, then transfer to a bowl. Stir in the cream and set aside.

4 To make the topping, beat together the yogurt and eggs and season with nutmeg, salt and pepper to taste. Stir in the cheese.

5 Brush a shallow ovenproof dish with oil. Spoon in half the pasta and cover it with half the meat sauce. Repeat these layers, spread the topping evenly over the dish and sprinkle the cheese on top.

6 Bake in a preheated oven at 190°C/ 375°F/Gas Mark 5, for 25 minutes, until the topping is golden brown and bubbling. Garnish with rosemary and serve immediately with a selection of raw vegetable crudités.

Tagliatelle with Pumpkin

This unusual pasta dish comes from the Emilia Romagna region of Italy – home of Parmesan cheese and Parma ham (prosciutto), among other world-famous gourmet treats. Why not serve it with a bottle of young, dry red Lambrusco?

Serves 4
500 g/1¼ lb pumpkin or butternut squash
2 tbsp olive oil
1 onion, finely chopped
2 garlic cloves, crushed
4–6 tbsp chopped fresh parsley
pinch of ground or freshly grated nutmeg
about 250 ml/8 fl oz/1 cup chicken or vegetable stock
115 g/4 oz Parma ham (prosciutto), cut into narrow strips
250 g/9 oz dried tagliatelle, green or white
150 ml/¼ pint/⅔ cup double (heavy) cream
salt and pepper
freshly grated Parmesan cheese, to serve

1 Peel the pumpkin or butternut squash. Scoop out and discard the seeds and membrane. Cut the flesh into 1-cm/½-inch dice.

2 Heat the oil in a pan and gently sauté the onion and garlic until soft. Add half the parsley and sauté for 1-2 minutes.

3 Add the pumpkin or squash and continue to cook for 2–3 minutes. Season well with salt, pepper and nutmeg. Add half the stock, bring to the boil, cover and simmer for about 10 minutes, or until the pumpkin is tender, adding more stock as necessary. Add the Parma ham (prosciutto) and continue to cook for a further 2 minutes, stirring frequently.

4 Meanwhile, cook the tagliatelle in a large saucepan of boiling salted water, for about 12 minutes, or until it is tender, but still firm to the bite. Drain thoroughly and turn into a warm dish.

5 Add the cream to the ham mixture and heat gently until really hot. Adjust the seasoning and spoon the mixture over the pasta. Sprinkle with the remaining parsley and serve immediately. Hand the grated Parmesan separately.

Chilli & (Bell) Pepper Pasta Salad

This roasted (bell) pepper and chilli sauce is sweet and spicy.
Add 2 tablespoons of red wine vinegar to the sauce and use
as a dressing for a cold pasta salad, if you wish.

Serves 4
2 red (bell) peppers, halved and seeded
1 small red chilli
2 garlic cloves
4 tomatoes, halved
50 g/2 oz/$^1/_2$ cup ground almonds
7 tbsp olive oil
675 g/1$^1/_2$ lb fresh pasta or
350 g/12 oz dried pasta
salt and pepper
fresh oregano leaves, to garnish

1 Place the (bell) peppers, skin side up, on a baking tray (cookie sheet) with the chilli and garlic. Cook under a preheated grill (broiler) for about 15 minutes, or until the skins are charred. After 10 minutes add the tomatoes, skin side up.

2 Place the (bell) peppers and chilli in a plastic bag and let sweat for 10 minutes.

3 Remove the skin from the (bell) peppers and chilli and slice the flesh into strips, using a sharp knife.

4 Peel the garlic and peel and seed the tomatoes.

5 Spread out the almonds on a baking tray (cookie sheet) and toast under the grill (broiler) for 2–3 minutes, until golden.

6 Put the (bell) pepper, chilli, garlic and tomatoes in a food processor and process to make a purée. Keep the motor running and slowly add the

olive oil to form a thick sauce. Alternatively, mash the mixture to a purée with a fork and beat in the olive oil, drop by drop.

7 Stir the toasted ground almonds into the mixture.

8 Warm the sauce in a saucepan until it is heated through.

9 Cook the pasta in a saucepan of boiling lightly salted water for 2–3 minutes if fresh, or for 8–12 minutes if dried, until it is tender, but still firm to the bite. Drain the pasta and transfer to a warm serving dish. Pour the sauce over the pasta and toss, with 2 forks, to mix. Garnish with fresh oregano leaves and serve immediately.

Sicilian Spaghetti

This delicious Sicilian dish originated as a handy way of using
up leftover cooked pasta. Any variety of long pasta could be used.

Serves 4
2 aubergines (eggplants), about 500 g/1¼ lb
150 ml/¼ pint/⅔ cup olive oil
350 g/12 oz finely minced (ground) lean beef
1 onion, chopped
2 garlic cloves, crushed
2 tbsp tomato purée (paste)
400 g/14 oz can chopped tomatoes
1 tsp Worcestershire sauce
1 tsp chopped fresh oregano or marjoram or ½ tsp dried oregano or marjoram
50 g/2 oz/½ cup pitted black olives, sliced
1 green, red or yellow (bell) pepper, seeded and chopped
175 g/6 oz dried spaghetti
125 g/4 oz/1⅓ cups grated Parmesan cheese
salt and pepper
fresh oregano or parsley, to garnish (optional)

1 Brush a 20-cm/8-inch loose-based
round cake tin (pan) with olive oil,
place a disc of baking parchment in
the base and brush with oil. Trim the
aubergines (eggplants) and cut into
slanting slices, 5 mm/¼ inch thick.
Heat some of the oil in a large frying
pan (skillet). Fry a few slices at a time
until lightly browned, turning once,
and adding more oil as necessary.
Drain thoroughly on kitchen paper
(paper towels).

2 Put the minced (ground) beef,
onion and garlic into a saucepan and
cook, stirring frequently, until

browned. Add the tomato purée
(paste), tomatoes, Worcestershire
sauce and oregano or marjoram and
season to taste with salt and pepper.
Simmer for 10 minutes, stirring
occasionally, then add the olives and
(bell) pepper and cook for a further
10 minutes.

3 Bring a large pan of salted water to
the boil. Cook the spaghetti for
12–14 minutes, until tender, but still
firm to the bite. Drain, turn into a
bowl and mix in the meat mixture and
Parmesan, tossing with 2 forks.

4 Lay overlapping slices of aubergine
(eggplant) evenly over the base of the
cake tin (pan) and up the sides. Add
the meat and spaghetti mixture,
pressing it down, and cover with the
remaining aubergine (eggplant) slices.

5 Stand the cake tin (pan) in a
roasting tin (pan) and cook in a
preheated oven at 200°C/ 400°F/Gas
Mark 6, for 40 minutes. Let stand for
5 minutes, then loosen around the
edges and invert on to a warm serving
dish. Remove the parchment. Sprinkle
with herbs before serving, if wished.

Spaghetti with Seafood Sauce

Frozen peeled prawns (shrimp) from the freezer can
become the star ingredient in this colourful and tasty dish.

Serves 4
250 g/9 oz/3 cups dried short-cut spaghetti, or long spaghetti broken into 15-cm/6-inch lengths
2 tbsp olive oil
300 ml/½ pint/1¼ cups chicken stock
1 tsp lemon juice
1 small cauliflower, cut into florets
2 carrots, thinly sliced
125 g/4 oz mangetout (snow peas), trimmed
50 g/2 oz/¼ cup butter
1 onion, sliced
250 g/9 oz courgettes (zucchini), thinly sliced
1 garlic clove, chopped
350 g/12 oz frozen peeled prawns (shrimp), thawed
2 tbsp chopped fresh parsley
25 g/1 oz/⅓ cup grated Parmesan cheese
salt and pepper
½ tsp paprika, to sprinkle
4 unpeeled prawns (shrimp), to garnish (optional)

1 Cook the spaghetti in a large saucepan of boiling salted water, adding 1 tablespoon of the olive oil for 8–12 minutes, until tender, but still firm to the bite. Drain, return to the pan and stir in the remaining olive oil. Cover and keep warm.

2 Bring the chicken stock and lemon juice to the boil. Add the cauliflower and carrots and cook for 3–4 minutes, until they are just tender. Remove with a slotted spoon and set aside. Add the mangetout (snow peas) and cook for 1–2 minutes, until they begin to soften. Remove with a slotted spoon and add to the other vegetables. Reserve the stock for future use.

3 Melt half of the butter in a frying pan (skillet) over a medium heat and sauté the onion and courgettes (zucchini) for about 3 minutes. Add the garlic and prawns (shrimp) and cook for a further 2–3 minutes, until thoroughly heated through.

4 Stir in the reserved vegetables and heat through. Season well, then stir in the remaining butter.

5 Transfer the spaghetti to a warm serving dish. Pour the sauce on top and add the parsley. Toss with 2 forks, until thoroughly coated. Sprinkle on the grated cheese and paprika, and garnish with unpeeled prawns (shrimp), if using. Serve immediately.

Pasta Vongole

Fresh clams are available from most good fish stores.
If you prefer, used canned clams, which are less messy to eat
but not so pretty to serve.

Serves 4
675 g/1½ lb fresh clams or 290 g/10 oz can clams, drained
2 tbsp olive oil
2 garlic cloves, finely chopped
400 g/14 oz mixed seafood, such as prawns (shrimp), squid and mussels, thawed if frozen
150 ml/¼ pint/⅔ cup white wine
150 ml/¼ pint/⅔ cup fish stock
675 g/1½ lb fresh pasta or 350 g/12 oz dried pasta
2 tbsp chopped tarragon
salt and pepper

1 If you are using fresh clams, scrub them clean under cold running water and discard any that are already open.

2 Heat the oil in a large frying pan (skillet). Add the garlic and clams and cook for 2 minutes, shaking the pan to ensure that all of the clams are coated in the oil.

3 Add the remaining seafood mixture to the pan and cook for a further 2 minutes.

4 Pour the wine and stock over the mixed seafood and garlic and bring to the boil. Cover the pan, reduce the heat and simmer for 8–10 minutes, or until the shells open. Discard any clams that do not open.

5 Meanwhile, cook the pasta in a saucepan of boiling lightly salted water for 2–3 minutes if fresh, or 8–12 minutes if dried, or until it is

cooked tender, but still firm to the bite. Drain well.

6 Stir the tarragon into the sauce and season to taste.

7 Transfer the pasta to a serving plate, pour the sauce on top and serve.

Pasta Shells with Mussels

Serve this aromatic seafood dish to family and friends who admit to a love of garlic. This dish would look particularly attractive made with green-lipped mussels.

Serves 4–6
400 g/14 oz/4²⁄₃ cup dried pasta shells
1 tbsp olive oil
SAUCE
1.5 kg/3¹⁄₂ lb mussels
250 ml/8 fl oz/1 cup dry white wine
2 large onions, chopped
115 g/4 oz/¹⁄₂ cup unsalted (sweet) butter
6 large garlic cloves, finely chopped
5 tbsp chopped fresh parsley
300 ml/¹⁄₂ pint/1¹⁄₄ cups double (heavy) cream
salt and pepper
crusty bread, to serve

1 Debeard and scrub the mussels under cold running water. Discard any mussels that do not close when sharply tapped with a knife. Put the mussels in a large pan with the white wine and half the onions. Cover the pan, and cook over a medium heat, shaking the pan frequently, for 3–5 minutes, until the mussels open.

2 Remove the pan from the heat, lift out the mussels with a slotted spoon, reserving the cooking liquid, and set aside until they are cool enough to handle. Discard any mussels that have not opened.

3 Melt the butter in a pan over a medium heat and sauté the remaining onion until translucent. Stir in the garlic and cook for 1 minute. Gradually stir in the reserved cooking liquid, blending it thoroughly. Stir in

the parsley and cream. Season to taste with salt and pepper and bring to simmering point.

4 Cook the pasta in a large pan of lightly salted boiling water, adding the oil for 8–12 minutes, until tender, but still firm to the bite. Drain in a colander, return to the pan, cover and keep warm.

5 Reserve a few mussels in their shells for garnish. Remove the remainder from their shells and gently stir them into the cream sauce. Tip the pasta into a warm serving dish, pour the mussel sauce on top and, using 2 large spoons, toss it thoroughly. Garnish with the reserved mussels in their shells. Serve immediately with warm, crusty bread.

Vermicelli with Clam Sauce

A quickly cooked recipe that transforms storecupboard ingredients
into a dish with style.

Serves 4
400 g/14 oz dried vermicelli, spaghetti, or other long pasta
1 tbsp olive oil
25 g/1 oz/2 tbsp butter
2 tbsp Parmesan shavings, to garnish
basil sprig, to garnish

SAUCE

1 tbsp olive oil
2 onions, chopped
2 garlic cloves, chopped
2 x 200 g/7 oz jars clams in brine
125 ml/4 fl oz/½ cup white wine
4 tbsp chopped fresh parsley
½ tsp dried oregano
pinch of freshly grated nutmeg
salt and pepper

1 Cook the pasta in boiling salted
water, adding the olive oil. When it is
tender, but still firm to the bite, drain,
return to the pan and add the butter.
Cover, shake the pan and keep warm.

2 To make the clam sauce, heat the
oil in a pan over a medium heat.
Add the onion and sauté until it is
translucent. Stir in the garlic and cook
for 1 minute.

3 Strain the liquid from one jar of
clams, pour it into the pan and add
the wine. Stir well, bring to
simmering point and simmer for
3 minutes. Drain the brine from the
second jar of clams and discard.

4 Add the shellfish and herbs to the
pan, and season with pepper and

nutmeg. Lower the heat and cook
until the sauce is heated through.

5 Transfer the pasta to a warmed
serving dish and pour the sauce on
top. Sprinkle with the Parmesan
shavings, garnish with the basil sprig
and serve immediately.

Spaghetti with Smoked Salmon

Made in moments, this is a special dish to astonish and delight
unexpected guests.

Serves 4
500 g/1¼ lb dried buckwheat spaghetti
2 tbsp olive oil
75 g/3 oz/³⁄₄ cup crumbled feta cheese
coriander (cilantro) or parsley, to garnish
SAUCE
300 ml/½ pint/1¼ cups double (heavy) cream
150 ml/¼ pint/²⁄₃ cup whisky or brandy
115 g/4 oz smoked salmon
pinch of cayenne pepper
2 tbsp chopped coriander (cilantro) or parsley
salt and pepper

1 Cook the spaghetti in a large pan of lightly salted boiling water, adding 1 tablespoon of the olive oil. When the pasta is tender, but still firm to the bite, drain in a colander. Return to the pan and sprinkle it with the remaining oil. Cover, shake the pan and keep warm.

2 In separate small pans, heat the cream and the whisky or brandy to simmering point. Do not let them come to the boil.

3 Combine the cream with the whisky or brandy. Cut the smoked salmon into thin strips and add to the cream mixture. Season with black pepper and cayenne pepper to taste, and stir in the chopped coriander (cilantro) or parsley.

4 Transfer the spaghetti to a warm serving dish, pour the sauce on top and toss thoroughly using 2 large forks. Scatter the crumbled feta cheese over the pasta and garnish with the coriander (cilantro) or parsley. Serve at once.

COOK'S VARIATION

If wished, cut ½ cucumber in half lengthways, seed and slice thinly. Sauté in a little butter for 2 minutes and add in step 3.

Spaghetti with Tuna & Parsley Sauce

This is a recipe to look forward to when parsley is at its
most prolific, in the growing season.

Serves 4
500 g/1¹/4 lb dried spaghetti
1 tbsp olive oil
25 g/1 oz/2 tbsp butter
black olives, to garnish
crusty bread, to serve
SAUCE
200 g/7 oz can tuna, drained
50 g/2 oz can anchovies, drained
250 ml/8 fl oz/1 cup olive oil
250 ml/8 fl oz/1 cup roughly chopped fresh, flat-leaf parsley
150 ml/¹/4 pint/²/3 cup crème fraîche
salt and pepper

1 Cook the spaghetti in a large pan of
salted boiling water, adding the olive
oil. When it is tender, but still firm to
the bite, drain in a colander and
return to the pan. Add the butter, toss
thoroughly to coat and keep warm.

2 Remove any bones from the tuna
and flake the flesh. Put it into a
blender or food processor with the
anchovies, olive oil and parsley and
process until the sauce is smooth.
Pour in the crème fraîche and process
for a few seconds to blend. Season.

3 Shake the pan of spaghetti over a
medium heat until it is thoroughly
warmed through.

4 Pour on the sauce and toss quickly,
using 2 forks. Transfer to warm
plates, garnish with the olives and
serve with warm, crusty bread.

Macaroni & Prawn (Shrimp) Bake

This adaptation of an eighteenth-century dish is baked until it is
golden brown and sizzling, then cut into wedges, like a cake.

Serves 4
350 g/12 oz/4 cups dried short pasta, such as short-cut macaroni
1 tbsp olive oil, plus extra for brushing
75 g/3 oz/6 tbsp butter, plus extra for greasing
2 small fennel bulbs, thinly sliced, fronds reserved
175 g/6 oz mushrooms, thinly sliced
175 g/6 oz cooked peeled prawns (shrimp)
Béchamel Sauce (see page 17)
pinch of cayenne
50 g/2 oz/²⁄₃ cup Parmesan cheese, grated
2 large tomatoes, sliced
1 tsp dried oregano
salt and pepper

1 Cook the pasta in a large pan of
boiling lightly salted water with
1 tablespoon of olive oil. When it is
tender, but still firm to the bite, drain
in a colander, return to the pan and
dot with 25 g/1 oz/2 tablespoons of
the butter. Shake the pan well, cover
and keep warm.

2 Melt the remaining butter in a pan
over a medium heat and sauté the
fennel for 3–4 minutes, until it begins
to soften. Stir in the mushrooms and
sauté for a further 2 minutes. Stir in
the prawns (shrimp), remove the pan
from the heat and set aside.

3 Make the Béchamel Sauce and add
the cayenne. Remove the pan from
the heat and stir in the vegetables,
prawns (shrimp) and pasta.

4 Grease a round, shallow ovenproof
dish with butter. Pour in the prawn
(shrimp) and pasta mixture. Sprinkle
the Parmesan cheese on top, and
arrange the tomato slices around the
edge of the dish. Brush the tomato

slices with olive oil and sprinkle with
the dried oregano.

5 Bake in a preheated oven at 180°C/
350°F/Gas Mark 4, for 25 minutes,
until golden brown. Serve hot.

Pasta & Sicilian Sauce

This Sicilian recipe of anchovies mixed with pine nuts and sultanas (golden raisins) in a tomato sauce is delicious with all types of chunky, hollow pasta, such as rigatoni or penne, as here.

Serves 4
450 g/1 lb tomatoes, halved
25 g/1 oz/¼ cup pine nuts
50 g/2 oz sultanas (golden raisins)
50 g/2 oz can anchovies, drained and halved lengthways
2 tbsp concentrated tomato purée (paste)
675 g/1½ lb fresh or 350 g/12 oz dried penne

7 Transfer the pasta to a warm serving dish, add the sauce and toss well with 2 forks. Serve immediately.

COOK'S VARIATION

Add 115 g/4 oz bacon, grilled (broiled) for 5 minutes until crispy, then chopped, instead of the anchovies, if you prefer.

1 Place the tomatoes on a baking tray (cookie sheet), skin side up, and cook under a preheated grill (broiler) for about 10 minutes. Let cool slightly, then peel off the skin and dice the flesh.

2 Place the pine nuts on a baking tray (cookie sheet) and lightly toast under the grill (broiler) for 2–3 minutes, or until golden.

3 Soak the sultanas (golden raisins) in a bowl of warm water for about 20 minutes. Drain thoroughly.

4 Place the tomatoes, pine nuts and sultanas (golden raisins) in a small pan and heat gently.

5 Add the anchovies and tomato purée (paste) and heat the sauce for a further 2–3 minutes, or until hot.

6 Cook the pasta in a saucepan of salted boiling water for 2–3 minutes if fresh, or for 8–12 minutes if dried, until tender, but still firm to the bite. Drain thoroughly.

Seafood Lasagne

Layers of cheese sauce, smoked cod and
wholewheat lasagne can be assembled overnight and
left ready to cook on the following day.

Serves 6
8 sheets wholewheat lasagne
500 g/1¼ lb smoked cod fillets
600 ml/1 pint/2½ cups milk
1 tbsp lemon juice
8 peppercorns
2 bay leaves
a few parsley stalks
50 g/2 oz/½ cup grated mature (sharp) Cheddar cheese
25 g/1 oz/⅓ cup grated Parmesan cheese
salt and pepper
a few prawns (shrimp), to garnish (optional)

SAUCE
50 g/2 oz/¼ cup butter, plus extra for greasing
1 large onion, sliced
1 green (bell) pepper, seeded and chopped
1 small courgette (zucchini), sliced
50 g/2 oz/½ cup plain (all-purpose) flour
150 ml/¼ pint/⅔ cup white wine
150 ml/¼ pint/⅔ cup single (light) cream
115 g/4 oz peeled cooked prawns (shrimp)
50 g/2 oz/½ cup grated mature (sharp) Cheddar cheese

1 Cook the lasagne in boiling, salted water until almost tender, according to the instructions on the packet. Drain and reserve.

2 Place the smoked cod, milk, lemon juice, peppercorns, bay leaves and parsley stalks in a frying pan (skillet). Bring to the boil, lower the heat, cover and simmer for 10 minutes.

3 Lift the fish from the pan with a slotted spoon. Skin and flake the flesh. Strain and reserve the cooking liquid.

4 To make the sauce, melt the butter in a pan and sauté the onion, (bell) pepper and courgette (zucchini) for 2–3 minutes. Stir in the flour and cook for 1 minute. Gradually stir in the reserved liquid, then stir in the wine, cream and prawns (shrimp). Simmer for 2 minutes. Remove from the heat, add the cheese, and season to taste.

5 Grease a shallow ovenproof dish. Pour in a quarter of the prawn (shrimp) sauce and spread evenly over the base. Cover the sauce with three sheets of lasagne, then add another quarter of the sauce.

6 Arrange the cod on top and cover with half the remaining sauce. Finish with the remaining lasagne, then the rest of the sauce. Sprinkle the Cheddar and Parmesan over the sauce.

7 Bake in the preheated oven at 190°C/375°F/Gas Mark 5, for 25 minutes, or until the top is golden brown and bubbling. Garnish with a few whole prawns (shrimp), if liked.

Squid & Macaroni Stew

This seafood dish is quick and easy to make, yet it results in a delicious mingling of flavours and is very satisfying to eat.

Serves 4–6

250 g/8 oz/2²/₃ cups dried short-cut macaroni, or other short pasta shapes

1 tbsp olive oil

salt and pepper

crusty bread, to serve

SAUCE

6 tbsp olive oil

2 onions, sliced

350 g/12 oz cleaned squid, cut into 4-cm/1¹/₂-inch strips

250 ml/8 fl oz/1 cup fish stock

150 ml/¹/₄ pint/²/₃ cup red wine

350 g/12 oz tomatoes, peeled and thinly sliced

2 tbsp tomato purée (paste)

1 tsp dried oregano

2 bay leaves

2 tbsp chopped fresh parsley

1 Cook the pasta for 3 minutes in a pan of boiling salted water, adding the oil. Drain in a colander, return to the pan, cover and keep warm.

2 To make the sauce, heat the oil in a pan over medium heat. Add the onion and sauté until translucent. Add the squid and stock, bring to the boil and simmer for 5 minutes. Pour in the wine and add the tomatoes, tomato purée (paste), oregano and bay leaves. Bring the sauce to the boil, season with salt and pepper to taste and cook, uncovered, for 5 minutes.

3 Add the pasta, stir well, cover the pan and continue simmering for 10 minutes, or until the macaroni is

tender, but still firm to the bite and the squid is cooked. By this time the sauce should be thick and syrupy. If it is too liquid, uncover the pan and continue cooking for a few minutes. Taste the sauce and adjust the seasoning if necessary.

4 Remove the bay leaves and stir in most of the parsley, reserving a little to garnish. Transfer to a warmed serving dish. Sprinkle on the remaining parsley and serve hot. Serve with warm, crusty bread such as ciabatta.

Green Garlic Tagliatelle

A rich pasta dish for garlic lovers everywhere.
It's quick and easy to prepare and full of flavour.

Serves 4
2 tbsp walnut oil
1 bunch spring onions (scallions), sliced
2 garlic cloves, thinly sliced
250 g/9 oz mushrooms, sliced
500 g/1¼ lb fresh green and white tagliatelle
250 g/9 oz frozen chopped leaf spinach, thawed and drained
115 g/4 oz/½ cup full-fat soft cheese with garlic and herbs
4 tbsp single (light) cream
50 g/2 oz/½ cup chopped, unsalted pistachio nuts
2 tbsp shredded fresh basil
salt and pepper
sprigs of fresh basil, to garnish
Italian bread, to serve

1 Gently heat the oil in a frying pan (skillet) and sauté the spring onions (scallions) and garlic for 1 minute, until just softened. Add the mushrooms, stir well, cover and cook gently for 5 minutes until softened.

2 Meanwhile, bring a large saucepan of lightly salted water to the boil and cook the pasta for 3–5 minutes, until tender, but still firm to the bite. Drain well and return to the saucepan.

3 Add the spinach to the mushrooms and heat through for 1–2 minutes. Add the soft cheese and allow to melt slightly. Stir in the cream and continue to heat without allowing it to come to the boil.

4 Pour the sauce over the pasta, season with salt and pepper to taste and mix well, using 2 forks. Heat gently, stirring, for 2–3 minutes.

5 Pile into a warm serving bowl and sprinkle with the pistachio nuts and shredded basil. Garnish with basil sprigs and serve with Italian bread.

Baked Aubergines (Eggplant) with Pasta

Combined with tomatoes and mozzarella, pasta makes a tasty filling for baked aubergine (eggplant) shells.

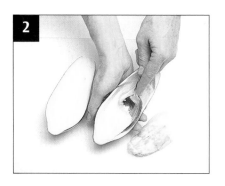

Serves 4

250 g/9 oz/3 cups dried penne, or other short pasta shapes

4 tbsp olive oil, plus extra for brushing

2 aubergines (eggplants)

1 large onion, chopped

2 garlic cloves, crushed

400 g/14 oz can chopped tomatoes

2 tsp dried oregano

50 g/2 oz mozzarella, thinly sliced

25 g/1 oz/⅓ cup grated Parmesan cheese

2 tbsp dry breadcrumbs

salt and pepper

salad leaves, to serve

1 Cook the pasta in a large pan of lightly salted boiling water, adding 1 tablespoon of the olive oil. When it is tender, but still firm to the bite, drain in a colander, return to the pan, cover and keep warm.

2 Cut the aubergines (eggplants) in half lengthways. Score around the inside with a sharp knife, then scoop out the flesh with a spoon, taking care not to pierce the skin. Brush the insides of the aubergine (eggplant) shells with olive oil. Chop the flesh and set it aside.

3 Heat the remaining oil in a frying pan (skillet) over a medium heat and sauté the onion until it is translucent. Add the garlic and sauté for 1 minute. Add the chopped aubergines (eggplants) and cook for 5 minutes, stirring frequently. Add the tomatoes and oregano, and season with salt and pepper. Bring to the boil and simmer for 10 minutes, or until the mixture is thick. Taste and adjust the seasoning if necessary. Remove from the heat and stir in the reserved pasta.

4 Brush a baking tray (cookie sheet) with oil and arrange the aubergine (eggplant) shells in a single layer. Divide half of the tomato mixture between the four shells. Arrange the mozzarella on top and cover with the remaining mixture, piling it into a mound. Mix together the Parmesan cheese and breadcrumbs, and sprinkle over the top of the filling, patting it lightly into the mixture.

5 Bake in a preheated oven at 200°C/400°F/Gas Mark 6, for 25 minutes, until the topping is golden brown. Serve hot, with a green salad.

Mediterranean Spaghetti

Delicious Mediterranean vegetables, cooked in a rich tomato sauce,
make an ideal topping for nutty wholewheat pasta.

Serves 4
2 tbsp olive oil
1 large red onion, chopped
2 garlic cloves, crushed
1 tbsp lemon juice
4 baby aubergines (eggplants), quartered
600 ml/1 pint/2½ cups passata (sieved tomatoes)
2 tsp caster (superfine) sugar
2 tbsp tomato purée (paste)
400 g/14 oz can artichoke hearts, drained and halved
115 g/4 oz/¾ cup stoned (pitted) black olives
350 g/12 oz dried wholewheat spaghetti
salt and pepper
sprigs of fresh basil, to garnish
olive bread, to serve

1 Heat 1 tablespoon of the olive oil in a large frying pan (skillet). Add the onion, garlic, lemon juice and aubergines (eggplants) and sauté over a medium heat for 4–5 minutes, until lightly browned.

2 Pour in the passata (sieved tomatoes), season with salt and pepper and add the sugar and tomato purée (paste). Bring to the boil, reduce the heat and simmer for 20 minutes.

3 Gently stir in the artichoke hearts and olives and cook for 5 minutes.

4 Meanwhile, bring a large saucepan of lightly salted water to the boil, and cook the spaghetti for 7–8 minutes, until tender, but still firm to the bite.

Drain well, toss in the remaining olive oil and season with salt and pepper.

5 Pile into a warm serving bowl and top with the vegetable sauce. Garnish with fresh basil sprigs and serve with olive bread.

COOK'S TIP

For extra colour, char-grill (charbroil) 2 red or orange (bell) peppers and add them with the artichoke hearts in step 3.

Tricolour Timballini

An unusual way of serving pasta, these cheese-flavoured moulds
are excellent served with a crunchy salad for a light lunch.

Serves 4
15 g/¹/₂ oz/1 tbsp butter or margarine, softened
50 g/2 oz/²/₃ cup dried white breadcrumbs
175 g/6 oz dried tricolour spaghetti
300 ml/¹/₂ pint/1¹/₄ cups Béchamel Sauce (see page 17)
1 egg yolk
115 g/4 oz/1 cup grated Gruyère (Swiss) cheese
salt and pepper
fresh flat leaf parsley, to garnish

SAUCE

2 tsp olive oil
1 onion, finely chopped
1 bay leaf
150 ml/¹/₄ pint/²/₃ cup dry white wine
150 ml/¹/₄ pint/²/₃ cup passata (sieved tomatoes)
1 tbsp tomato purée (paste)

1 Grease four 180 ml/6 fl oz/³/₄ cup moulds (molds) or ramekins with the butter or margarine. Evenly coat the insides with half of the breadcrumbs.

2 Break the spaghetti into 5-cm/ 2-inch lengths. Bring a saucepan of lightly salted water to the boil and cook the spaghetti for 8–12 minutes, until tender, but still firm to the bite. Drain well and put in a bowl.

3 Mix the Béchamel Sauce, egg yolk, cheese and seasoning into the cooked pasta and pack into the moulds (molds).

4 Sprinkle with the remaining breadcrumbs and place on a baking

tray (cookie sheet). Bake in a preheated oven at 220°C/425°F/Gas Mark 7, for 20 minutes, until golden. Remove from the oven and let stand for 10 minutes.

5 Meanwhile, make the sauce. Heat the oil in a saucepan, add the onion and bay leaf and sauté gently for 2–3 minutes until just softened.

6 Stir in the wine, passata (sieved tomatoes), tomato purée (paste) and seasoning. Bring to the boil and simmer for 20 minutes, until thickened. Discard the bay leaf.

7 Run a palette knife (spatula) around the inside of the moulds (molds) or ramekins. Turn on to serving plates, garnish and serve with the sauce.

Vegetable Pasta Stir-Fry

East meets West in this delicious dish. Prepare all the vegetables and cook the pasta in advance, then the dish can be cooked in a few minutes.

Serves 4
400 g/14 oz/4²/₃ cups dried wholewheat pasta shells, or other short pasta shapes
1 tbsp olive oil
2 carrots, thinly sliced
115 g/4 oz baby corn cobs
3 tbsp peanut oil
2.5-cm/1-inch piece fresh ginger root, thinly sliced
1 large onion, thinly sliced
1 garlic clove, thinly sliced
3 celery sticks, thinly sliced
1 small red (bell) pepper, seeded and sliced into matchstick strips
1 small green (bell) pepper, seeded and sliced into matchstick strips
salt
steamed mangetout (snow peas), to serve

SAUCE
1 tsp cornflour (cornstarch)
2 tbsp water
3 tbsp soy sauce
3 tbsp dry sherry
1 tsp clear honey
dash of hot pepper sauce (optional)

1 Cook the pasta in a large pan of boiling lightly salted water, adding the tablespoon of olive oil. When tender, but still firm to the bite, drain the pasta in a colander, return to the pan, cover and keep warm.

2 Cook the carrots and baby corn cobs in boiling, salted water for 2 minutes. Drain in a colander, plunge into cold water to prevent further cooking and drain again.

3 Heat the peanut oil in a large frying pan (skillet) over medium heat. Add the ginger and stir-fry for 1 minute, to flavour the oil. Remove with a slotted spoon and discard.

4 Add the onion, garlic, celery and (bell) peppers to the oil and stir-fry over a medium heat for 2 minutes. Add the carrots and baby corn cobs, and stir-fry for a further 2 minutes, then stir in the reserved pasta.

5 Put the cornflour (cornstarch) in a small bowl and mix to a smooth paste with the water. Stir in the soy sauce, sherry and honey.

6 Pour the sauce into the pan, stir well and cook for 2 minutes, stirring once or twice. Taste the sauce and season with hot pepper sauce if wished. Serve with a steamed green vegetable, such as mangetout (snow peas).

Pasta with Green Vegetable Sauce

The different shapes and textures of the vegetables make a mouth-watering presentation in this light and summery dish.

Serves 4
250 g/9 oz/3 cups gemelli or other pasta shapes
1 tbsp olive oil
2 tbsp chopped fresh parsley
2 tbsp freshly grated Parmesan cheese
salt and pepper

SAUCE

1 head green broccoli, cut into florets
2 courgettes (zucchini), sliced
250 g/9 oz asparagus spears, trimmed
115 g/4 oz mangetout (snow peas), trimmed
115 g/4 oz frozen peas
25 g/1 oz/2 tbsp butter
3 tbsp vegetable stock
5 tbsp double (heavy) cream
pinch of freshly grated nutmeg

1 Cook the pasta in a large pan of salted boiling water, adding the olive oil. When tender, but still firm to the bite, drain in a colander and return to the pan, cover and keep warm.

2 Steam the broccoli, courgettes (zucchini), asparagus spears and mangetout (snow peas) over a pan of boiling, salted water until just beginning to soften. Remove from the heat and plunge into cold water to prevent further cooking. Drain and set aside.

3 Cook the peas in boiling, salted water for 3 minutes, then drain. Refresh in cold water and drain again.

4 Put the butter and vegetable stock in a pan over a medium heat. Add all the vegetables, except the asparagus spears, and toss carefully with a wooden spoon to heat through.

5 Stir in the cream, allow the sauce just to heat through and season with salt, pepper and nutmeg to taste.

6 Transfer the pasta to a warm serving dish and stir in the chopped parsley. Spoon the sauce over the pasta, and sprinkle with the Parmesan cheese. Arrange the asparagus spears in a pattern on top. Serve hot.

Vegetarian Pasta & Bean Casserole

A satisfying winter dish, this vegetable, pasta and bean casserole
with a crunchy topping is a slow-cooked, one-pot meal.

Serves 6
250 g/9 oz/1⅓ cups dried haricot (navy) beans, soaked overnight and drained
250 g/9 oz/3 cups dried penne, or other short pasta shapes
6 tbsp olive oil
900 ml/1½ pints/3¾ cups vegetable stock
2 large onions, sliced
2 garlic cloves, chopped
2 bay leaves
1 tsp dried oregano
1 tsp dried thyme
5 tbsp red wine
2 tbsp tomato purée (paste)
2 celery stalks, sliced
1 fennel bulb, sliced
115 g/4 oz mushrooms, sliced
250 g/9 oz tomatoes, sliced
1 tsp dark muscovado sugar
4 tbsp dry white breadcrumbs
salt and pepper
TO SERVE
salad leaves
crusty bread

1 Put the beans in a large pan, cover them with water and bring to the boil. Boil the beans rapidly for 20 minutes, then drain.

2 Cook the pasta for 3 minutes in a large pan of boiling salted water, adding 1 tablespoon of the oil. Drain in a colander and set aside.

3 Put the beans in a large flameproof casserole, pour in the vegetable stock and stir in the remaining olive oil, the onions, garlic, bay leaves, oregano, thyme, red wine and tomato purée (paste), mixing thoroughly.

4 Bring to the boil over a medium heat, cover the casserole and cook in a preheated oven at 180°C/350°F/Gas Mark 4 for 2 hours.

5 Add the reserved pasta, the celery, fennel, mushrooms and tomatoes and season with salt and pepper.

6 Stir in the sugar and sprinkle the breadcrumbs on top. Cover the casserole and continue cooking for 1 hour. Serve hot, with salad leaves and plenty of crusty bread.

Vermicelli Flan

Lightly cooked vermicelli is pressed into a flan ring and baked
with a creamy mushroom filling.

Serves 4
250 g/9 oz vermicelli or spaghetti
1 tbsp olive oil
25 g/1 oz/2 tbsp butter, plus extra for greasing
salt
tomato and basil salad, to serve
SAUCE
50 g/2 oz/¹/₄ cup butter
1 onion, chopped
150 g/5 oz button mushrooms, trimmed
1 green (bell) pepper, seeded and sliced into thin rings
150 ml/¹/₄ pint/²/₃ cup milk
3 eggs, lightly beaten
2 tbsp double (heavy) cream
1 tsp dried oregano
pinch of finely grated nutmeg
freshly ground black pepper
1 tbsp freshly grated Parmesan cheese

1 Cook the pasta in a large pan of salted boiling water, adding the olive oil. When tender, but still firm to the bite, drain in a colander. Return the pasta to the pan, add the butter and shake the pan well.

2 Grease a 20-cm/8-inch loose-based flan tin (pan). Press the pasta on to the base and around the sides to form a flan case (shell).

3 Heat the butter in a frying pan (skillet) over a medium heat and sauté the onion until it is translucent. Remove with a slotted spoon and spread in the flan base.

4 Add the mushrooms and (bell) pepper rings to the pan and turn them in the butter until glazed. Fry for 2 minutes on each side, then arrange in the flan base.

5 Beat together the milk, eggs and cream, stir in the oregano, and season with nutmeg and pepper. Pour the mixture carefully over the vegetables and sprinkle the cheese on top.

6 Bake the flan in a preheated oven at 180°C/ 350°F/Gas Mark 4, for 40–45 minutes, until the filling is set. Slide on to a serving plate and serve.

Steamed Pasta Pudding

A tasty mixture of creamy fish and pasta cooked in a bowl, unmoulded (unmolded) and drizzled with tomato sauce presents macaroni in a new guise.

Serves 4
115 g/4 oz/1⅓ cups dried short-cut macaroni, or other short pasta shapes
1 tbsp olive oil
15 g/½ oz/1 tbsp butter, plus extra for greasing
500 g/1¼ lb white fish fillets, such as cod or haddock
a few parsley stalks
6 black peppercorns
125 ml/4 fl oz/½ cup double (heavy) cream
2 eggs, separated
2 tbsp chopped fresh dill, or parsley
pepper
pinch of freshly grated nutmeg
50 g/2 oz/⅔ cup grated Parmesan cheese
Basic Tomato Sauce (see page 17), to serve
dill or parsley sprigs, to garnish

1 Cook the pasta in a large pan of salted boiling water, adding the oil. When tender, but still firm to the bite, drain in a colander, return to the pan, add the butter, cover and keep warm.

2 Place the fish in a frying pan (skillet) with the parsley stalks, peppercorns and just enough water to cover. Bring to the boil, cover, and simmer for 10 minutes. Lift out the fish with a fish slice, reserving the cooking liquid. Skin the fish and cut into bite-size pieces.

3 Transfer the pasta to a large bowl and stir in the cream, egg yolks and dill. Stir in the fish, taking care not to break it up, and enough reserved

liquid to make a moist but firm mixture. It should fall easily from a spoon, but not be too runny. Beat the egg whites until stiff, but not dry, then fold into the mixture.

4 Grease a heatproof bowl or pudding basin and spoon in the mixture to within 4 cm/1½ inches of the rim. Cover the top with greased greaseproof (wax) paper and a cloth, or with foil, and tie firmly around the rim. Do not use foil if you cook the pudding in a microwave.

5 Stand the pudding on a trivet in a large pan of boiling water to come halfway up the sides. Cover and steam for 1½ hours, topping up the boiling water as needed, or cook in a microwave on maximum power for 7 minutes.

6 Run a knife around the inside of the bowl and invert on to a warm serving dish. Pour some tomato sauce over the top and serve the rest separately. Garnish with the herb sprigs.

Fish Dishes

With its long coastline, islands and inland lakes Italy has a wealth of fish and seafood. In fact, after pasta, fish is probably the most important source of food. An immense variety is available from fresh anchovies and sardines to tuna and swordfish, and from mussels and clams to sea urchins and squid. A visit to an Italian fish market, with its colourful, shiny display of the sea's

harvest nestling in crushed ice, is an unforgettable experience.

Mediterranean fish may not always be easy to obtain elsewhere. While it is always better to buy fresh fish, preferably only a few hours out of the sea or river, frozen imports are available. If buying fresh fish, look for shiny scales, bright eyes, firm, plump flesh and pink gills. If fish is being filleted for you, take the heads and trimmings home so that you can make fish stock.

Squid Casserole

Squid is often served fried in Italy, but here it is casseroled
with tomatoes and (bell) peppers to give a rich sauce.

Serves 4
1 kg/2¹/₄ lb squid, cleaned or 675 g/1¹/₂ lb squid rings, thawed if frozen
3 tbsp olive oil
1 large onion, thinly sliced
2 garlic cloves, crushed
1 red (bell) pepper, seeded and sliced
1–2 sprigs of fresh rosemary
150 ml/¹/₄ pint/²/₃ cup dry white wine and 250 ml/8 fl oz/1 cup water, or 350 ml/12 fl oz/1¹/₂ cups water or fish stock
400 g/14 oz can chopped tomatoes
2 tbsp tomato purée (paste)
1 tsp paprika
salt and pepper
fresh sprigs of rosemary or parsley, to garnish

1 Cut the squid bodies into 1-cm/
¹/₂-inch slices and cut the tentacles
into 5-cm/2-inch lengths. If using
frozen squid rings, make sure they are
fully thawed and well drained.

2 Heat the oil in a flameproof
casserole and sauté the onion and
garlic gently until soft. Add the squid,
increase the heat and continue to
cook for about 10 minutes, until
sealed and beginning to colour lightly.
Add the red (bell) pepper, rosemary
and wine (if using), and water or
stock and bring to the boil. Cover and
simmer gently for 45 minutes.

3 Remove and discard the sprigs of
rosemary. Add the tomatoes, tomato

purée (paste), seasonings and paprika.
Continue to simmer gently for
45–60 minutes, or cover the casserole
tightly and cook in a preheated oven
at 180°C/350°F/Gas Mark 4, for
45–60 minutes, until tender.

4 Stir the sauce thoroughly, taste and
adjust the seasoning if necessary and
serve immediately.

Stuffed Squid

Whole squid are stuffed with a mixture of fresh herbs and
sun-dried tomatoes and then cooked in a wine sauce.

Serves 4
8 squid, cleaned and gutted but left whole
6 canned anchovies, chopped
2 garlic cloves, chopped
2 tbsp chopped rosemary leaves
2 sun-dried tomatoes, chopped
150 g/5 oz/2½ cups breadcrumbs
1 tbsp olive oil
1 onion, finely chopped
200 ml/7 fl oz/¾ cup white wine
200 ml/7 fl oz/¾ cup fish stock
cooked rice, to serve

1 Remove the tentacles from the
squid and finely chop. Set aside the
squid bodies.

2 Pound the anchovies, garlic,
rosemary and tomatoes to a paste in a
mortar with a pestle.

3 Add the breadcrumbs and the
chopped squid tentacles and mix
thoroughly to form a thick paste. If
the mixture is too dry to combine
properly, add 1 teaspoon of water.

4 Spoon the paste into the body sacs
of the squid, then tie a length of
cotton around the end of each sac to
fasten them. Do not overfill the sacs
because they will expand during
cooking and might burst.

5 Heat the olive oil in a heavy-based
frying pan (skillet). Add the onion and
cook over a medium heat, stirring
constantly, for about 3–4 minutes, or
until golden.

6 Add the stuffed squid to the pan
and cook for 3–4 minutes or until
brown all over.

7 Add the wine and stock and bring to
the boil. Reduce the heat, cover and
simmer for 15 minutes.

8 Remove the lid and cook for a
further 5 minutes, until the squid is

tender and the juices have reduced
slightly. Serve the stuffed squid with
cooked rice.

COOK'S TIP

If you cannot buy whole squid, use
squid pieces and stir the paste into
the sauce with the wine and stock.

Roasted Seafood

Vegetables become deliciously sweet and juicy when they are roasted, and they go particularly well with fish and seafood. This dish would be just right for an *al fresco* summer supper.

Serves 4
600 g/1 lb 5 oz new potatoes
3 red onions, cut into wedges
2 courgettes (zucchini), sliced into chunks
8 garlic cloves, peeled
2 lemons, cut into wedges
4 sprigs rosemary
4 tbsp olive oil
350 g/12oz unpeeled raw prawns (shrimp)
2 small squid, chopped into rings
4 tomatoes, quartered

1 Scrub the potatoes. Cut any large potatoes in half. Place the potatoes in a large roasting tin (pan), together with the onions, courgettes (zucchini), garlic, lemon and rosemary.

2 Pour the olive oil over the vegetables and toss them well to coat thoroughly.

3 Cook in a preheated oven at 200°C/400°F/Gas Mark 6, for about 40 minutes, turning occasionally, until the potatoes are tender.

4 Once the potatoes are tender, add the prawns (shrimp), squid and tomatoes, tossing to coat them in the oil, and roast for 10 minutes. All the vegetables should be cooked through and slightly charred for full flavour.

5 Transfer to warm individual serving plates and serve hot.

COOK'S VARIATION

Most vegetables are suitable for roasting in the oven. Try adding 450 g/1 lb pumpkin, squash or aubergine (eggplant), if you prefer.

COOK'S TIP

If you cannot obtain raw prawns (shrimp), use cooked ones and add them 2–3 minutes before the end of the cooking time.

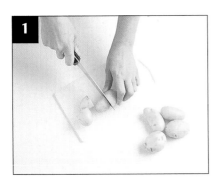

Mussel Casserole

Mussels are not difficult to cook, just a little messy to eat.
The flavours are worth it, however, and serving this dish
with a finger bowl helps to keep things clean!

Serves 4
1 kg/2¹/₄ lb mussels
150 ml/¹/₄ pint/²/₃ cup white wine
1 tbsp oil
1 onion, finely chopped
3 garlic cloves, chopped
1 red chilli, finely chopped
125 ml/4 fl oz/¹/₂ cup passata (sieved tomatoes)
1 tbsp chopped marjoram
toast or crusty bread, to serve

1 Scrub the mussels to remove any mud or sand.

2 Remove the beards from the mussels by pulling away the hairy bit between the two shells. Rinse the mussels in a bowl of clean water. Discard any mussels that do not close immediately when sharply tapped with the back of a knife – they are dead and should not be eaten.

3 Place the mussels in a large saucepan. Pour in the wine and cook, shaking the pan occasionally, for 5 minutes, until the shells open. Remove and discard any mussels that do not open.

4 Remove the mussels from the saucepan with a slotted spoon. Strain the cooking liquid through a fine strainer and reserve.

5 Heat the oil in a large frying pan (skillet). Add the onion, garlic and chilli and sauté for 4–5 minutes, or until softened.

6 Add the reserved cooking liquid to the pan, bring to the boil and cook for 5 minutes, or until reduced.

7 Stir in the passata (sieved tomatoes), marjoram and mussels and cook until hot.

8 Transfer to warm individual serving bowls and serve with toast or plenty of crusty bread to mop up the juices.

Pan-Fried Prawns (Shrimp) with Garlic

A luxurious dish which makes an impressive starter or light meal.

Serves 4
4 garlic cloves
20–24 unpeeled large raw prawns (shrimp)
115 g/4 oz/$\frac{1}{2}$ cup butter
4 tbsp olive oil
6 tbsp brandy
salt and pepper
2 tbsp chopped fresh parsley
8 lemon wedges, to garnish
ciabatta or other Italian bread, to serve

1 Peel and thinly slice the garlic.

2 Wash the prawns (shrimp) and pat dry with kitchen paper (paper towels).

3 Melt the butter with the oil in a large frying pan (skillet), add the garlic and prawns (shrimp), and cook over a high heat, stirring constantly, for 3–4 minutes, until the prawns (shrimp) are pink.

4 Sprinkle with brandy and season with salt and pepper to taste. Sprinkle with parsley and transfer to warm individual serving plates. Garnish with the lemon wedges and serve with ciabatta or other Italian bread, if wished.

COOK'S TIP

Finely sliced garlic has a less dominant flavour than crushed garlic and will not overwhelm the other ingredients.

Orange Mackerel

Mackerel is an oily fish and can be quite rich, but when it is stuffed with oranges and toasted ground almonds it is tangy and light.

Serves 4
2 tbsp oil
4 spring onions (scallions), chopped
2 oranges
50 g/2 oz/¹/₂ cup ground almonds
1 tbsp oats
50 g/2 oz/¹/₂ cup mixed green and black olives, stoned (pitted) and chopped
8 mackerel fillets
salt and pepper
crisp salad, to serve

1 Heat the oil in a frying pan (skillet). Add the spring onions (scallions) and sauté over a medium heat for about 2 minutes, until translucent.

2 Finely grate the rind of the oranges, then, using a sharp knife, cut away the remaining skin and white pith.

3 Using a sharp knife, segment the oranges by cutting down either side of the lines of pith to loosen each segment. Do this over a plate so that you can reserve any juices. Cut each orange segment in half.

4 Lightly toast the almonds under a preheated grill (broiler) for about 2–3 minutes, or until golden. Watch them carefully, as they will brown very quickly.

5 Mix the spring onions (scallions), orange rind and segments, toasted almonds, oats and chopped olives together in a bowl and season to taste with salt and pepper.

6 Divide the orange mixture between the fish, spooning it along the centre of each mackerel fillet. Roll up each fillet, securing it in place with a cocktail stick (toothpick).

7 Bake in a preheated oven at 190°C/375°F/Gas Mark 5 for 25 minutes, until the fish are tender. Transfer to warm individual serving plates and serve immediately with a crisp salad.

Baked Sea Bass

Sea bass is a delicious white-fleshed fish. If you are cooking two small fish,
they can be grilled (broiled), but a single large fish is better baked in the oven.

Serves 4
1.4 kg/3 lb sea bass or
2 x 750 g/1¹/₂ lb sea bass, gutted
2–4 sprigs fresh rosemary
¹/₂ lemon, thinly sliced
2 tbsp olive oil

GARLIC SAUCE

2 tsp coarse sea salt
2 tsp capers
2 garlic cloves, crushed
4 tbsp water
2 fresh bay leaves
1 tsp lemon juice or wine vinegar
2 tbsp olive oil
pepper

TO GARNISH

bay leaves
lemon wedges

1 Scrape off the scales from the fish
and cut off the sharp fins. Make
diagonal cuts along both sides. Wash
and dry thoroughly. Place a sprig of
rosemary in the cavity of each of the
smaller fish with half the lemon
slices, or 2 sprigs and all of the lemon
slices in the large fish.

2 To grill (broil), place the fish in a
foil-lined pan, brush lightly with
1–2 tablespoons oil and grill (broil)
under a preheated grill (broiler) for
about 5 minutes each side, or until
cooked through, turning carefully.

3 To bake, place the fish in a foil-
lined dish or roasting tin (pan)
brushed with oil, and brush the fish

with the rest of the oil. Cook in a
preheated oven at 190°C/375°F/Gas
Mark 5 for about 30 minutes if using
2 small fish, or 45–50 minutes if using
1 large fish, until the thickest part of
the fish is opaque.

4 For the sauce, crush the salt and
capers with the garlic in a mortar with
a pestle if available and then gradually
work in the water. Alternatively, put
the ingredients into a food processor
or blender and process until smooth.

5 Bruise the bay leaves and remaining
sprigs of rosemary and put in a bowl.
Add the garlic mixture, lemon juice or
vinegar and oil and pound together
until the flavours are released. Season
to taste with pepper.

6 Transfer the fish to a warm serving
dish and, if wished, remove the skin.
Spoon some of the sauce over the fish,
garnish with fresh bay leaves and
lemon wedges and serve immediately
with the remaining sauce.

Marinated Fish

Marinating fish, for even a short period, adds a subtle flavour to the flesh
and makes simply grilled (broiled) or fried fish a delicious dish.

Serves 4
4 mackerel
4 tbsp chopped marjoram
2 tbsp extra virgin olive oil
finely grated rind and juice of 1 lime
2 garlic cloves, crushed
salt and pepper
lime wedges, to garnish
salad leaves, to serve

1 Under gently running cold water,
scrape the mackerel, from tail to head,
with a fish scaler or the blunt side of
a knife to remove any scales.

2 Using a sharp knife, make a slit in
the stomach of the fish and cut
horizontally along until the knife will
go no further very easily. Gut the fish
and rinse under water. Pat dry with
kitchen paper (paper towels). You may
prefer to remove the heads before
cooking, but it is not necessary.

3 Using a sharp knife, cut
4–5 diagonal slashes on each side of
the fish. Place the fish in a single
layer in a shallow, non-metallic dish.

4 To make the marinade, mix
together the marjoram, olive oil, lime
rind and juice and garlic in a bowl.
Season to taste with salt and pepper.

5 Pour the mixture over the fish.
Marinate in the refrigerator for
30 minutes.

6 Cook the mackerel, under a
preheated grill (broiler), for

5–6 minutes on each side, brushing
occasionally with the reserved
marinade, until golden.

7 Transfer the fish to warm serving
plates. Pour over any remaining
marinade, garnish with lime wedges
and serve with salad leaves.

COOK'S TIP

If the lime is too hard to squeeze,
microwave on high power for
30 seconds to release the juice. This
dish is also excellent cooked
on the barbecue.

Grilled (Broiled) Stuffed Sole

A delicious mixture of sun-dried tomatoes and fresh lemon
thyme are used to stuff whole sole.

Serves 4
1 tbsp olive oil
25 g/1 oz/2 tbsp butter
1 small onion, finely chopped
1 garlic clove, chopped
3 sun-dried tomatoes, chopped
2 tbsp lemon thyme
50 g/2 oz/1 cup breadcrumbs
1 tbsp lemon juice
4 small sole, gutted and cleaned
salt and pepper
lemon wedges, to garnish
green salad leaves, to serve

1 Heat the oil and butter in a frying pan (skillet) over a low heat until it just begins to froth.

2 Add the onion and garlic to the frying pan (skillet) and sauté, stirring frequently, for 5 minutes, until just softened and translucent. Remove the pan from the heat.

3 To make the stuffing, mix the tomatoes, thyme, breadcrumbs and lemon juice in a bowl, and season to taste with salt and pepper.

4 Add the stuffing mixture to the pan, and stir to mix.

5 Using a sharp knife, carefully pare the skin from the bone inside the gut hole of each fish to make a pocket.

6 Carefully spoon the tomato and herb stuffing into the pockets, dividing it equally between them.

7 Cook the fish, under a preheated grill (broiler), for 6 minutes on each side, or until golden brown.

8 With a fish slice, transfer the stuffed fish to warm individual serving plates. Garnish with lemon wedges and serve immediately with fresh green salad leaves.

COOK'S TIP

Lemon thyme (Thymus x citriodorus) has a delicate lemon scent and flavour. Ordinary thyme can be used instead, but mix it with 1 teaspoon of lemon rind to add extra flavour.

Sole Fillets in Marsala & Cream

A rich wine and cream sauce makes this an excellent dinner party dish. You can make the stock the day before, so it takes only minutes to cook and serve the fish.

Serves 4
STOCK
600 ml/1 pint/2^1/$_2$ cups water
bones and skin from the sole
1 onion, peeled and halved
1 carrot, peeled and halved
3 fresh bay leaves
SAUCE
1 tbsp olive oil
15 g/^{1}/$_2$ oz/1 tbsp butter
4 shallots, finely chopped
115 g/4 oz baby button mushrooms, wiped and halved
1 tbsp peppercorns, lightly crushed
8 sole fillets
125 ml/4 fl oz/^{1}/$_2$ cup Marsala
150 ml/^{1}/$_4$ pint/^{2}/$_3$ cup double (heavy) cream

1 To make the stock, place the water, fish bones and skin, onion, carrot and bay leaves in a saucepan and bring to the boil.

2 Reduce the heat and simmer for 1 hour, or until the stock has reduced to about 150 ml/^{1}/$_2$ pint/^{2}/$_3$ cup. Strain the stock through a fine strainer, discarding the bones and vegetables, and set aside.

3 To make the sauce, heat the oil and butter in a frying pan (skillet). Add the shallots and cook, stirring, for 2–3 minutes, or until just softened.

4 Add the mushrooms to the frying pan (skillet) and cook, stirring, for a further 2–3 minutes, or until they are just beginning to brown.

5 Add the peppercorns and sole fillets to the frying pan (skillet). Fry the sole fillets for 3–4 minutes on each side or until golden brown.

6 Pour the wine and stock over the fish and leave to simmer for 3 minutes. Remove the fish with a fish slice or a slotted spoon, set aside and keep warm.

7 Increase the heat and boil the mixture in the pan for about 5 minutes or until the sauce has reduced and thickened.

8 Pour in the cream, return the fish to the pan and heat through. Serve with the cooked vegetables of your choice.

Italian Cod

Cod fillets are roasted with herbs and topped with a lemon
and rosemary crust – a fragrant combination that immediately evokes the
Mediterranean. This dish is a delicious main course.

Serves 4
25 g/1 oz/2 tbsp butter
50 g/2 oz/1 cup wholemeal (whole-wheat) breadcrumbs
25 g/1 oz/¼ cup chopped walnuts
grated rind and juice of 2 lemons
2 sprigs rosemary, stalks removed
2 tbsp chopped parsley
4 cod fillets, each about 150 g/5 oz
1 garlic clove, crushed
3 tbsp walnut oil
1 small red chilli, diced
salad leaves, to serve

1 Melt the butter in a large frying pan (skillet). Remove the frying pan (skillet) from the heat and add the breadcrumbs, walnuts, the rind and juice of 1 lemon, half the rosemary and half the parsley. Stir the mixture thoroughly.

2 Press the breadcrumb mixture over the top of the cod fillets. Place the cod fillets in a single layer in a shallow, foil-lined roasting tin (pan).

3 Bake in a preheated oven at 200°C/400°F/Gas Mark 6 for 25–30 minutes.

4 Mix the garlic, the remaining lemon rind and juice, rosemary, parsley and chilli in a bowl. Beat in the walnut oil and mix to combine. Drizzle the dressing over the cod fillets as soon as they are cooked.

5 Transfer to serving plates and serve immediately with salad leaves.

COOK'S VARIATION

If preferred, the walnuts may be omitted from the crust. In addition, extra virgin olive oil can be used instead of walnut oil, if you prefer.

COOK'S TIP

The 'hotness' of chillies varies, so use them with caution. As a general guide, the smaller the chilli the hotter it will be.

Trout in Red Wine

This recipe from Trentino is best when the fish
are freshly caught, but it is a good way to cook any trout,
giving it an interesting flavour.

Serves 4
4 fresh trout, about 300 g/10¹/₂ oz each
250 ml/8 fl oz/1 cup red or white wine vinegar
300 ml/¹/₂ pint/1¹/₄ cups red or dry white wine
150 ml/¹/₄ pint/²/₃ cup water
1 carrot, sliced
2–4 bay leaves
thinly pared rind of 1 lemon
1 small onion, very thinly sliced
4 sprigs fresh parsley
4 sprigs fresh thyme
1 tsp black peppercorns
6–8 cloves
75 g/3 oz/6 tbsp butter
1 tbsp chopped fresh mixed herbs
salt and pepper

GARNISH

sprigs of herbs
lemon slices

1 Gut the trout but leave their heads on. Dry on kitchen paper (paper towels) and lay the fish head to tail in a shallow container just large enough to hold them.

2 Bring the wine vinegar to the boil and pour slowly all over the fish. Marinate in the refrigerator for about 20 minutes.

3 Put the wine, water, carrot, bay leaves, lemon rind, onion, parsley, thyme, peppercorns and cloves into a pan with a good pinch of sea salt and heat gently.

4 Drain the fish thoroughly, discarding the vinegar. Place the fish in a fish kettle or large frying pan (skillet) so they touch. When the wine mixture boils, strain it gently over the fish, so they are about half covered. Cover the pan and simmer over a very low heat for 15 minutes.

5 Carefully remove the fish from the pan, draining off as much of the liquid as possible, and arrange them on a warm serving dish. Keep warm.

6 Boil the cooking liquid hard until reduced to about 4–6 tablespoons. Melt the butter in a small saucepan and strain into the cooking liquid. Adjust the seasoning and spoon the sauce over the fish. Sprinkle with chopped mixed herbs and garnish with lemon and sprigs of herbs.

Sardinian Red Mullet

Red mullet has a beautiful pink skin, which is enhanced in this dish
by being cooked in red wine and orange juice. It may be served chilled or warm.

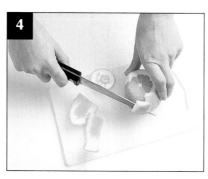

Serves 4
50 g/2 oz/$^1/_3$ cup sultanas (golden raisins)
150 ml/$^1/_4$ pint/$^2/_3$ cup red wine
2 tbsp olive oil
2 medium onions, sliced
1 courgette (zucchini), cut into 5-cm/2-inch sticks
2 oranges
2 tsp coriander seeds, lightly crushed
4 red mullet, boned and filleted
50g/2 oz can anchovy fillets, drained
2 tbsp chopped, fresh oregano
salt and pepper

1 Place the sultanas (golden raisins) in a bowl. Add the red wine and set aside to soak for 10 minutes.

2 Heat the oil in a large frying pan (skillet). Add the onions and sauté for 2 minutes.

3 Add the courgettes (zucchini) to the pan and sauté, stirring occasionally, for 3 minutes, or until tender.

4 Using a zester, pare long, thin strips from 1 of the oranges. Using a sharp knife, remove the skin from both the oranges, then segment the oranges by slicing between the lines of pith.

5 Add the orange zest and the crushed coriander seeds to the frying pan (skillet). Add the red wine, sultanas (golden raisins), red mullet and anchovies to the pan and simmer for 10–15 minutes, or until the fish is cooked through.

6 Stir in the oregano and set aside to cool. Transfer the mixture to a large bowl, cover and chill in the refrigerator for at least 2 hours to allow the flavours to mingle.

7 Transfer the fish to serving plates and serve immediately or heat through and serve warm.

COOK'S TIP

There are at least two varieties of red mullet. The type with the best flavour and texture is sometimes called golden mullet. It is usually available all year round – frozen, if not fresh.

Herrings with Hot Pesto Sauce

By making a simple pesto sauce, but omitting the cheese, it is possible to heat
the paste without it becoming stringy, so it can be used as a hot sauce.

Serves 4
4 herrings or small mackerel, cleaned and gutted
2 tbsp olive oil
225 g/9 oz tomatoes, peeled, seeded and chopped
8 canned anchovy fillets, chopped
about 30 fresh basil leaves
50 g/2 oz/$^1/_2$ cup pine nuts
2 garlic cloves, crushed

1 Cook the herrings or mackerel under a preheated grill (broiler) for about 8-10 minutes on each side, or until the skin is slightly charred on both sides.

2 Meanwhile, heat 1 tablespoon of the olive oil in a large saucepan.

3 Add the tomatoes and anchovies to the saucepan and cook, stirring frequently, over a medium heat for 5 minutes.

4 Meanwhile, place the basil, pine nuts, garlic and remaining olive oil in a food processor and process to form a smooth paste. Alternatively, pound the ingredients by hand in a mortar with a pestle.

5 Add the pesto mixture to the saucepan containing the tomato and anchovy mixture and lower the heat. Heat through, stirring constantly.

6 Spoon a little of the pesto sauce on to warm individual serving plates. Arrange the fish on top and pour the rest of the pesto sauce over the fish. Serve immediately.

COOK'S TIP

Try barbecuing (grilling) the fish for an extra charbroiled flavour, if you prefer.

Sardine & Potato Bake

Fresh sardines are now readily available,
so this traditional dish from Liguria can be enjoyed by all.

Serves 4
1 kg/2¼ lb potatoes
1 kg/2¼ lb sardines, defrosted if frozen
1 tbsp olive oil, plus extra for oiling
1 onion, chopped
2–3 garlic cloves, crushed
2 tbsp chopped fresh parsley
350 g/12 oz ripe tomatoes, peeled and sliced or 400 g/14 oz can peeled tomatoes, partly drained and chopped
1–2 tbsp chopped fresh Italian herbs, such as oregano, thyme, rosemary and marjoram
150 ml/¼ pint/⅔ cup dry white wine
salt and pepper

1 Put the potatoes in a pan of salted water, bring to the boil, cover and simmer for 10 minutes, then drain. When cool enough to handle, cut into slices about 6 mm/¼ inch thick.

2 Gut and clean the sardines. Cut off their heads and tails and then slit open the length of the belly. Turn the fish over so the skin is upwards and press firmly along the backbone to loosen it. Turn over and carefully remove the backbone. Wash the fish in cold water, drain well and dry them on kitchen paper (paper towels).

3 Heat the olive oil in a pan and sauté the onion and garlic until soft, but not coloured.

4 Arrange the potatoes in a well-oiled ovenproof dish and sprinkle with the onions and then the parsley and plenty of seasoning.

5 Arrange the open sardines over the potatoes, skin side down, then cover with the tomatoes and sprinkle with the rest of the herbs. Pour in the white wine and season to taste with salt and pepper.

6 Cook uncovered in a preheated oven at 190°C/180°F/Gas Mark 5, for about 40 minutes, until the fish is tender. If the casserole seems to be drying out, add another couple of tablespoons of wine. Serve hot.

Fresh Baked Sardines

Here, fresh sardines are baked with eggs, herbs and vegetables to form a dish similar to an omelette.

Serves 4
2 tbsp olive oil
2 large onions, sliced into rings
3 garlic cloves, chopped
2 large courgettes (zucchini), cut into sticks
3 tbsp fresh thyme, stalks removed
8 sardine fillets or about 1 kg/ 2¼ lb whole sardines, filleted
75 g/3 oz/1 cup grated Parmesan cheese
4 eggs, beaten
150 ml/¼ pint/⅔ cup milk
salt and pepper

7 Bake in a preheated oven at 180°C/350°F/Gas Mark 4 for 20–25 minutes, or until golden and set.

8 Serve the fresh baked sardines hot, straight from the oven.

COOK'S VARIATION

If you cannot find sardines that are large enough to fillet, use small mackerel instead.

1 Heat 1 tablespoon of the oil in a frying pan (skillet). Add the onions and garlic and sauté for 2–3 minutes.

2 Add the courgettes (zucchini) and cook for 5 minutes, until golden.

3 Stir 2 tablespoons of the thyme into the mixture.

4 Place half of the onions and courgettes (zucchini) in the base of a large ovenproof dish. Top with the sardine fillets and half the grated Parmesan cheese.

5 Place the remaining onions and courgettes (zucchini) on top and sprinkle with the remaining thyme.

6 Mix the eggs and milk together in a bowl and season to taste with salt and pepper. Pour the mixture over the vegetables and sardines in the dish. Sprinkle the remaining Parmesan cheese over the top.

Small Pancakes with Smoked Fish

These are delicious as a starter or light supper dish and
you can vary the filling with whichever fish you prefer.

Makes 12 pancakes
PANCAKES
115 g/4 oz/1 cup plain (all-purpose) flour
¹/₂ tsp salt
1 egg, beaten
300 ml/¹/₂ pint/1¹/₄ cups milk
1 tbsp oil, for frying
SAUCE
450 g/1 lb smoked haddock fillets, skinned
300 ml/¹/₂ pint/1¹/₄ cups milk
40 g/1¹/₂ oz/3 tbsp butter or margarine
40 g/1¹/₂ oz/¹/₃ cup plain (all-purpose) flour
300 ml/¹/₂ pint/1¹/₄ cups fish stock
75 g/3 oz/1 cup grated Parmesan cheese
115 g/4 oz frozen peas, thawed
115 g/4 oz peeled cooked prawns (shrimp)
50 g/2 oz/¹/₂ cup grated Gruyère (Swiss) cheese
salt and pepper

1 To make the batter, sift the flour
and salt into a bowl and make a well
in the centre. Add the egg and, using a
wooden spoon, begin to draw in the
flour. Slowly add the milk and beat to
form a smooth batter. Set aside.

2 Place the fish in a large frying pan
(skillet), add the milk and bring to the
boil. Simmer for 10 minutes, or until
the fish begins to flake. Drain,
reserving the milk, and flake the fish.

3 Melt the butter in a pan. Add
the flour and cook, stirring, for 2–3
minutes. Remove the pan from the
heat and stir in the reserved milk and

fish stock to make a sauce. Return to
the heat and bring to the boil, stirring.
Stir in the Parmesan and season.

4 Grease a frying pan (skillet) with
oil. Add 2 tablespoons of the pancake
batter, swirling it around, and cook for
2–3 minutes. Loosen the sides with a
palette knife (spatula) and flip over the
pancake. Cook for 2–3 minutes until
golden. Repeat, stacking the pancakes

interleaved with sheets of baking
parchment. Keep warm in the oven.

5 Stir the flaked fish, peas and prawns
(shrimp) into half of the sauce and use
to fill each pancake. Put the pancakes
in an ovenproof dish, cover with the
remaining sauce, top with the Gruyère
(Swiss) cheese and bake in a preheated
oven at 190°C/375°F/Gas Mark 5 for 20
minutes, until golden.

Skewered Monkfish with Caper Sauce

Monkfish is a very meaty-textured fish. It cooks extremely
well, as it doesn't flake like most other fish.

Serves 4
675 g/1¹/₂ lb monkfish tail
finely grated rind and juice 1 small lemon
2 tbsp olive oil
small bunch of fresh bay leaves
1 small lemon, cut into wedges
green salad, to serve
SAUCE
6 tbsp olive oil
1 garlic clove, finely chopped
finely grated rind and juice 1 small lemon
1 tbsp chopped fresh parsley
2 tbsp capers, drained and chopped
3 anchovy fillets, finely chopped
pepper

1 Wash the monkfish and pat dry with kitchen paper (paper towels). Carefully trim away the pinky grey membrane and slice either side of the central bone to give 2 thick fillets.

2 Cut the monkfish into 2.5-cm/ 1-inch cubes and place in a shallow dish. Toss in the lemon rind and juice and the olive oil.

3 Drain the fish, reserving the juices, and thread on to four bamboo skewers, threading a few bay leaves and wedges of lemon in between the fish cubes.

4 Preheat a grill (broiler). Place the skewers on a rack and cover the ends of the skewers with foil to prevent them from burning. Brush the fish

with some of the reserved juices and cook for 3 minutes. Turn over, brush again and cook for a further 3–4 minutes, until tender and cooked through. Alternatively, cook on a barbecue, turning and brushing with the reserved juices, for 6–8 minutes.

5 Meanwhile, mix together all the ingredients for the sauce in a small serving bowl and set aside.

6 Drain the skewers and transfer to warm serving plates. Serve with the sauce and a green salad.

Celery & Salt Cod Casserole

Salt cod is dried and salted in order to preserve it. It has an unusual
and quite strong flavour, which goes particularly well with celery in this dish.

Serves 4
250 g/9 oz salt cod fillets, soaked overnight
1 tbsp oil
4 shallots, finely chopped
2 garlic cloves, chopped
3 celery sticks, chopped
400 g/14 oz can tomatoes, chopped
150 ml/$^1/_4$ pint/$^2/_3$ cup fish stock
50 g/2 oz/$^1/_2$ cup pine nuts
2 tbsp roughly chopped tarragon
2 tbsp capers
crusty bread or mashed potato, to serve

1 Drain the salt cod, rinse it under plenty of cold running water and drain again thoroughly. Remove and discard any skin and bones. Pat the fish dry with kitchen paper (paper towels) and cut it into chunks.

2 Heat the oil in a large frying pan (skillet). Add the shallots and garlic and sauté for 2–3 minutes. Add the celery and sauté for a further 2 minutes, then add the tomatoes and stock.

3 Bring the mixture to the boil, reduce the heat and simmer for 5 minutes.

4 Add the fish and cook for 10 minutes or until tender.

5 Meanwhile, place the pine nuts on a baking tray (cookie sheet). Place under a preheated grill (broiler) and toast for 2–3 minutes, or until golden.

6 Stir the tarragon, capers and pine nuts into the fish casserole and heat gently to warm through.

7 Transfer to warm serving plates and serve immediately with fresh crusty bread or mashed potato.

COOK'S TIP

Salt cod is a useful ingredient to keep in the storecupboard and once soaked, can be used in the same way as any other fish.

Salt Cod Fritters

These tasty little fried cakes of mashed salt cod mixed with fennel and a little chilli make an excellent snack or main course served with vegetables and a chilli relish.

Serves 4
115 g/4 oz self-raising flour
1 egg, beaten
150 ml/¼ pint/⅔ cup milk
250 g/9 oz salt cod fillets, soaked overnight
1 small red onion, finely chopped
1 small fennel bulb, finely chopped
1 fresh red chilli, finely chopped
2 tbsp oil
TO SERVE
crisp salad, chilli relish, cooked rice and fresh vegetables

hot oil. Cook the fritters, in batches, for 3–4 minutes on each side, until golden and slightly puffed. Keep warm while cooking the remaining mixture.

7 Serve immediately with salad and chilli relish for a light meal or with vegetables and rice.

COOK'S TIP

If you prefer larger fritters, use 2 tablespoons of batter per fritter and cook for slightly longer.

1 Sift the flour into a large mixing bowl. Make a well in the centre and add the egg.

2 Using a wooden spoon, gradually draw in the flour, slowly adding the milk, and mix to form a smooth batter. Let stand for 10 minutes.

3 Drain the salt cod and rinse it under cold running water. Drain thoroughly again.

4 Remove and discard the skin and any bones from the fish, then mash the flesh with a fork.

5 Place the fish in a large bowl and combine with the onion, fennel and chilli. Add the mixture to the batter and blend together.

6 Heat the oil in a frying pan (skillet) and, taking about 1 tablespoon of the mixture at a time, spoon it into the

Meat & Poultry Dishes

Meat and poultry are quite expensive in Italy, so they are prepared and cooked with special care. Meat and poultry dishes are often served in their cooking juices rather than with the addition of extra sauces. Pork is the most frequently eaten meat, but veal is popular too and Tuscan steak is unmatched anywhere in the world. Spring lamb is traditionally served on Easter

Sunday, following the long Lent fast. Spit-roasted with fresh rosemary and other herbs or cooked in the oven in garlic, wine and

herbs, it is worth waiting forty days to eat it.

Meat is usually sold already boned, often cut across the grain. No part is wasted – what cannot be served at the table is used for making stocks and soups.

Chicken tends to be regarded as a luxury, although there are some superb classic dishes: Chicken with Green Olives from Apulia, Roman Chicken and Balsamic Chicken from Emilia Romagna.

Beef in Barolo

Barolo is a famous wine from the Piedmont area of Italy.
Its mellow flavour is the key to this dish, so don't stint on the quality of the wine.

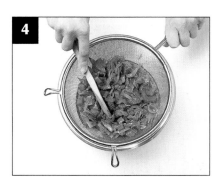

Serves 6
4 tbsp oil
1 kg/2¼ lb piece boned rolled rib of beef, or piece of silverside (round)
2 garlic cloves, crushed
4 shallots, sliced
1 tsp chopped fresh rosemary
1 tsp chopped fresh oregano
2 celery sticks, sliced
1 large carrot, diced
2 cloves
1 bottle Barolo wine
freshly grated nutmeg
salt and pepper
broccoli, carrots and new potatoes, to serve

1 Heat the oil in a flameproof casserole. Add the beef and cook until browned all over. Remove the meat from the casserole.

2 Add the garlic, shallots, rosemary, oregano, celery, carrot and cloves to the casserole and sauté, stirring frequently, for 5 minutes.

3 Return the meat to the casserole, placing it on top of the vegetables. Pour in the wine. Bring to the boil, lower the heat, cover and simmer for 2 hours, until the beef is tender. Remove the meat from the casserole and let stand for 5–10 minutes.

4 Meanwhile, rub the contents of the casserole through a strainer or work in a food processor, adding a little hot beef stock if necessary. Season to taste with nutmeg, salt and pepper.

5 Slice the beef and arrange on a warm serving plate.

6 Spoon a little sauce on top of the beef and serve immediately with broccoli, carrots and new potatoes (or other vegetables of your choice) and the remaining sauce.

COOK'S TIP

Resting the meat after cooking will make it easier to carve, as well as allowing you sufficient time to prepare the sauce. Carve thick or thin slices, as you prefer.

Rich Beef Stew

This slow-cooked beef stew is flavoured with
oranges, red wine and porcini mushrooms.

Serves 4
1 tbsp oil
15 g/¹⁄₂ oz/1 tbsp butter
225 g/8 oz baby onions, peeled and halved
600 g/1 lb 5 oz stewing steak, diced into 4-cm/1¹⁄₂-inch chunks
300 ml/¹⁄₂ pint/1¹⁄₄ cups beef stock
150 ml/¹⁄₄ pint/²⁄₃ cup red wine
4 tbsp chopped oregano
1 tbsp sugar
1 orange
25 g/1 oz dried porcini or other dried mushrooms
225 g/8 oz fresh plum tomatoes
cooked rice or potatoes, to serve

1 Heat the oil and butter in a large frying pan (skillet). Add the onions and sauté for 5 minutes, or until golden. Remove with a slotted spoon, set aside and keep warm.

2 Add the steak to the pan and cook, stirring, for 5 minutes or until browned all over.

3 Return the onions to the frying pan (skillet) and add the beef stock, red wine, oregano and sugar, stirring to mix well. Transfer the mixture to a casserole dish.

4 Pare the rind from the orange and cut it into thin strips. Remove any remaining pith and slice the orange flesh into rings. Add the orange rings and the rind to the casserole. Cook in a preheated oven at 180°C/350°F/Gas Mark 4, for 1¹⁄₄ hours.

5 Soak the porcini mushrooms for 30 minutes in a small bowl containing 4 tablespoons of warm water.

6 Peel and halve the tomatoes. Add the tomatoes, porcini mushrooms and their soaking liquid to the casserole. Cook for a further 20 minutes, until the meat is tender and the juices have

thickened. Serve immediately with cooked rice or potatoes.

COOK'S VARIATION

Instead of fresh tomatoes, try using 8 sun-dried tomatoes, cut into wide strips, if you prefer.

Beef Olives in Rich Gravy

Wafer-thin slices of tender beef enclose a rich garlic and
bacon stuffing, flavoured with the tang of orange.

Serves 4
8 ready-prepared beef olives
4 tbsp chopped fresh parsley
4 garlic cloves, finely chopped
115 g/4 oz smoked bacon, finely chopped
grated rind of $^1/_2$ small orange
2 tbsp olive oil
300 ml/$^1/_2$ pint/$1^1/_4$ cups dry red wine
1 bay leaf
1 tsp sugar
50 g/2 oz/$^1/_2$ cup stoned (pitted) black olives, drained
salt and pepper

GARNISH

orange slices

chopped fresh parsley

1 Unroll the beef olives and flatten out as thinly as possible using a meat mallet or rolling pin. Trim the edges to neaten.

2 Mix together the parsley, garlic, bacon, orange rind and salt and pepper to taste. Spread this mixture evenly over each beef olive.

3 Roll up each beef olive tightly, then secure with a cocktail stick (toothpick). Heat the oil in a frying pan (skillet) and fry the beef on all sides for 10 minutes.

4 Drain the beef olives, reserving the pan juices, and keep warm. Pour the wine into the juices, add the bay leaf, sugar and salt and pepper to taste.

Bring to the boil and boil rapidly for 5 minutes to reduce slightly.

5 Return the cooked beef to the pan, together with the olives and heat through for a further 2 minutes.

Remove and discard the bay leaf and cocktail sticks (toothpicks).

6 Transfer the beef olives and sauce to a serving dish, and serve garnished with orange slices and parsley.

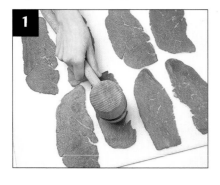

Pizzaiola Steak

This has a Neapolitan sauce, using the delicious fresh red tomatoes
so abundant in that area, but canned tomatoes make an excellent alternative.

Serves 4
2 x 400 g/14 oz cans peeled tomatoes or 675 g/1½ lb fresh tomatoes
4 tbsp olive oil
2–3 garlic cloves, crushed
1 onion, finely chopped
1 tbsp tomato purée (paste)
1½ tsp chopped fresh marjoram or oregano or ¾ tsp dried marjoram or oregano
4 thin sirloin or rump steaks
2 tbsp chopped fresh parsley
1 tsp sugar
salt and pepper
fresh herbs, to garnish (optional)
sauté potatoes, to serve

1 If using canned tomatoes, process them in a food processor, then rub them through a strainer to remove the seeds. If using fresh tomatoes, peel, seed and chop finely.

2 Heat half of the oil in a frying pan (skillet). Add the garlic and onions and sauté for 5 minutes, or until soft.

3 Add the tomatoes, tomato purée (paste) and marjoram or oregano to the pan and season to taste with salt and pepper. If using fresh tomatoes, add 4 tablespoons of water. Simmer very gently, stirring occasionally, for 8–10 minutes.

4 Meanwhile, trim the steaks if necessary and season with salt and pepper. Heat the remaining oil in a frying pan (skillet) and fry the steaks quickly on both sides to seal, then

continue until cooked to your liking – 2 minutes for rare, 3–4 minutes for medium, or 5 minutes for well done. Alternatively, cook the steaks under a preheated grill (broiler) after brushing lightly with oil.

5 When the sauce has thickened a little, adjust the seasoning and stir in the chopped parsley and sugar.

6 Pour off the excess fat from the frying pan (skillet) with the steaks and add the tomato sauce. Reheat gently. Transfer the steaks to a warm serving dish, spooning the sauce over and around them. Garnish with fresh herbs, such as marjoram or sage, if liked. Serve immediately, with sauté potatoes and a green vegetable or salad leaves.

Pork with Lemon & Garlic

This is a simplified version of a traditional dish from
the Marche region, on the east coast of Italy. Pork fillet pockets are stuffed
with ham (prosciutto) and herbs.

Serves 4
450 g/1 lb pork fillet (tenderloin)
50 g/2 oz/½ cup chopped almonds
2 tbsp olive oil
115 g/4 oz raw ham (prosciutto), finely chopped
2 garlic cloves, chopped
1 tbsp fresh oregano, chopped
finely grated rind of 2 lemons
4 shallots, finely chopped
200 ml/7 fl oz/¾ cup ham or chicken stock
1 tsp sugar

1 Using a sharp knife, cut the pork fillet (tenderloin) into 4 equal pieces. Place the pork between sheets of greaseproof (wax) paper and pound each piece with a meat mallet or the end of a rolling pin to flatten it.

2 Cut a horizontal slit in each piece of pork to make a pocket.

3 Place the almonds on a baking tray (cookie sheet). Lightly toast the almonds under a preheated grill (broiler) for about 2–3 minutes, or until golden.

4 Mix the almonds with 1 tablespoon of the olive oil, the chopped ham (prosciutto), garlic, oregano and the finely grated rind from 1 lemon. Spoon the mixture into the pockets of the pork.

5 Heat the remaining oil in a large frying pan (skillet). Add the shallots and sauté for 2 minutes.

6 Add the pork to the frying pan (skillet) and cook over a medium heat for 2 minutes on each side, or until browned all over.

7 Add the stock to the pan and bring to the boil. Lower the heat, cover and simmer for 45 minutes, or until the pork is tender. Remove the meat from the pan, place on warm individual serving plates and keep warm.

8 Using a zester, pare the remaining lemon. Add the rind and the sugar to the pan, bring back to the boil and boil for 3–4 minutes, or until reduced and syrupy. Pour the sauce over the pork and serve immediately.

Pork Wrapped in Prosciutto

A sophisticated roast with Mediterranean flavours
is ideal served with a pungent olive paste.

Serves 4
500 g/1¼ lb pork fillet (tenderloin)
small bunch of fresh basil leaves, washed
2 tbsp freshly grated Parmesan cheese
2 tbsp sun-dried tomato paste
6 thin slices Parma ham (prosciutto)
1 tbsp olive oil
salt and pepper
sage sprigs, to garnish
salad leaves, to serve

OLIVE PASTE

115 g/4 oz/1 cup stoned (pitted) black olives
4 tbsp olive oil
2 garlic cloves, peeled

1 Trim away any excess fat and membrane from the pork fillet (tenderloin). Slice the pork lengthways down the middle, taking care not to cut all the way through.

2 Open out the pork and season the inside with salt and pepper. Lay the basil leaves down the centre. Mix the cheese and sun-dried tomato paste and spread on top of the basil.

3 Press the pork back together. Wrap the ham (prosciutto) around the pork, overlapping, to cover. Place on a rack in a roasting tin (pan), seam side down, and brush well with olive oil. Bake in a preheated oven at 190°C/375°F/Gas Mark 5, for 30–40 minutes, until tender and cooked through. Remove from the oven and let stand for 10 minutes.

4 For the olive paste, place all the ingredients in a food processor and process until smooth. Alternatively, for a coarser paste, finely chop the olives and garlic and mix with the oil.

5 Drain the cooked pork and slice it thinly. Arrange the slices on individual serving plates, garnish with sage sprigs and serve, accompanied with the olive paste and salad leaves.

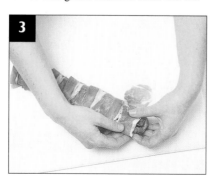

Pork Chops with Fennel & Juniper

The addition of juniper and fennel to the pork chops gives
an unusual and delicate flavour to this dish.

Serves 4
¹/₂ fennel bulb
1 tbsp juniper berries
about 2 tbsp olive oil
finely grated rind and juice of 1 orange
4 pork chops, each about 150 g/5 oz
fresh bread and a crisp salad, to serve

1 Using a sharp knife, trim any damaged or discoloured outer layers from the fennel bulb. Finely chop the fennel, discarding the green parts.

2 Grind the juniper berries in a mortar with a pestle. Mix the crushed juniper berries with the fennel, olive oil and orange rind.

3 Using a sharp knife, score a few cuts all over each chop.

4 Arrange the pork chops in a single layer in a roasting tin (pan) or an ovenproof dish. Spoon the fennel and juniper mixture over the top.

5 Carefully pour the orange juice over the top of each pork chop, cover with cling film (plastic wrap) and marinate in the refrigerator for a minimum of 2 hours.

6 Cook the pork chops, under a preheated grill (broiler), turning occasionally, for 10–15 minutes, until the meat is tender and cooked through. Test by piercing the meat

with the point of a sharp knife. The meat is cooked through when the juices run clear.

7 Transfer the pork chops to warm, individual serving plates and serve immediately with a crisp, fresh green salad and plenty of fresh crusty bread to mop up the delicious cooking juices.

COOK'S TIP

Juniper berries are most commonly associated with gin, but they are often added to meat dishes in Italy for a delicate citrus flavour. They can be bought dried from most health food shops and some larger supermarkets.

Pork Chops with Sage

The fresh, aromatic taste of sage is the perfect counterbalance
to the richness of pork.

Serves 4
2 tbsp flour
1 tbsp chopped fresh sage or 1 tsp dried
4 lean boneless pork chops, trimmed of excess fat
2 tbsp olive oil
15 g/$^1/_2$ oz/1 tbsp butter
2 red onions, thinly sliced and pushed out into rings
1 tbsp lemon juice
2 tsp caster (superfine) sugar
4 plum tomatoes, quartered
salt and pepper
green salad, to serve

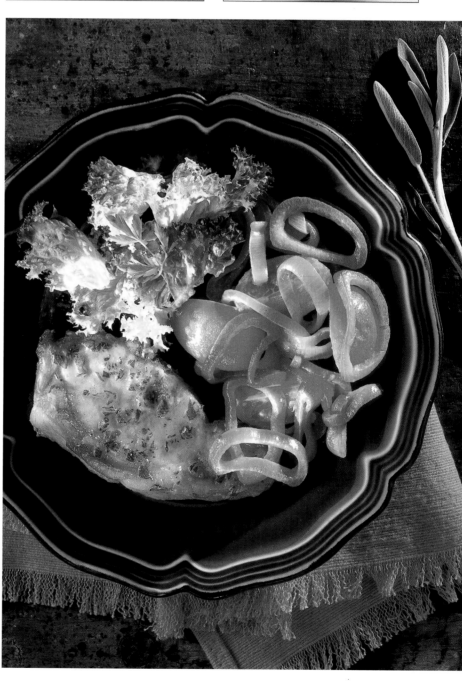

1 Mix the flour, sage and salt and pepper on a plate. Lightly dust the pork chops on both sides with the seasoned flour.

2 Heat the oil and butter in a frying pan (skillet). Add the chops and cook for 6–7 minutes on each side, until tender and cooked through.

3 Remove the chops from the pan, drain well, set aside and keep warm. Reserve the pan juices.

4 Toss the onion in the lemon juice. Return the pan to the heat. Add the onion, sugar and tomatoes and sauté for 5 minutes, until tender.

5 Place the pork chops on individual serving plates and spoon the tomato and onion mixture beside them. Serve immediately with a green salad.

Pork Cooked in Milk

This traditional dish of boneless pork cooked with garlic
and milk can be served hot or cold.

Serves 4
800 g/1¾ lb boneless leg of pork
1 tbsp oil
25 g/1 oz/2 tbsp butter
1 onion, chopped
2 garlic cloves, chopped
75 g/3 oz pancetta or bacon, diced
1.2 litres/2 pints/5 cups milk
1 tbsp green peppercorns, crushed
2 fresh bay leaves
2 tbsp marjoram
2 tbsp thyme

1 Using a sharp knife, remove the fat
from the pork. Shape the meat into a
neat form, tying it in place with a
length of string.

2 Heat the oil and butter in a large
saucepan. Add the onion, garlic and
pancetta to the pan and sauté for
2–3 minutes.

3 Add the pork to the pan and cook,
turning occasionally, until it is
browned all over.

4 Pour in the milk, add the
peppercorns, bay leaves, marjoram
and thyme and cook over a low heat
for 1¼–1½ hours, or until tender.
Watch the liquid carefully for the last
15 minutes of the cooking time
because it tends to reduce very
quickly and could easily burn. If the
liquid reduces and the pork is still not
tender, add another 125 ml/4 fl oz/
½ cup milk and continue cooking.
Reserve the cooking liquid.

5 Remove the pork from the
saucepan. Using a sharp knife, cut the
meat into slices.

6 Transfer the pork slices to serving
plates and serve immediately with
the sauce (see Cook's Tip).

COOK'S TIP

As the milk reduces naturally
in this dish, it forms a thick
and creamy sauce, which
curdles slightly, but tastes delicious.

Neapolitan Pork Steaks

An Italian version of grilled (broiled) pork steaks,
this dish is easy to make and delicious to eat.

Serves 4
2 tbsp olive oil
1 garlic clove, chopped
1 large onion, sliced
400 g/14 oz can tomatoes
2 tsp yeast extract
4 pork loin steaks, each about 130 g/4^1/$_2$ oz
75 g/3 oz/^{3}/$_4$ cup stoned (pitted) black olives
2 tbsp fresh basil, shredded
freshly grated Parmesan cheese, to garnish
green vegetables, such as broccoli and green beans, to serve

1 Heat the oil in a large frying pan (skillet). Add the onions and garlic and sauté, stirring, for 3–4 minutes or until they just begin to soften.

2 Add the tomatoes and yeast extract to the frying pan (skillet) and simmer for about 5 minutes, or until the sauce starts to thicken.

3 Cook the pork steaks, under a preheated grill (broiler), for 5 minutes on both sides, until the the the meat is golden and cooked through. Set the pork steaks aside and keep warm.

4 Add the olives and shredded basil to the sauce in the frying pan (skillet) and stir to combine.

5 Transfer the steaks to warm serving plates. Top the steaks with the sauce, sprinkle with freshly grated Parmesan cheese and serve immediately.

COOK'S TIP

Parmesan is a mature and exceptionally hard cheese produced in Italy. You need to add only a little as it has a very strong flavour.

COOK'S TIP

Some types of canned tomatoes are flavoured with onion, chillies or herbs. However, it is usually better to add your own flavourings.

Roman Pan-fried Lamb

Chunks of tender lamb, pan-fried with garlic and
stewed in red wine are a real Roman dish.

Serves 4
1 tbsp oil
15 g/ $^1/_2$ oz/1 tbsp butter
500 g/1$^1/_4$ lb boneless lamb (shoulder or leg), cut in 2.5-cm/1-inch chunks
4 garlic cloves, peeled
3 sprigs thyme, stalks removed
6 canned anchovy fillets
150 ml/$^1/_4$ pint/$^2/_3$ cup red wine
150 ml/$^1/_2$ pint/$^2/_3$ cup lamb or vegetable stock
1 tsp sugar
50 g/2 oz/$^1/_2$ cup stoned (pitted) black olives, halved
2 tbsp chopped parsley, to garnish
mashed potato, to serve

1 Heat the oil and butter in a large frying pan (skillet). Add the lamb and cook, stirring, for 4–5 minutes, until the meat is browned all over.

2 Using a pestle and mortar, grind together the garlic, thyme and anchovies to make a smooth paste.

3 Add the wine and lamb or vegetable stock to the frying pan (skillet). Stir in the garlic and anchovy paste, together with the sugar.

4 Bring the mixture to the boil, reduce the heat, cover and simmer for 30–40 minutes, or until the lamb is tender. For the last 10 minutes of the cooking time, remove the lid to allow the sauce to reduce slightly.

5 Stir the olives into the sauce and mix to combine.

6 Transfer the lamb, together with the sauce to a warm serving dish and garnish with the freshly chopped parsley. Serve the pan-fried lamb immediately with creamy mashed potatoes, if you like.

COOK'S TIP

Roman dishes are characteristically robust, with plenty of herbs and seasonings.

Lamb with Olives

This is a very simple dish that is quick to prepare. The fresh chilli
gives this ideal supper dish a real kick.

Serves 4
1.2 kg/2½ lb boneless leg of lamb
6 tbsp olive oil
2 garlic cloves, crushed
1 onion, sliced
1 small fresh red chilli, seeded and finely chopped
175 ml/6 fl oz/¾ cup dry white wine
175 g/6 oz/1 cup stoned (pitted) black olives
salt
chopped fresh parsley, to garnish

1 Using a sharp knife, cut the lamb
into 2.5-cm/1-inch cubes.

2 Heat the oil in a frying pan (skillet).
Add the garlic, onion and chilli and
sauté, stirring frequently, for
5 minutes.

3 Add the wine and meat and cook
for 5 minutes.

4 Stir in the olives, then transfer the
mixture to a casserole. Cook in a
preheated oven at 180°C/350°F/Gas
Mark 4, for about 1 hour 20 minutes,
until the meat is tender. Season to
taste with salt, and serve garnished
with chopped fresh parsley.

COOK'S TIP

Black olives are quite easy to stone
(pit) with a sharp knife, but for a
neater job and for green olives, use
a olive or cherry stoner (pitter). It is
also known as a chasse noyer.

Lamb Noisettes with Bay & Lemon

These lamb chops quickly become more elegant when the
bone is removed to make noisettes.

Serves 4
4 lamb chops
1 tbsp oil
15 g/¹/₂ oz/1 tbsp butter
150 ml/¹/₄ pint/²/₃ cup white wine
150 ml/¹/₂ pint/²/₃ cup lamb or vegetable stock
2 bay leaves
pared rind of 1 lemon
salt and pepper

7 Transfer the lamb to individual serving plates. Remove the string from each noisette and serve immediately with the sauce.

COOK'S TIP

Any one of Italy's excellent, slightly sweet rosé wines would also complement the lamb in this dish.

1 Using a sharp knife, carefully remove the bone from each lamb chop, keeping the meat intact. Alternatively, ask the butcher to prepare the lamb noisettes for you.

2 Shape the meat into rounds and secure with lengths of string.

3 Heat the oil and butter together in a frying pan (skillet) until the mixture starts to froth. Add the lamb noisettes and cook for 2–3 minutes on each side, or until browned all over.

4 Remove the frying pan (skillet) from the heat, drain off all of the fat and discard.

5 Return the frying pan (skillet) to the heat. Add the white wine, lamb or vegetable stock, bay leaves and lemon rind to the frying pan (skillet) and cook for 20–25 minutes, or until the lamb is tender.

6 Season the lamb noisettes and the sauce with a little salt and pepper to taste.

Pot Roasted Leg of Lamb

This dish from the Abruzzi region uses a slow
cooking method which ensures that the meat absorbs the
flavourings and becomes very tender.

Serves 4
1.75 kg/4 lb leg of lamb
3–4 sprigs fresh rosemary
115 g/4 oz bacon
4 tbsp olive oil
2–3 garlic cloves, crushed
2 onions, sliced
2 carrots, sliced
2 celery sticks, sliced
300 ml/$^1/_2$ pint/1$^1/_4$ cups dry white wine
1 tbsp tomato purée (paste)
300 ml/$^1/_2$ pint/1$^1/_4$ cups stock
350 g/12 oz tomatoes, peeled, quartered and seeded
1 tbsp chopped fresh parsley
1 tbsp chopped fresh oregano or marjoram
salt and pepper
fresh rosemary sprigs, to garnish

1 Wipe the joint of lamb all over and trim off any excess fat, then season with salt and pepper, rubbing well in. Lay the sprigs of rosemary over the lamb, cover evenly with the bacon slices and tie in place with fine string.

2 Heat the oil in a frying pan (skillet). Add the lamb and fry, turning it several times, for about 10 minutes, until browned all over. Remove from the pan.

3 Transfer the oil from the pan to a large flameproof casserole and sauté the garlic and onion together for 3–4 minutes, until beginning to soften. Add the carrots and celery, and cook for a few minutes longer.

4 Lay the lamb on top of the vegetables and press it down well to partly submerge. Pour the wine over the lamb and add the tomato purée (paste). Bring to the boil and simmer for 3–4 minutes. Add the stock, tomatoes and herbs and season with salt and pepper. Bring back to the boil for a further 3–4 minutes.

5 Cover the casserole tightly and cook in a preheated oven at 180°C/350°F/

Gas Mark 4 for 2–2$^1/_2$ hours, until cooked through and very tender.

6 Remove the lamb from the casserole and if wished, take off the bacon and herbs along with the string. Place the lamb on a warm serving dish and keep warm. Strain the juices, skimming off any excess fat, and serve in a jug. The vegetables may be arranged around the lamb or put into a serving dish. Garnish with fresh sprigs of rosemary.

Liver with Wine Sauce

Liver is popular in Italy and is served in many ways.
Tender calf's liver is traditional and the best to use for this recipe,
but you could use lamb's liver.

Serves 4
4 slices calf's liver or 8 slices lamb's liver, about 500 g/1¼ lb
flour, for coating
1 tbsp olive oil
25 g/1 oz/2 tbsp butter
1 garlic clove, crushed
115 g/4 oz lean bacon, cut into narrow strips
1 onion, chopped
1 celery stick, thinly sliced
150 ml/½ pint/⅔ cup red wine
150 ml/½ pint/⅔ cup beef stock
pinch of ground allspice
1 tsp Worcestershire sauce
1 tsp chopped fresh sage or ½ tsp dried sage
3–4 tomatoes, peeled, quartered and seeded
salt and pepper
fresh sage leaves, to garnish
new potatoes or sauté potatoes, to serve

1 Wipe the liver, season with salt and pepper and coat lightly in flour, shaking off the surplus.

2 Heat the oil and butter together in a frying pan (skillet). Add the liver and fry until well sealed on both sides and just cooked through. Take care not to overcook it or it will become tough. Remove the liver from the pan, cover and keep warm, but do not allow it to dry out.

3 Add the bacon to the fat left in the pan, with the garlic, onion and celery. Fry gently until the onion is soft.

4 Add the wine, stock, allspice, Worcestershire sauce and sage and season to taste with salt and pepper. Bring to the boil and simmer for 3–4 minutes. Cut each tomato segment in half. Add to the sauce and continue to cook for 2–3 minutes.

5 Spoon a little of the sauce on to individual serving plates, top with the slices of liver and spoon the remaining sauce over them. Garnish with fresh sage leaves and serve immediately with boiled tiny new potatoes or sauté potatoes.

Escalopes with Italian Sausage & Capers

Anchovies are often used to enhance flavour, particularly in meat dishes.
Either veal or turkey escalopes can be used for this pan-fried dish.

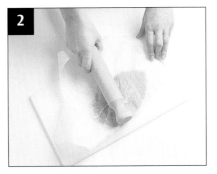

Serves 4
1 tbsp olive oil
6 canned anchovy fillets, drained
1 tbsp capers, drained
1 tbsp fresh rosemary leaves
finely grated rind and juice of 1 orange
75 g/3 oz Italian sausage, diced
3 tomatoes, peeled and chopped
4 turkey or veal escalopes, each about 125 g/4^1/$_2$ oz
salt and pepper
crusty bread or cooked polenta, to serve

COOK'S TIP

Polenta is typical of northern Italian cuisine. It is often fried or toasted and used to mop up the juices of the main course.

COOK'S VARIATION

Try using 4-minute steaks, slightly flattened, instead of the turkey or veal. Cook them for 4–5 minutes on top of the sauce in the pan.

1 Heat the oil in a large frying pan (skillet). Add the anchovies, capers, fresh rosemary, orange rind and juice, Italian sausage and tomatoes to the pan and cook, stirring occasionally, for 5–6 minutes.

2 Meanwhile, place the turkey or veal escalopes between sheets of greaseproof (wax) paper. Pound the meat with a meat mallet or the end of a rolling pin to flatten it.

3 Add the meat to the mixture in the frying pan (skillet). Season to taste with salt and pepper, cover and cook for 3–5 minutes on each side, slightly longer if the meat is thicker.

4 Transfer the escalopes to individual serving plates and serve with fresh crusty bread or cooked polenta.

Barbecued Chicken

You need a bit of brute force to prepare the chicken,
but once marinated, it's an easy and tasty candidate for the barbecue (grill).

Serves 4
1.5 kg/3 lb chicken
grated rind of 1 lemon
4 tbsp lemon juice
2 sprigs rosemary
1 small fresh red chilli, finely chopped
150 ml/¼ pint/⅔ cup olive oil
green salad, to serve

1 Split the chicken down the breast bone and open it out. Trim off excess fat, and remove the wing and leg tips. Break the leg and wing joints to enable you to pound it flat. This ensures that it cooks evenly.

2 Cover the split chicken with cling film (plastic wrap) and pound it as flat as possible with a rolling pin.

3 Mix the lemon rind and juice, rosemary sprigs, chilli and olive oil together in a small bowl. Place the chicken in a large dish and pour the marinade over it, turning the chicken to coat it evenly. Cover the dish and marinate for at least 2 hours.

4 Cook the chicken over a hot barbecue (the coals should be white, and red when fanned) for about 30 minutes, turning it regularly, until the skin is golden and crisp. To test if it is cooked, pierce one of the chicken thighs with the point of a skewer or sharp knife; if it is ready, the juices will run clear, not pink. Cut into serving portions and serve with a green salad.

Chicken Marengo

Napoleon's chef was ordered to cook a meal
after the battle of Marengo in 1800. He gathered everything possible
to make a feast, and this was the result.

Serves 4
1 tbsp olive oil
8 chicken pieces
300 ml/½ pint/1¼ cups passata (sieved tomatoes)
200 ml/7 fl oz/¾ cup white wine
2 tsp dried mixed herbs
8 slices white bread
40 g/1½ oz butter, melted
2 garlic cloves, crushed
115 g/4 oz mixed mushrooms (such as button, oyster and ceps)
50 g/2 oz/½ cup stoned (pitted) black olives, chopped
1 tsp sugar
fresh basil, to garnish

1 Using a sharp knife, remove the bone from each of the chicken pieces.

2 Heat the oil in a large frying pan (skillet). Add the chicken pieces and cook, turning occasionally, for 4–5 minutes, or until browned all over.

3 Add the passata (sieved tomatoes), wine and mixed herbs to the frying pan (skillet). Bring to the boil and simmer for 30 minutes, or until the chicken is tender and the juices run clear when a skewer is inserted into the thickest part of the meat.

4 Mix the melted butter and crushed garlic together. Lightly toast the slices of bread and brush them with the garlic butter.

5 Add the remaining oil to a separate frying pan (skillet). Add the

mushrooms and sauté for 2–3 minutes, or until just brown.

6 Add the olives and sugar to the chicken mixture and warm through.

7 Transfer the chicken and sauce to serving plates. Serve with the bruschetta (fried bread) and fried mushrooms.

COOK'S TIP

If you have time, marinate the chicken pieces in the wine and herbs in the refrigerator for 2 hours. This will make the chicken more tender and accentuate the wine flavour of the sauce.

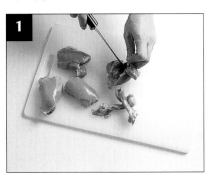

Roman Chicken

This classic Roman dish makes an ideal light meal. It is equally good cold
and could be taken on a picnic.

Serves 4
4 tbsp olive oil
6 chicken pieces
2 garlic cloves, crushed with 1 tsp salt
1 large red onion, sliced
4 large mixed red, green and yellow (bell) peppers, seeded and cut into strips
115 g/4 oz/1 cup stoned (pitted) green olives
1/2 quantity Tomato Sauce (see page 37)
300 ml/1/2 pint/1 1/4 cups hot chicken stock
2 sprigs fresh marjoram
salt and pepper
crusty bread, to serve

1 Heat half of the oil in a flameproof casserole. Add the chicken pieces and cook, turning frequently, until browned on all sides. Remove the chicken pieces and set aside.

2 Add the remaining oil to the casserole. Add the garlic and onion and sauté for 3–5 minutes, until softened. Stir in the (bell) peppers, olives and tomato sauce.

3 Return the chicken to the casserole and add the stock and marjoram. Cover the casserole and simmer for about 45 minutes, until the chicken is tender. Season to taste with salt and pepper and serve with plenty of crusty bread to mop up the juices.

Parma-wrapped Chicken

Your guests will be delighted when they discover that there is
a delicious surprise inside these chicken breast parcels!

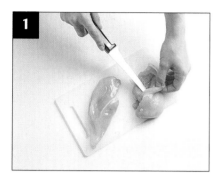

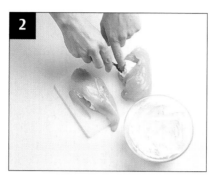

Serves 4
4 skinless chicken breasts
115 g/4 oz full-fat soft cheese, flavoured with herbs and garlic
8 slices Parma ham (prosciutto)
150 ml/¼ pint/⅔ cup red wine
150 ml/¼ pint/⅔ cup chicken stock
1 tbsp brown sugar

7 Boil the sauce until reduced and thickened. Remove the string from the chicken and discard. Cut the chicken into slices and arrange on a warm serving plate. Pour the sauce over the chicken and serve.

COOK'S VARIATION

Try adding 2 finely chopped sun-dried tomatoes to the soft cheese in step 2, if you prefer.

1 Using a sharp knife, make a horizontal slit along the length of each chicken breast to form a pocket.

2 Beat the cheese with a wooden spoon to soften it. Spoon the cheese into the pockets of the chicken breasts, dividing it equally.

3 Wrap 2 slices of Parma ham (prosciutto) around each chicken breast and secure in place with lengths of string.

4 Pour the red wine and chicken stock into a large frying pan (skillet) and bring to the boil. When the mixture is just starting to boil, add the brown sugar and stir until it has dissolved completely.

5 Add the chicken breasts to the mixture in the frying pan (skillet). Simmer for 12–15 minutes, or until the chicken is tender and the juices run clear when a skewer is inserted into the thickest part of the meat.

6 Remove the chicken from the pan, set aside and keep warm.

Chicken with Green Olives

Superb olives are grown in Apulia, where this recipe originates,
and they are a popular flavouring for poultry and game there.

Serves 4
4 chicken breasts, part boned
25 g/1 oz/2 tbsp butter
2 tbsp olive oil
1 large onion, finely chopped
2 garlic cloves, crushed
2 (bell) peppers, red, yellow or green, seeded and cut into large pieces
225 g/8 oz large closed cup mushrooms, sliced or quartered
175 g/6 oz tomatoes, peeled and halved
150 ml/¼ pint/⅔ cup dry white wine
125–175 g/4–6 oz/1–1½ cups stoned (pitted) green olives
4–6 tbsp double (heavy) cream
salt and pepper
chopped flat leaf parsley, to garnish
pasta or boiled new potatoes, to serve

1 Season the chicken with salt and pepper. Heat the oil and butter in a frying pan (skillet), add the chicken and fry until browned all over. Remove the chicken from the pan.

2 Add the onion and garlic to the pan and sauté until the onion is beginning to soften. Add the (bell) peppers and mushrooms to the pan and continue to cook for a few minutes longer.

3 Add the tomatoes and plenty of seasoning to the pan and then transfer the vegetable mixture to a casserole. Place the chicken on the bed of vegetables.

4 Add the wine to the frying pan (skillet) and bring to the boil. Pour the wine over the chicken and cover the casserole tightly. Cook in a preheated oven at 180°C/350°F/Gas Mark 4, for 50 minutes.

5 Add the olives to the chicken, then pour in the cream. Re-cover and return to the oven for 10–20 minutes, or until the chicken is very tender.

6 Adjust the seasoning if necessary. Transfer the pieces of chicken to a warm serving dish. Surround them with the vegetables and spoon the sauce over the top. Sprinkle with parsley to garnish and serve immediately with pasta or tiny new potatoes.

Chicken with Balsamic Vinegar

A rich caramelized sauce, flavoured with balsamic vinegar and wine,
gives this chicken dish a piquant flavour.

Serves 4
4 boneless chicken thighs
2 garlic cloves, crushed
200 ml/7 fl oz/³/₄ cup red wine
3 tbsp white wine vinegar
1 tbsp oil
15 g/¹/₂ oz/1 tbsp butter
4 shallots
3 tbsp balsamic vinegar
2 tbsp fresh thyme
salt and pepper
cooked polenta or rice, to serve

1 Using a sharp knife, make a few slashes in the skin of the chicken. Brush the chicken with the crushed garlic and arrange in a single layer in a non-metallic dish.

2 Pour the wine and wine vinegar over the chicken and season to taste with salt and pepper. Cover and marinate in the refrigerator overnight.

3 Remove the chicken pieces with a slotted spoon, draining well, and reserve the marinade.

4 Heat the oil and butter in a frying pan (skillet). Add the shallots and sauté for 2–3 minutes, or until they begin to soften.

5 Add the chicken pieces to the pan and cook, turning them frequently, for 3–4 minutes, until browned all over. Reduce the heat and add half of the reserved marinade. Cover and cook for 15–20 minutes, adding more marinade when necessary.

6 Once the chicken is tender, add the balsamic vinegar and thyme and cook for a further 4 minutes.

7 Transfer the chicken and sauce to warm serving plates and serve with polenta or rice.

COOK'S TIP

To make the chicken pieces look a little neater, use wooden skewers to hold them together or secure them with a length of string.

Chicken Scallops

Served in scallop shells, this makes a stylish presentation for a
dinner-party first course or a light lunch.

Serves 4
175 g/6 oz/2 cups dried short-cut macaroni, or other short pasta shapes
3 tbsp vegetable oil, plus extra for brushing
1 onion, finely chopped
3 slices unsmoked lean bacon, chopped
115 g/4 oz button mushrooms, thinly sliced or chopped
175 g/6 oz/$^3/_4$ cup diced cooked chicken
175 ml/6 fl oz/$^3/_4$ cup crème fraîche
4 tbsp dry breadcrumbs
25 g/2 oz/$^1/_2$ cup grated mature (sharp) Cheddar cheese
salt and pepper
flat leaf parsley sprigs, to garnish

1 Cook the pasta in a large pan of boiling salted water to which you have added 1 tablespoon of the oil. When the pasta is tender, but still firm to the bite, drain in a colander, return to the pan and cover.

2 Heat the remaining oil in a pan over medium heat and sauté the onion until it is translucent. Add the chopped bacon and mushrooms and cook, stirring occasionally, for a further 3–4 minutes.

3 Stir in the pasta, chicken and crème fraîche and season to taste with salt and pepper.

4 Brush four large, clean scallop shells with oil. Spoon in the chicken mixture and smooth the surface to make neat mounds.

5 Mix together the breadcrumbs and cheese, and sprinkle over the top of the shells. Press the topping lightly into the chicken mixture, and cook under a preheated grill (broiler) for 4–5 minutes, until golden brown and bubbling. Garnish with parsley, and serve immediately.

Pan-Cooked Chicken with Artichokes

Artichokes are a familiar ingredient in Italian cookery.
In this dish, they add a delicate flavour to chicken.

Serves 4
4 chicken breasts, part boned
25 g/1 oz/2 tbsp butter
2 tbsp olive oil
2 red onions, cut into wedges
2 tbsp lemon juice
150 ml/^{1}/$_4$ pint/^{2}/$_3$ cup dry white wine
150 ml/^{1}/$_4$ pint/^{2}/$_3$ cup chicken stock
2 tsp plain (all-purpose) flour
400 g/14 oz can artichoke halves, drained and halved
salt and pepper
chopped fresh parsley, to garnish

1 Season the chicken with salt and freshly ground black pepper. Heat the oil and 15 g/^{1}/$_2$ oz/1 tablespoon of the butter in a large frying pan (skillet). Add the chicken and fry for 4–5 minutes on each side, until lightly golden. Remove the chicken from the pan using a slotted spoon.

2 Toss the onion in the lemon juice, and add to the frying pan (skillet). Sauté, stirring, for 3–4 minutes, until just beginning to soften.

3 Return the chicken to the pan. Pour in the wine and stock, bring to the boil, cover and simmer gently for 30 minutes.

4 Remove the chicken from the pan, reserving the cooking juices, and keep warm. Bring the juices to the boil, and boil rapidly for 5 minutes.

5 Blend the remaining butter with the flour to form a paste. Reduce the heat so that the juices are just simmering. Add the paste a little at a time, stirring until each addition has been fully incorporated.

6 Adjust the seasoning, stir in the artichoke hearts and cook for a further 2 minutes. Pour over the chicken and garnish with parsley.

Italian Sausage & Bean Casserole

In this traditional Tuscan dish, Italian sausages are cooked
with cannellini beans and tomatoes.

Serves 4
1 green (bell) pepper
8 Italian sausages
1 tbsp olive oil
1 large onion, chopped
2 garlic cloves, chopped
225g/8 oz fresh tomatoes, skinned and chopped or 400 g/14 oz can tomatoes, chopped
2 tbsp sun-dried tomato paste
400g/14 oz can cannellini beans
mashed potatoes or rice, to serve

1 Seed the (bell) pepper and cut it
into thin strips.

2 Prick the Italian sausages all over
with a fork. Cook the sausages, under
a preheated grill (broiler), for about
10–12 minutes, turning occasionally,
until brown all over. Set aside and
keep warm.

3 Heat the oil in a large frying pan
(skillet). Add the onion, garlic and
(bell) pepper and cook, stirring
occasionally, for 5 minutes, or until
softened, but not coloured.

4 Add the tomatoes to the frying pan
(skillet) and simmer, stirring
occasionally, for about 5 minutes, or
until the mixture is slightly reduced
and thickened.

5 Stir the sun-dried tomato paste,
cannellini beans and Italian sausages
into the mixture. Cook for about
4–5 minutes, or until the mixture is
piping hot. If the mixture is becoming

too dry during cooking, add 4–5
tablespoons of water.

6 Transfer the Italian sausage and
bean casserole to warm individual
serving plates and serve with mashed
potatoes or cooked rice.

COOK'S TIP

Italian sausages are coarse in
texture and have quite a strong
flavour. They can be found in
specialist sausage shops, Italian
delicatessens and some larger
supermarkets. They are replaceable
in this recipe only by game
sausages.

Saltimbocca

Literally translated *saltimbocca* means 'jump in the mouth',
and this quick, tasty veal dish almost does that.

Serves 4
4 thin veal escalopes
8 fresh sage leaves
4 thin slices Parma ham (prosciutto), twice the size of the veal
flour, for dredging
2 tbsp olive oil
25 g/1 oz/2 tbsp butter
4 tbsp white wine
4 tbsp chicken stock
4 tbsp Marsala
salt and pepper
fresh sage leaves, to garnish

1 Either leave the escalopes as they are or cut them in half. Place the pieces of veal on a sheet of cling film (plastic wrap) or baking parchment, keeping them well apart, and cover with another piece.

2 Using a meat mallet or rolling pin beat the escalopes gently until at least double in size and very thin.

3 Lightly season the escalopes with salt and pepper and place two fresh sage leaves on the large slices, or one leaf on each of the smaller slices. Then lay the Parma ham (prosciutto) slices evenly over the veal escalopes to cover the sage and fit the veal almost exactly.

4 Secure the Parma ham (prosciutto) to the veal with cocktail sticks (toothpicks). If preferred, the large slices can be folded in half first. Dredge lightly with a little flour.

5 Heat the olive oil and butter in a large frying pan (skillet) and fry the escalopes for 4 minutes if single, or for 5–6 minutes if double, until golden brown on both sides and just cooked through. Take care not to overcook. Transfer to a serving dish.

6 Add the wine, stock and Marsala to the pan and bring to the boil, stirring well to loosen all the sediment from the base. Boil until reduced by almost half. Adjust the seasoning and pour the sauce over the veal. Garnish with fresh sage leaves and serve.

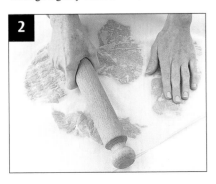

Vitello Tonnato

Veal dishes are the speciality of Lombardy,
this dish being one of the more sophisticated.

Serves 4
675 g/1¹/₂ lb boneless leg of veal, rolled
2 bay leaves
10 black peppercorns
2–3 cloves
¹/₂ tsp salt
2 carrots, sliced
1 onion, sliced
2 celery sticks, sliced
about 750 ml/1¹/₄ pints/3 cups stock or water
150 ml/¹/₄ pint/²/₃ cup dry white wine (optional)
75 g/3 oz canned tuna fish, well drained
50 g/2 oz can anchovy fillets, drained
150 ml/¹/₄ pint/²/₃ cup olive oil
2 tsp bottled capers, drained
2 egg yolks
1 tbsp lemon juice
salt and pepper
GARNISH
capers
lemon wedges
fresh herbs

1 Put the veal in a saucepan with the bay leaves, peppercorns, cloves, salt and vegetables. Add sufficient stock or water and the wine (if using) just to cover the veal. Bring to the boil, remove any scum from the surface, then cover the pan and simmer gently for about 1 hour, until tender. Allow to cool completely in the cooking liquid, then drain thoroughly. If time allows, chill the veal in the refrigerator to make it easier to carve.

2 For the tuna sauce, thoroughly mash the tuna with 4 anchovy fillets, 1 tablespoon oil and the capers. Add the egg yolks and rub through a strainer or process in a food processor until smooth.

3 Stir in the lemon juice, then beat in the rest of the oil, a few drops at a time, until the sauce is smooth and has the consistency of thick cream. Season with salt and pepper to taste.

4 Slice the veal thinly and arrange on a serving platter in overlapping slices. Spoon the sauce over the veal. Then cover the dish with cling film (plastic wrap) and chill in the refrigerator for 8 hours or overnight.

5 Before serving, uncover the veal carefully. Arrange the remaining anchovy fillets and the capers in a decorative pattern on top, and garnish with lemon wedges and herbs.

Orange Mascarpone Chicken

A creamy citrus sauce gives this chicken a delicious flavour.
If you have time, marinate overnight.

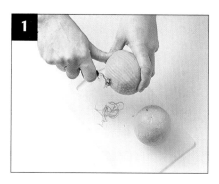

Serves 4
2 oranges
2 tbsp Marsala or medium sherry
4 skinless chicken breasts
25 g/1 oz/2 tbsp butter
150 ml/$^1/_4$ pint/$^2/_3$ cup chicken stock
4 tbsp mascarpone cheese
salt and pepper
green beans and boiled new potatoes, to serve

1 Using a zester remove the rind from 1 of the oranges and squeeze the juice. Mix the rind and juice with the Marsala or sherry. Slice the other orange into rings and then cut each ring into 4.

2 Make diagonal slits across each chicken breast and brush with the orange and Marsala mixture. Cover and marinate in the refrigerator for at least 30 minutes.

3 Melt the butter in a large frying pan (skillet), add the chicken and cook for 4–5 minutes, until browned on both sides. Add the marinade, orange segments and stock, bring to the boil and simmer gently for 20–25 minutes. To test whether the chicken is tender, insert a skewer into the thickest part of the meat – the juices will run clear when cooked through.

4 Stir in the mascarpone cheese, season to taste with salt and pepper and heat through for 2–3 minutes. Transfer to serving plates and serve with green beans and new potatoes.

Rice, Polenta & Gnocchi

Rice is to the north of Italy what pasta is to the south and is prepared in a wide variety of ways. It is never served as just an accompaniment to meat or fish dishes. Risotto rice, such as arborio, has a shorter grain than most other rices and a capacity to absorb a considerable amount of liquid without becoming soggy. Preparing risotto can be quite time consuming, but the result is

deliciously creamy.

Polenta, a kind of porridge made from cornmeal or polenta flour, is also a traditional northern dish. It may be served soft and freshly cooked or allowed to set and then fried or grilled (broiled) and served with a sauce. Once it was necessary to stir polenta almost constantly for at least an hour, but virtually instant polenta is now available.

Gnocchi are small dumplings, often served as an appetizer in northern Italy. They can be made from a variety of ingredients and are poached or baked and served with sauce.

Polenta

Polenta – a kind of cornmeal porridge – is prepared and
served in a variety of ways and can be eaten
hot or cold, and as a sweet or savoury dish.

Serves 4
1.5 litres/2¹/₂ pints/6¹/₄ cups water
1¹/₂ tsp salt
300 g/10¹/₂ oz/2¹/₄ cups polenta or cornmeal flour
vegetable oil, for frying and oiling
2 beaten eggs (optional)
115 g/4 oz/2 cups fresh fine white breadcrumbs (optional)
2 quantities Basic Tomato Sauce (see page 17)

MUSHROOM SAUCE

3 tbsp olive oil
225 g/8 oz mushrooms, sliced
2 garlic cloves, crushed
150 ml/¹/₄ pint/²/₃ cup dry white wine
4 tbsp double (heavy) cream
2 tbsp chopped fresh mixed herbs
salt and pepper

1 Bring the water and salt to the boil
in a large saucepan and gradually
sprinkle in the polenta or cornmeal
flour, stirring all the time to prevent
lumps forming.

2 Simmer the mixture very gently,
stirring frequently, for about
30–35 minutes, until the polenta
becomes very thick and starts to draw
away from the sides of the pan. It is
likely to splatter, in which case
partially cover the pan with a lid.

3 Oil a shallow tin (pan), about 28 ×
18 cm/11 × 7 inches, and spoon in the
polenta. Spread it out evenly, using a
wet spatula. Cool, then let stand for a
few hours at room temperature.

4 Cut the polenta into 30–36 squares.
Heat the oil in a frying pan (skillet)
and fry the polenta squares, in
batches, turning them several times,
for about 5 minutes, until golden
brown all over. Alternatively, dip each
piece of polenta in beaten egg and coat
in breadcrumbs before frying it in the
hot oil. Drain and keep warm while
you cook the remaining batches.

5 To make the mushroom sauce, heat
the oil in a pan and sauté the
mushrooms with the crushed garlic
for 3–4 minutes. Add the wine, season
well and simmer for 5 minutes. Add
the cream and chopped herbs and
simmer for 1–2 minutes.

6 Serve the polenta with either the
tomato sauce or mushroom sauce.

Chilli Polenta Chips (Fries)

Polenta is used in Italy in the same way as potatoes
and rice. On its own it has little flavour, but combined with butter,
garlic and herbs, it is completely transformed.

Serves 4
350 g/12 oz/2½ cups instant polenta
2 tsp chilli powder
1 tbsp olive oil
150 ml/5 fl oz/⅔ cup soured cream
1 tbsp chopped parsley
salt and pepper

1 Place 1.5 litres/2½ pints/6¼ cups of water in a saucepan and bring to the boil. Add 2 teaspoons of salt and then add the polenta in a steady stream, stirring constantly.

2 Reduce the heat slightly and continue stirring for about 5 minutes. It is essential to stir the polenta, otherwise it will stick and burn. The polenta should have a thick consistency at this point and should be stiff enough to hold the spoon upright in the pan.

3 Add the chilli powder to the polenta mixture and stir well. Season to taste with a little salt and pepper.

4 Spread the polenta out on a board or baking tray (cookie sheet) to about 4 cm/1½ inch thick. Cool and let stand until set.

5 Cut the cooled polenta mixture into thin wedges.

6 Heat 1 tablespoon of oil in a pan. Add the polenta wedges and fry for 3–4 minutes on each side, until golden and crispy. Alternatively, brush with melted butter and cook

under a preheated grill (broiler) for 6–7 minutes, until golden. Drain the cooked polenta on kitchen paper (paper towels).

7 Mix the soured cream with parsley and place in a small serving bowl.

8 Serve the polenta with the soured cream and parsley dip.

COOK'S TIP

Easy-cook instant polenta is widely available in supermarkets and is quick to make. It will keep for up to 1 week in the refrigerator. The polenta can also be baked in a preheated oven, at 200°C/400°F/ Gas Mark 6, for 20 minutes.

Polenta Kebabs (Kabobs)

Here, skewers of thyme-flavoured polenta, wrapped
in Parma ham (prosciutto), are grilled (broiled) or barbecued.

Serves 4
750 ml/1¹/₄ pints/3 cups water
175 g/6 oz/1¹/₄ cups instant polenta
2 tbsp fresh thyme, stalks removed
8 slices Parma ham (prosciutto), about 75 g/3 oz
1 tbsp olive oil
salt and pepper
green salad, to serve

1 Bring the water to the boil in a large saucepan. Add 1 teaspoon salt and then add the polenta in a steady stream, stirring constantly.

2 Reduce the heat and continue stirring for about 5 minutes, until the polenta is thick and sticky enough to hold the spoon upright in the pan. It is essential to keep stirring, otherwise the polenta will stick and burn. Add the fresh thyme and season to taste with pepper.

3 Spread out the polenta on a board or baking tray (cookie sheet) to about 2.5 cm/1 inch thick. Set aside to cool, then let stand at room temperature until set.

4 Using a sharp knife, cut the cooled polenta into 2.5-cm/1-inch cubes.

5 Cut the slices of Parma ham (prosciutto) into 2 pieces lengthways. Wrap a piece around each of the polenta cubes.

6 Thread the wrapped polenta cubes on to skewers.

7 Brush the kebabs (kabobs) with a little olive oil and cook under a preheated grill (broiler), turning frequently, for 7–8 minutes. Alternatively, barbecue the kebabs (kabobs) until golden. Transfer to serving plates and serve with a green salad.

COOK'S VARIATION

Try flavouring the polenta with oregano, basil or marjoram instead of the thyme. Use 3 tablespoons of chopped herbs to every 350 g/ 12 oz/2¹/₄ cups instant polenta.

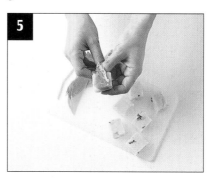

Lazy Polenta with Rabbit Stew

Polenta can be served fresh, as in this dish, as well as cooled,
sliced and fried or grilled (broiled).

Serves 4
300 g/10¹/₂ oz/2 cups polenta or cornmeal
1 tbsp coarse sea salt
1.2 litres/2 pints/5 cups water
4 tbsp olive oil
2 kg/4 lb rabbit pieces
3 garlic cloves, peeled
3 shallots, sliced
150 ml/¹/₄ pint/²/₃ cup red wine
1 carrot, sliced
1 celery stick, sliced
2 bay leaves
1 sprig rosemary
3 tomatoes, peeled and diced
75 g/3 oz/³/₄ cup stoned (pitted) black olives
salt and pepper

1 Grease an ovenproof dish with a little butter. Mix the polenta, salt and water in a large saucepan, beating well. Bring to the boil and simmer, stirring vigorously, for 10 minutes. Turn the polenta into the buttered dish and bake in a preheated oven at 190°C/375°F/Gas Mark 5 for 40 minutes.

2 Meanwhile, heat the oil in a large pan and fry the rabbit, garlic and shallots, stirring frequently, for 10 minutes, until the rabbit is browned all over. Stir in the wine and cook for a further 5 minutes.

3 Add the carrot, celery, bay leaves, rosemary, tomatoes, olives and 300 ml/¹/₂ pint/1¹/₄ cups water. Cover the pan and simmer for 45 minutes, until the rabbit is tender. Season.

4 Remove the polenta from the oven, cut 4 portions and place them on warm individual serving plates. Ladle the rabbit stew around the polenta and serve immediately.

COOK'S TIP

You could also make this stew with chicken pieces, if preferred.

Smoked Cod Polenta

Using polenta as a crust for a gratin dish gives a lovely
crispy outer texture and a smooth inside. It works especially well
with smoked fish and chicken.

Serves 4
1.5 litres/2¹/₂ pints/6¹/₄ cups water
350 g/12 oz/2¹/₂ cups instant polenta
200 g/7 oz chopped frozen spinach, thawed
50 g/2 oz/4 tbsp butter
50 g/2 oz/¹/₂ cup grated pecorino cheese
200 ml/7 fl oz/³/₄ cup milk
450 g/1 lb smoked cod fillet, skinned
4 eggs, beaten
salt and pepper

1 Bring the water to the boil in a large
pan. Add 2 teaspoons of salt and the
polenta in a steady stream, stirring
constantly. Lower the heat slightly
and simmer, stirring constantly, for
about 5 minutes, or until the polenta
is thick and sticky enough to hold the
spoon upright. It is essential to keep
stirring to prevent it from burning.

2 Stir the spinach, butter and half the
pecorino cheese into the polenta.
Season to taste with salt and pepper.

3 Divide the polenta among
4 individual ovenproof dishes,
spreading it evenly across the bases
and up the sides.

4 Bring the milk to the boil in a large
frying pan (skillet). Add the fish and
cook, turning once, for 8–10 minutes,
or until tender. Remove the fish with
a slotted spoon.

5 Remove the pan from the heat.
Strain the milk and mix with the eggs.
Set aside.

6 Using a fork, flake the fish and
place it in the centre of the dishes.

7 Pour the milk and egg mixture over
the fish.

8 Sprinkle the remaining grated
cheese on top and bake in a preheated
oven at 190°C/375°F/Gas Mark 5 for
25–30 minutes, or until set and
golden. Serve hot.

Rice & Peas

This famous Venetian dish is best with fresh peas. If you can get
them – and willing helpers to shell them – do use them: you will need
1 kg/2 lb. Add to the pan with the stock.

Serves 4
1 tbsp olive oil
50 g/2 oz/^{1}/$_4$ cup butter
50 g/2 oz/^{1}/$_3$ cup diced pancetta or unsmoked bacon
1 small onion, chopped
1.5 litres/2^1/$_2$ pints/6^1/$_4$ cups hot chicken stock
200 g/7 oz/1 cup risotto rice
3 tbsp chopped fresh parsley
225 g/8 oz/1^1/$_4$ cups frozen or canned petits pois
50 g/2 oz/^{2}/$_3$ cup grated Parmesan cheese pepper

1 Heat the oil with half of the butter
over a medium heat. Add the pancetta
or bacon and onion, and fry, stirring
frequently, for 5 minutes. Add the hot
stock (and fresh peas if using) and
bring to the boil.

2 Stir in the rice and season to taste
with pepper. Cook, stirring
occasionally, for about 20–30 minutes,
until the rice is tender.

3 Add the parsley and frozen or
canned petits pois and cook for
8 minutes, until the peas are
thoroughly heated.

4 Stir in the remaining butter and the
Parmesan cheese. Transfer to a warm
serving dish and serve immediately,
with freshly ground black pepper.

Risotto-stuffed (Bell) Peppers

Sweet roasted (bell) peppers are delightful containers for a creamy risotto and especially good topped with mozzarella cheese.

Serves 4
4 red or orange (bell) peppers
1 tbsp olive oil
1 large onion, finely chopped
350 g/12 oz/1¾ cups arborio (risotto) rice, washed
about 15 strands saffron
150 ml/¼ pint/⅔ cup white wine
900 ml/1½ pints/3¾ cups hot vegetable or chicken stock
50 g/2 oz/4 tbsp butter
50 g/2 oz/⅔ cup grated pecorino cheese
50 g/2 oz Italian sausage, such as felino salame or other coarse Italian salame, chopped
200 g/7 oz mozzarella cheese, sliced

1 Cut the (bell) peppers in half, retaining some of the stalk. Remove the seeds. Place the (bell) peppers, cut side up, under a preheated grill (broiler) for 12–15 minutes, until softened and charred.

2 Meanwhile, heat the oil in a large frying pan (skillet). Add the onion and sauté for 3–4 minutes, until softened and translucent. Add the rice and saffron, stirring to coat in the oil, and cook for 1 minute.

3 Add the wine and stock, a ladleful at a time, making sure that all of the liquid has been absorbed before adding the next ladleful. When all of the liquid has been absorbed, the rice should be cooked and tender. Test by tasting a grain – if it is still crunchy, add a little more water and continue cooking. It should take at least 15 minutes to cook.

4 Stir in the butter, pecorino cheese and the chopped Italian sausage.

5 Spoon the risotto into the (bell) peppers. Top with a slice of mozzarella cheese and grill (broil) for about 4–5 minutes, or until the cheese is bubbling. Serve hot.

COOK'S VARIATION

Use tomatoes instead of the (bell) peppers, if you prefer. Halve 4 large tomatoes and scoop out the seeds. Follow steps 2–5, as there is no need to roast them.

Milanese Risotto

Italian rice is a round, short-grained variety with a nutty flavour,
which is essential for a good risotto. Arborio is one of the best ones to use.

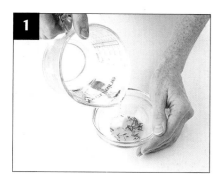

Serves 4
¹/₂ tsp saffron threads
1 large onion, finely chopped
1–2 garlic cloves, crushed
75 g/3 oz/6 tbsp butter
350 g/12 oz/1³/₄ cups arborio or other short-grain Italian rice
150 ml/¹/₄ pint/²/₃ cup dry white wine
1.2 litres/2 pints/5 cups boiling stock (chicken, beef or vegetable)
75 g/3 oz/1 cup grated Parmesan cheese
salt and pepper

Simmer for 1–2 minutes until piping
hot and thoroughly mixed.

6 Cover the pan tightly and let stand
for 5 minutes off the heat. Give a good
stir and serve at once.

COOK'S TIP

This is the classical accompaniment
to serve with veal dishes, but it also
goes well with pork.

1 Put the saffron in a small bowl,
cover with 3–4 tablespoons boiling
water and let soak while you are
cooking the risotto.

2 Sauté the onion and garlic in 50 g/
2 oz/4 tbsp of the butter until soft, but
not coloured, then add the rice and
continue to cook for a few minutes
until all the grains are coated in oil
and beginning to colour lightly.

3 Add the wine to the rice and
simmer gently, stirring from time to
time, until it has all been absorbed.

4 Add the boiling stock, a little at a
time (about 150 ml/¹/₄ pint/²/₃ cup),
cooking until the liquid has been fully
absorbed before adding more, and
stirring frequently.

5 When all the stock has been
absorbed, the rice should be tender,
but not soft and soggy. Add the
saffron liquid, Parmesan, remaining
butter and plenty of seasoning.

Genoese Seafood Risotto

The Genoese risotto is cooked in a different way from any of the other risottos.
First, you cook the rice, then you prepare a sauce, then you mix
the two together. The results are just as delicious though!

Serves 4
1.2 litres/2 pints/5 cups hot fish or chicken stock
350 g/12 oz/1¾ cups arborio (risotto) rice, washed
50 g/2 oz/4 tbsp butter
2 garlic cloves, chopped
250 g/9 oz mixed seafood, preferably raw, such as prawns (shrimp), squid, mussels and clams
2 tbsp chopped oregano, plus extra for garnishing
50 g/2 oz/⅔ cup grated pecorino or Parmesan cheese

6 Stir in the grated pecorino or Parmesan cheese and mix well.

7 Transfer the risotto to warm serving dishes and serve immediately.

1 In a large saucepan, bring the stock to the boil. Add the rice and cook for about 12 minutes, stirring, until the rice is tender, or cook according to the instructions on the packet. Drain thoroughly, reserving any excess cooking liquid.

2 Heat the butter in a large frying pan (skillet) over a medium heat and add the garlic, stirring.

3 Add the raw mixed seafood to the pan (skillet) and cook for 5 minutes. If the seafood is already cooked, fry for 2–3 minutes.

4 Stir the chopped oregano into the seafood mixture.

5 Add the cooked rice to the pan and cook, stirring constantly, for about 2–3 minutes, or until hot. Add the reserved stock if the mixture becomes too sticky.

Wild Mushroom Risotto

This creamy risotto is flavoured with a mixture of wild and cultivated mushrooms and thyme. Wild mushrooms each have their own distinctive flavours, but they can be quite expensive, so you can always use a mixture with chestnut (crimini) or button mushrooms instead.

Serves 4
2 tbsp olive oil
1 large onion, finely chopped
1 garlic clove, crushed
200 g/7 oz mixed wild and cultivated mushrooms, such as oyster, porcini, chanterelles and button, wiped and sliced if large
250 g/9 oz/1¼ cups arborio (risotto) rice, washed
pinch of saffron threads
750 ml/1¼ pints/3 cups hot vegetable stock
150 ml/5 fl oz/²/₃ cup white wine
115 g/4 oz/1¹/₃ cups Parmesan cheese, grated, plus extra, for serving
2 tbsp chopped thyme
salt and pepper

1 Heat the oil in a large frying pan (skillet). Add the onions and garlic and sauté for 3–4 minutes, or until softened and translucent.

2 Add the mushrooms to the pan and cook for a further 3 minutes, or until they are just beginning to brown.

3 Add the rice and saffron to the pan and stir to coat the rice in the oil.

4 Mix the stock and the wine and add to the pan, a ladleful at a time. Stir the rice mixture and wait until the liquid has been fully absorbed before adding more liquid, a ladleful at a time.

5 When all the wine and stock has been incorporated, the rice should be cooked. Test by tasting a grain – if it is still crunchy, add a little more water and continue cooking. It should take at least 15 minutes to cook.

6 Stir in the cheese and thyme, and season with pepper.

7 Transfer the risotto to warm serving dishes and serve sprinkled with extra Parmesan cheese.

Gnocchi Romana

This is a traditional recipe from Piedmont.
For a less rich version, omit the eggs. Serve as a starter,
or as a main meal with a crisp salad.

Serves 4
750 ml/1¼ pints/3 cups milk
¼ tsp freshly grated nutmeg
75 g/3 oz/6 tbsp butter, plus extra for greasing
225 g/8 oz/1⅓ cups semolina
115 g/4 oz/1⅓ cups grated Parmesan cheese
2 eggs, beaten
50 g/2 oz/½ cup grated Gruyère (Swiss) cheese
salt and pepper
basil sprigs, to garnish

1 Bring the milk to the boil, remove from the heat and stir in the seasoning, nutmeg and 25 g/1 oz/ 2 tablespoons of butter. Gradually add the semolina, beating to prevent lumps forming, and return to a low heat. Simmer gently, stirring constantly, for about 10 minutes, until very thick.

2 Beat 50 g/2 oz/⅔ cup of Parmesan cheese into the semolina, followed by the eggs. Continue beating until the mixture is quite smooth.

3 Spread out the semolina mixture in an even layer on a sheet of baking parchment or in a large oiled baking tin (pan), smoothing the surface with a wet spatula – it should be about 1 cm/½ inch thick. Cool, then chill for about 1 hour, until firm.

4 Cut the gnocchi into rounds about 4 cm/1½ inches in diameter, using a plain greased pastry (cookie) cutter.

5 Thoroughly grease a shallow ovenproof dish, or four individual dishes. Lay the gnocchi trimmings in the base of the dish and cover with overlapping rounds of gnocchi. Melt the remaining butter and drizzle it all over the gnocchi, then sprinkle first with the remaining Parmesan and then with the Gruyère (Swiss) cheese.

6 Cook the gnocchi in a preheated oven at 200°C/400°F/Gas Mark 4 for 25–30 minutes until the top is crisp and golden brown. Serve at once.

Potato Gnocchi with Tomato Sauce

This dish is typical of the fertile farmlands of the Piedmont region in northern Italy. Freshly made potato gnocchi are delicious, especially when they are topped with a fragrant tomato sauce.

Serves 4
350 g/12 oz floury (mealy) potatoes (those suitable for baking or mashing), halved
75 g/3 oz/²/₃ cup self-raising flour, sifted plus extra for dusting
2 tsp dried oregano
2 tbsp oil
1 large onion, chopped
2 garlic cloves, chopped
400 g/14 oz can chopped tomatoes
¹/₂ vegetable stock (bouillon) cube dissolved in 6 tbsp boiling water
salt and pepper
2 tbsp basil, shredded, plus whole leaves to garnish
grated Parmesan cheese, to serve

1 Bring a large pan of water to the boil. Add the potatoes and cook for 12–15 minutes, or until tender. Drain and let cool.

2 Peel and then mash the potatoes with salt and pepper to taste, the flour and oregano. Mix together with your hands to form a dough.

3 Heat the oil in a pan. Add the onions and garlic and sauté for 3–4 minutes. Add the tomatoes and stock and cook, uncovered, for 10 minutes. Season with salt and pepper to taste.

4 Roll the potato dough into a sausage about 2.5 cm/1 inch in diameter. Cut the sausage into 2.5-cm/1-inch lengths. Dust your hands with flour, then press a fork

into each piece to create a series of ridges on one side and the indent of your index finger on the other.

5 Bring a large saucepan of water to the boil and cook the gnocchi, in batches, for 2–3 minutes. They should rise to the surface when cooked. Drain thoroughly, transfer to serving plates and keep warm.

6 Stir the basil into the tomato sauce and pour it over the gnocchi. Garnish with basil leaves, sprinkle with Parmesan cheese and serve.

COOK'S VARIATION

Try serving the gnocchi with pesto sauce for a change.

Potato Gnocchi with Garlic & Herb Sauce

These little potato dumplings are a traditional Italian appetizer but, served with a salad and bread, they make a substantial meal.

Serves 4–6

1 kg/2¼ lb potatoes, cut into
1-cm/½-inch pieces

50 g/2 oz/¼ cup butter

1 egg, beaten

300 g/10½ oz/2⅔ cups plain
(all-purpose) flour

salt

SAUCE

125 ml/4 fl oz/½ cup olive oil

2 garlic cloves, very finely chopped

1 tbsp chopped fresh oregano

1 tbsp chopped fresh basil

salt and pepper

TO SERVE

freshly grated Parmesan cheese (optional)

mixed salad

warm ciabatta or other Italian bread

1 Cook the potatoes in boiling salted water for about 10 minutes, or until tender. Drain well.

2 Rub the hot potatoes through a strainer into a large bowl. Add 1 teaspoon of salt, the butter, egg and 150 g/5 oz/1¼ cups of the flour. Mix well to bind together.

3 Turn on to a lightly floured surface and knead, gradually adding the remaining flour, until a smooth, soft, slightly sticky dough is formed.

4 Dust your hands with flour and roll the dough into 2-cm/¾-inch thick rolls. Cut into 1-cm/½-inch pieces. Press the top of each one with the

floured prongs of a fork and spread the gnocchi out on a floured tea towel (dish cloth).

5 Bring a large saucepan of salted water to a simmer. Add the gnocchi and cook, in batches, for 2–3 minutes, until they rise to the surface.

6 Remove with a slotted spoon and arrange in a warm, greased serving dish. Cover and keep warm.

7 To make the garlic and herb sauce, put the oil and garlic in a saucepan and season to taste with salt and pepper. Cook over a low heat, stirring constantly, for 3–4 minutes, until the garlic is golden. Remove the pan from the heat and stir in the herbs. Pour the sauce over the gnocchi and serve immediately, sprinkled with Parmesan, if liked, and accompanied by salad and warm ciabatta or other Italian bread.

Spinach and Ricotta Gnocchi

The combination of spinach, ricotta and pine nuts features in many Italian recipes.
Try not to handle the mixture too much when making these gnocchi,
as this will make the dough a little heavy.

Serves 4
1 kg/2¼ lb spinach
350 g/12 oz/1½ cups ricotta
115 g/4 oz/1⅓ cups grated pecorino cheese
3 eggs, beaten
¼ tsp freshly grated nutmeg
plain (all-purpose) flour, for dusting
115 g/4 oz/½ cup unsalted (sweet) butter
25 g/1 oz/¼ cup pine nuts
50 g/2 oz/⅓ cup raisins
salt and pepper

1 Wash and drain the spinach well and cook in a covered saucepan without any additional liquid for about 8 minutes, until softened. Place in a colander and press well to remove as much liquid as possible. Either rub through a strainer or process in a food processor.

2 Combine the spinach purée with the ricotta, half the pecorino, the eggs and nutmeg and season to taste with salt and pepper, mixing lightly but thoroughly. Work in enough flour, lightly and quickly, to make the mixture easy to handle.

3 Shape the dough into small lozenge shapes, and dust lightly with flour.

4 Add a dash of oil to a large pan of salted water and bring to the boil. Add the gnocchi carefully and boil for about 2 minutes, until they float to the top. Using a slotted spoon, transfer to a buttered ovenproof dish. Keep warm until required.

5 Melt the butter in a frying pan (skillet). Add the pine nuts and raisins and sauté until the nuts start to brown slightly, but do not allow the butter to burn. Pour the mixture over the gnocchi and serve sprinkled with the remaining pecorino.

COOK'S VARIATION

You can vary the cheeses used in this recipe. Try mascarpone instead of ricotta or grana padano instead of pecorino.

Garlic Mushroom Polenta

Any mushrooms can be used for this savoury polenta
accompaniment, but wild mushrooms will add a stronger flavour.

Serves 4–6
75 g/3 oz/6 tbsp butter
3 garlic cloves, crushed
75 g/3 oz mushrooms, wiped and sliced
2 sprigs thyme, stalks removed
115 g/4 oz/³/₄ cup instant polenta
600 ml/1 pint/2¹/₂ cups water
1 tsp salt
pepper
1 tbsp oil

1 Melt 50 g/2 oz/4 tbsp of the butter in a saucepan over a medium heat.

2 Add the garlic and mushrooms and sauté for 4–5 minutes, until just soft.

3 Add the thyme to the mixture, stir well and set aside.

4 In a large saucepan, bring the water to the boil.

5 Add the polenta to the saucepan of boiling water, stirring constantly. Leave to simmer, stirring constantly, for 4–5 minutes, or until the mixture is thick and starts to leave the side of the pan.

6 Stir the remaining butter into the polenta and season to taste with salt and pepper.

7 Add the mushroom and garlic mixture to the polenta, and stir to combine. Although the mixture is still quite wet, it is now ready to serve.

8 Transfer the garlic mushroom polenta to serving bowls and serve immediately.

COOK'S TIP

Try adding 50 g/2 oz chopped salami to the polenta in step 7.

Blue Cheese Risotto

Gorgonzola, one of Italy's most famous cheeses, is a semi-soft cheese made from cow's milk and aged for at least 2 months – often for much longer.

Serves 4–6
1 tbsp olive oil
1 red onion, cut into wedges
2 garlic cloves, crushed
1 red (bell) pepper, diced
350 g/12 oz/1¾ cups arborio or other short-grained Italian rice
600 ml/1 pint/2½ cups chicken or vegetable stock
150 ml/¼ pint/⅔ cup white wine
150 ml/¼ pint/⅔ cup water
150 g/5 oz Gorgonzola cheese, cubed
about 15 basil leaves, torn

1 Heat the oil in a large frying pan (skillet) and sauté the onion and garlic for 3–4 minutes. Add the (bell) pepper and sauté for a further 2–3 minutes, until just soft.

2 Add the rice and stir until all of the grains are coated in oil.

3 Mix together the stock, wine and water and add about 150 ml/¼ pint/⅔ cup of the liquid to the pan. When this has been completely absorbed, add a further 150 ml/¼ pint/⅔ cup. Continue until all the liquid has been absorbed and the rice is tender. It will take 15–20 minutes.

4 Remove the pan from the heat and stir in the Gorgonzola cheese and basil. Transfer to a warm serving dish and serve immediately.

Pizzas & Breads

Next to pasta, pizza must be the best-known Italian dish and exists with an almost infinite variety of toppings. Pizza bases can be made from a variety of ingredients, although bread dough is probably the most traditional. Most, but not all, pizzas are topped with home-made tomato sauce before other ingredients, ranging from mushrooms to seafood, and from

vegetables to nuts, are added. Grated or thinly sliced cheese usually tops the other ingredients. Mozzarella is

traditionally used because it melts easily and forms long, elastic strings, but other cheeses can be used.

Bread is an integral part of any Italian meal and a range of specially flavoured breads may be prepared. You can buy a range of Italian breads with sun-dried tomatoes or olives from supermarkets, but these do not compare with freshly baked, home-cooked loaves.

Tomato Sauce

Using canned chopped tomatoes for this dish saves time, and they are preferable to plum tomatoes which tend to be a little watery. This is a good basic sauce for spreading over your pizza base when making your own pizza.

Makes 180 ml/6 fl oz/¾ cup
1 small onion, chopped
1 garlic clove, crushed
1 tbsp olive oil
200 g/7 oz can chopped tomatoes
2 tsp tomato purée (paste)
½ tsp sugar
½ tsp dried oregano
1 bay leaf
salt and pepper

1 Sauté the onion and garlic gently in the oil for 5 minutes, until softened, but not browned.

2 Add the tomatoes, tomato purée (paste), sugar, oregano, bay leaf and seasoning. Stir well.

3 Bring to the boil, cover and simmer gently for 20 minutes, stirring occasionally, until the sauce has become quite thick.

4 Remove the bay leaf and adjust the seasoning to taste. Let cool completely before using. This sauce keeps well in a screw-top jar in the refrigerator for up to 1 week.

COOK'S VARIATION

For a stronger herb flavour, stir in 1–2 tablespoons chopped fresh oregano, parsley, basil, thyme, marjoram or chives. You could use a mixture of herbs, but do not use more than three different varieties.

Special Tomato Sauce

This sauce is made with fresh tomatoes. Use the plum variety whenever available and always choose the reddest ones for the best flavour. This delicious sauce is ideal to use when you have a little more time to make more of an effort when making your pizza.

Makes 180 ml/6 fl oz/¾ cup
1 small onion, chopped
1 small red (bell) pepper, seeded and chopped
1 garlic clove, crushed
2 tbsp olive oil
225 g/8 oz tomatoes
1 tbsp tomato purée (paste)
1 tsp light brown sugar
2 tsp chopped fresh basil
½ tsp dried oregano
1 bay leaf
salt and pepper

1 Sauté the onion, (bell) pepper and garlic gently in the oil for 5 minutes, until softened, but not browned.

2 Cut a cross in the base of each tomato and place them in a bowl. Pour in boiling water and leave for about 45 seconds. Drain, and then plunge in cold water. The skins will slide off easily.

3 Chop the tomatoes, discarding any hard cores. Add to the onion mixture with the tomato purée (paste), sugar, herbs and seasoning. Stir well. Bring to the boil, cover and simmer gently for 30 minutes, stirring occasionally, until the sauce has thickened.

4 Remove the bay leaf and adjust the seasoning to taste. Let cool completely before using.

5 This sauce will keep well in a screw-top jar in the refrigerator for up to 1 week.

Bread Dough Base

Traditionally, pizza bases are made from bread dough;
this recipe will give you a base similar to an Italian pizza.

Makes one 25-cm/10-inch pizza
15 g/¹/₂ oz fresh yeast or 1 tsp easy-blend (active dry) yeast
6 tbsp tepid water
¹/₂ tsp sugar
1 tbsp olive oil
175 g/6 oz plain (all-purpose) flour
1 tsp salt

1 Combine the fresh yeast with the water and sugar in a bowl.

2 Leave the mixture to rest in a warm place for 10–15 minutes, until frothy on the surface. Stir in the olive oil.

3 Sift the flour and salt into a large bowl. Make a well in the centre and pour in the fresh yeast liquid. If using easy-blend (active dry) yeast, add it to the bowl and pour in the water and oil. Omit the sugar if using easy-blend (active dry) yeast.

4 Using lightly floured hands or a wooden spoon, mix together to form a dough. Turn out on to a floured work surface (counter) and knead vigorously for about 5 minutes, until smooth and elastic.

5 Place the dough in a large greased plastic bag and set aside in a warm place for about 1 hour, or until doubled in size.

6 Turn the dough out on to a lightly floured work surface (counter) and knock back (punch down) by punching the dough. This releases

any air bubbles which would make the pizza uneven. Knead 4 or 5 times. The dough is now ready to use.

COOK'S TIP

You can make the dough in a food processor, using easy-blend (active dry) yeast. Process for 3–4 minutes, then knead for 2–3 minutes.

Scone (Biscuit) Base

If you do not have time to wait for bread dough
to rise, a scone (biscuit) base is ideal.

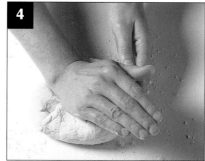

Makes one 25-cm/10-inch base
175 g/6 oz/1$\frac{1}{2}$ cups self-raising flour
$\frac{1}{2}$ tsp salt
25 g/1 oz/2 tbsp butter
125 ml/4 fl oz/$\frac{1}{2}$ cup milk

1 Sift the flour and salt together into a mixing bowl.

2 Add the butter and rub it in with your fingertips until the mixture resembles fine breadcrumbs.

3 Make a well in the centre of the flour and butter mixture and pour in nearly all the milk at once. Mix in quickly with a knife. Add the remaining milk only if necessary to mix to form a soft dough.

4 Turn the dough out on to a floured work surface (counter) and knead by turning and pressing with the heel of your hand 3 or 4 times.

5 Either roll out or press the dough into a 25-cm/10-inch round on a lightly greased baking tray (cookie sheet) or pizza pan. Push up the edge slightly all around to form a ridge and use immediately.

COOK'S TIP

You can vary the taste of your scone (biscuit) base by adding a little grated cheese or $\frac{1}{2}$ tsp dried oregano or mixed herbs to the mixture after rubbing in the butter.

Potato Base

This is an unusual pizza base made from mashed potatoes
and flour and is a great way to use up any leftover boiled potatoes.

Makes one 25-cm/10-inch base
225 g/8 oz boiled potatoes
50 g/2 oz/¼ cup butter or margarine
115 g/4 oz/1 cup self-raising flour
½ tsp salt

1 If the potatoes are hot, mash them, then stir in the butter until it has melted and is distributed evenly throughout. Set aside to cool. Sift the flour and salt together and stir into the mashed potato to form a soft dough.

2 If the potatoes are cold, mash them without adding the butter. Sift the flour and salt into a mixing bowl. Add the butter and rub it in with your fingertips until the mixture resembles fine breadcrumbs. Stir the mixture into the mashed potatoes to form a soft dough.

3 Either roll out or press the dough into a 25-cm/10-inch round on a lightly greased baking tray (cookie sheet) or pizza pan, pushing up the edge slightly all round to form a ridge before adding the topping. This base is tricky to lift before it is cooked, so you will find it easier to handle if you roll it out directly on to the baking tray (cookie sheet).

4 If the base is not required for cooking immediately, cover with cling film (plastic wrap) and leave to chill for up to 2 hours.

Pizza Margherita

Pizza means 'pie' in Italian. The traditional fresh bread dough is not difficult to make but it does take a little time.

Serves 4
DOUGH
7 g/¹⁄₄ oz dried yeast
1 tsp sugar
250 ml/8 fl oz/1 cup hand-hot water
350 g/12 oz/3 cups strong flour
1 tsp salt
1 tbsp olive oil
TOPPING
400 g/14 oz can tomatoes, chopped
2 garlic cloves, crushed
2 tsp dried basil
1 tbsp olive oil
2 tbsp tomato purée (paste)
115 g/4 oz mozzarella cheese, finely diced
2 tbsp freshly grated Parmesan cheese
salt and pepper

1 Mix together the yeast, sugar and 4 tbsp of the warm water. Leave the yeast mixture in a warm place for 15 minutes, or until frothy.

2 Sift the flour and salt together into a mixing bowl. Make a well in the centre, add the oil, the yeast mixture and the remaining water. Using a wooden spoon, mix to form a dough.

3 Turn the dough out on to a lightly floured surface and knead vigorously for about 4–5 minutes, or until smooth and elastic.

4 Return the dough to the bowl, cover with an oiled sheet of cling film (plastic wrap) and set aside to rise in a warm place for 30 minutes, or until doubled in size.

5 Turn out the dough and knead again for 2 minutes. Stretch the dough with your hands, then place on an oiled baking tray (cookie sheet), pushing out the edges until even and to the shape required. The dough should be no more than 6 mm/¹⁄₄ inch thick because it will rise during cooking.

6 To make the topping, place the tomatoes, garlic, dried basil, olive oil and salt and pepper to taste in a large

frying pan (skillet) and simmer over a low heat for 20 minutes, or until the sauce has thickened. Stir in the tomato purée (paste), remove from the heat and cool slightly.

7 Spread the topping evenly over the pizza base. Top with the diced mozzarella cheese and grated Parmesan cheese and bake in a preheated oven at 200°C/400°F/Gas Mark 6 for 20–25 minutes. Serve hot.

Calabrian Pizza

Traditionally, this pizza has a double layer of dough to make it robust and filling.
Alternatively, it can be made as a single pizza (as shown here).

Serves 4–6

425 g/15 oz/3³/₄ cups plain
(all-purpose) flour

¹/₂ tsp salt

1 sachet easy-blend (active dry) yeast

2 tbsp olive oil

about 275 ml/9 fl oz/generous
1 cup warm water

FILLING / TOPPING

2 tbsp olive oil

2 garlic cloves, crushed

1 red (bell) pepper,
seeded and sliced

1 yellow (bell) pepper,
seeded and sliced

115 g/4 oz/¹/₂ cup ricotta cheese

175 g/6 oz jar sun-dried
tomatoes, drained

3 hard-boiled (hard-cooked) eggs,
thinly sliced

1 tbsp chopped fresh mixed herbs

115 g/4 oz salami, cut into strips

150–175 g/5–6 oz/1¹/₄–1¹/₂ cups grated
mozzarella cheese

milk, to glaze

salt and pepper

1 Sift the flour and salt into a bowl and mix in the easy-blend (active dry) yeast. Add the olive oil and enough warm water to mix to a smooth pliable dough. Knead for about 10–15 minutes by hand, or process for 5 minutes in a food processor.

2 Shape the dough into a ball, place in a lightly oiled plastic bag and set aside in a warm place for 1–1¹/₂ hours, or until doubled in size.

3 For the filling, heat the oil in a frying pan (skillet) and sauté the garlic and (bell) peppers until soft.

4 Knead the dough and roll out half to 30 × 25 cm/12 × 10 inches. Place on an oiled baking sheet (cookie sheet).

5 Season the dough and spread with the ricotta, then cover with sun-dried tomatoes, hard-boiled (hard-cooked) eggs, herbs and the (bell) pepper mixture. Arrange the salami strips on top and sprinkle with the cheese.

6 Roll out the remaining dough and place over the filling, sealing the edges well, or use to make a second pizza. Set aside to rise for 1 hour in a warm place. An uncovered pizza will take only about 30–40 minutes to rise.

7 Prick the double pizza with a fork about 20 times, brush the top with milk and cook in a preheated oven, 180°C/350°F/Gas Mark 4, for about 50 minutes, or until lightly browned. The uncovered pizza will take only 35–40 minutes. Serve hot.

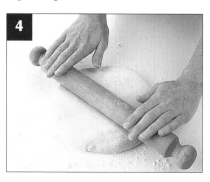

Pizza with Creamy Ham & Cheese Sauce

This is a traditional pizza which uses a pastry case and béchamel sauce to make a type of savoury flan. Grating the pastry gives it a lovely nutty texture.

Serves 4
250 g/9 oz flaky pastry, well chilled
40 g/1¹/₂ oz/3 tbsp butter
1 red onion, chopped
1 garlic clove, chopped
40 g/1¹/₂ oz strong flour
300 ml/¹/₂ pint/1¹/₄ cups milk
50 g/2 oz/²/₃ cup finely grated Parmesan cheese, plus extra for sprinkling
2 eggs, hard-boiled (hard-cooked), cut into quarters
115 g/4 oz Italian pork sausage, such as feline salame, cut into strips
salt and pepper
sprigs of fresh thyme, to garnish

1 Fold the sheet of flaky pastry in half and coarsely grate it into 4 individual flan tins (muffin pans), 10 cm/4 inches across. Using a floured fork, press the pastry flakes down lightly so that they are even, there are no holes and the pastry comes up the sides of the tin (pan).

2 Line with foil and bake in a preheated oven at 220°C/425°F/Gas Mark 7 for 10 minutes. Reduce the heat to 200°C/400°F/Gas Mark 6, remove the foil and cook for a further 15 minutes, or until golden and set.

3 Heat the butter in a pan and sauté the onion and garlic for 5–6 minutes, or until softened.

4 Stir in the flour. Gradually stir in the milk to make a thick sauce. Season with salt and pepper and then stir in the Parmesan cheese. Do not

reheat once the cheese has been added or the sauce will be stringy.

5 Spread the sauce over the pastry cases (shells). Decorate with the egg and strips of sausage.

6 Sprinkle a little extra grated Parmesan cheese over the top, return to the oven and bake for 5 minutes, just to heat through.

7 Serve immediately, garnished with sprigs of fresh thyme.

COOK'S TIP

This pizza is just as delicious cold, but do not prepare it too far in advance of serving, as the pastry will become soggy and unappetizing.

Three Cheese & Artichoke Pizza

Sliced artichokes combined with mature (sharp) Cheddar,
Parmesan and blue cheeses give a really delicious topping to this pizza.

Serves 2-4

Bread Dough Base (see page 192)
Special Tomato Sauce (see page 191)
50 g/2 oz blue cheese, sliced
115 g/4 oz artichoke hearts
in oil, sliced
1/2 small red onion, chopped
40 g/1 1/2 oz/1/3 cup grated mature
(sharp) Cheddar cheese
2 tbsp freshly grated Parmesan
1 tbsp chopped fresh thyme
oil from artichokes,
for drizzling
salt and pepper

TO SERVE

salad leaves
cherry tomatoes, halved

1 Roll out or press the dough into a 25-cm/10-inch round on a lightly floured work surface (counter). Place the base on a large greased baking tray (cookie sheet) or pizza pan and push up the edge slightly all around to form a ridge. Cover and set aside in a warm place for 10 minutes, until risen.

2 Spread the tomato sauce over the base almost to the edge. Arrange the blue cheese on the tomato sauce, followed by the artichoke hearts and red onion.

3 Mix together the Cheddar cheese, Parmesan cheese and thyme and sprinkle the mixture over the pizza. Drizzle a little of the oil from the jar of artichokes over the pizza and season with salt and pepper to taste.

4 Bake in a preheated oven at 200°C/400°F/Gas Mark 6, for 18–20 minutes, or until the edge is crisp and golden and the cheese is bubbling.

5 Mix the salad leaves and cherry tomatoes together and serve with the pizza.

COOK'S TIP

Dolcelatte would be an excellent choice for the blue cheese, as it has a delicate, but still piquant, flavour that will not overpower the artichoke hearts.

Gorgonzola Pizza

This unusual combination of blue Gorgonzola cheese and pears produces
a colourful pizza. The wholemeal (whole-wheat) base adds a nutty flavour and texture.

Serves 4
DOUGH
7 g/¼ oz dried yeast
1 tsp sugar
250 ml/8 fl oz/1 cup hand-hot water
175 g/6 oz/1½ cups wholemeal (whole-wheat) flour
175 g/6 oz/1½ cups strong white flour
1 tsp salt
1 tbsp olive oil
TOPPING
400 g/14 oz/3 cups peeled and cubed pumpkin or squash
1 tbsp olive oil
1 pear, cored, peeled and sliced
115 g/4 oz Gorgonzola cheese
1 sprig fresh rosemary, to garnish

1 Mix together the yeast, sugar and 4 tablespoons of the water and set aside in a warm place for 15 minutes, or until frothy.

2 Mix both the flours with the salt in a large mixing bowl and make a well in the centre. Add the olive oil, the yeast mixture and the remaining water. Using a wooden spoon, mix to form a dough.

3 Turn the dough out on to a floured surface and knead for 4–5 minutes, or until smooth.

4 Return the dough to the bowl, cover with an oiled sheet of cling film (plastic wrap) and set aside to rise for 30 minutes, or until doubled in size.

5 Remove the dough from the bowl and knead for 2 minutes. Roll out the dough to form a long oval shape, then place it on an oiled baking tray (cookie sheet), pushing out the edges until even. The dough should be no more than 6 mm/¼ inch thick because it will rise during cooking. Push up the edge slightly all around.

6 To make the topping, place the pumpkin in a shallow roasting tin (pan). Drizzle with the olive oil and cook under a preheated grill (broiler) for 20 minutes, or until soft and lightly golden.

7 Top the dough with the pear and pumpkin, brushing with the oil from the tin (pan). Sprinkle the Gorgonzola on top. Bake in a preheated oven, at 200°C/400°F/Gas Mark 6, for 15 minutes, or until the base is golden. Garnish with a sprig of rosemary and serve.

Funny Faces Pizza

These individual pizzas have faces made from
sliced vegetables and pasta. Children love pizzas and
will enjoy making their own funny faces.

Serves 4
Bread Dough Base (see page 192)
25 g/1 oz spaghetti or egg noodles
Tomato Sauce (see page 190)
8 slices peperoni
8 thin slices celery
4 slices button mushrooms
4 slices yellow (bell) pepper
4 slices mozzarella cheese
4 slices courgette (zucchini)
olive oil, for drizzling
8 cooked or canned peas

1 Divide the dough into four. Roll
each piece out into a 13-cm/5-inch
diameter round and place on greased
baking trays (cookie sheets). Cover
and set aside to rise slightly in a
warm place for about 10 minutes.

2 Cook the spaghetti or egg noodles
according to the packet instructions.

3 Divide the tomato sauce evenly
between each pizza base and spread
out almost to the edges.

4 To make the faces, use peperoni
slices for the main part of the eyes,
celery for the eyebrows, mushrooms
for the noses and (bell) pepper slices
for the mouths.

5 Cut the mozzarella and courgette
(zucchini) slices in half. Use the
cheese for the cheeks and the
courgettes (zucchini) for the ears.

6 Drizzle a little olive oil over each
pizza and bake in a preheated oven at

200°C/400°F/Gas Mark 6, for 12–15
minutes, until the edges are crisp and
golden and the cheese is bubbling.

7 Transfer the pizzas to serving plates
and place the peas in the centre of the
eyes. Drain the spaghetti or noodles
and arrange around the tops of the
pizzas for hair. Serve immediately.

COOK'S TIP

Other adaptable ingredients for
making pizza faces include sliced
olives, anchovies, tomato slices and
strips of bacon. Other types of
pasta, such as fusilli – coloured or
plain – can add to the fun.

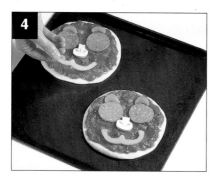

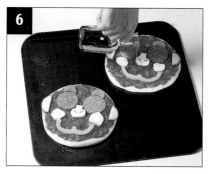

Mini-pizzas

Known as *pizette* in Italy, these tiny pizzas taste as good as they look. This quantity will make 8 individual pizzas, or 16 cocktail pizzas to go with drinks, but you may well find demand outstripping supply.

Makes 8

1 portion Bread Dough Base
(see page 192)

TOPPING

2 courgettes (zucchini)

125 ml/4 fl oz/½ cup passata
(sieved tomatoes)

75 g/3 oz/½ cup diced pancetta

50 g/2 oz/½ cup stoned (pitted) black
olives, chopped

1 tbsp mixed dried herbs

2 tbsp olive oil

salt and pepper

4 Bake in a preheated oven at 200°C/400°F/Gas Mark 6 for 15 minutes, or until crispy and the topping is cooked. Season to taste, transfer to a warm serving dish and serve hot.

COOK'S TIP

Small round pitta breads could be substituted for the pizza dough if you are short of time or you are preparing a large quantity. Brush the edges of the breads with a little olive oil before adding the topping and bake for 10–15 minutes, until the topping is cooked.

1 Knead the dough for 2 minutes and divide it into 8 balls. Roll out each portion thinly to form rounds or squares, then place them on an oiled baking tray (cookie sheet), pushing out the edges until even. The dough should be no more than 6 mm/¼ inch thick because it will rise during cooking. Push up the edges slightly all around to form a rim.

2 To make the topping, grate the courgettes (zucchini) finely.

3 Spread 2–3 teaspoons of the passata (sieved tomatoes) over each of the pizza bases and top each with the grated courgettes (zucchini), diced pancetta and chopped olives. Season to taste with pepper, a sprinkling of mixed dried herbs and drizzle with olive oil.

Spicy Meatball Pizza

Small minced (ground) beef meatballs, spiced with chillies and cumin seeds, are baked on a scone (biscuit) base.

Serves 2–4
250 g/8 oz minced (ground) lean beef
25 g/1 oz jalapeño chillies in brine, drained and chopped
1 tsp cumin seeds
1 tbsp chopped fresh parsley
1 tbsp beaten egg
3 tbsp olive oil
Scone (Biscuit) Base (see page 193)
Tomato Sauce (see page 190)
25 g/1 oz canned pimiento, sliced
2 slices bacon, cut into strips
50 g/2 oz/½ cup grated mature (sharp) Cheddar
olive oil, for drizzling
salt and pepper
chopped fresh parsley, to garnish

1 Mix the beef, chillies, cumin seeds, parsley and egg together in a bowl and season to taste with salt and pepper. Divide the mixture into 12 portions. Form them into meatballs with the palms of your hands. Cover and chill in the refrigerator for 1 hour.

2 Heat the oil in a large frying pan (skillet). Add the meatballs and fry, turning frequently, until browned all over. Remove with a slotted spoon or fish slice and drain on kitchen paper (paper towels).

3 Roll out or press the dough into a 25-cm/10-inch round on a lightly floured work surface (counter). Place on a greased baking tray (cookie sheet) or pizza pan and push up the

edge slightly all around to form a rim. Spread the pizza base with the tomato sauce almost to the edge.

4 Arrange the meatballs on the pizza with the pimiento and bacon. Sprinkle the cheese on top and drizzle with a little olive oil. Season to taste with salt and pepper.

5 Bake in a preheated oven at 200°C/400°F/Gas Mark 6, for 18–20 minutes, or until the edge is golden and crisp. Serve immediately, garnished with chopped parsley.

American Hot Chilli Beef Pizza

This deep-pan pizza is topped with minced (ground) beef,
red kidney beans and jalapeño chillies, which are small, green and very hot.

Serves 2–4
DOUGH BASE
20 g/³/₄ oz fresh yeast or 1¹/₂ tsp easy-blend (active dry) yeast
125 ml/4 fl oz/¹/₂ cup tepid water
1 tsp sugar
3 tbsp olive oil
225 g/8 oz/2 cups plain (all-purpose) flour
1 tsp salt
TOPPING
1 small onion, thinly sliced
1 garlic clove, crushed
¹/₂ yellow (bell) pepper, seeded and chopped
1 tbsp olive oil
175 g/6 oz lean minced (ground) beef
¹/₂ tsp chilli powder
¹/₂ tsp ground cumin
200 g/7 oz can red kidney beans, drained
Tomato Sauce (see page 190)
25 g/1 oz jalapeño chillies, sliced
50 g/2 oz mozzarella, thinly sliced
50 g/2 oz/¹/₂ cup grated mature (sharp) Cheddar or Monterey Jack
olive oil, for drizzling
salt and pepper
chopped parsley, to garnish

1 Make the deep-pan dough base following the same method as the Bread Dough Base (see page 192).

2 Roll out or press the dough into a 23-cm/9-inch round on a lightly floured surface. Place on a large greased baking tray (cookie sheet) and push up the edge to form a rim. Cover and leave to rise for 10 minutes.

3 Sauté the onion, garlic and (bell) pepper gently in the oil for 5 minutes, until soft, but not browned. Increase the heat slightly and add the minced (ground) beef, chilli and cumin. Cook for 5 minutes, stirring occasionally. Remove from the heat and stir in the kidney beans. Season with salt and pepper to taste.

4 Spread the tomato sauce over the pizza base almost to the edge and top with the chilli beef mixture.

5 Top with the sliced chillies and mozzarella and sprinkle the grated cheese over the top. Drizzle with a little olive oil and season.

6 Bake in a preheated oven at 200°C/400°F/Gas Mark 6, for 18–20 minutes, or until the crust is golden and the cheese is bubbling. Serve immediately sprinkled with chopped parsley.

Breakfast Pizza

Sausages, bacon and mushrooms on a bread base
topped with a fried egg will probably see you through the day.

Serves 4
Bread Dough Base (see page 192)
12 skinless cocktail sausages
3 tbsp oil
Tomato Sauce (see page 190)
150 g/5 oz can baked beans
4 slices bacon
50 g/2 oz baby button mushrooms, wiped and quartered
1 small tomato, cut into 8 wedges
50 g/2 oz/½ cup grated mature (sharp) Cheddar
4 eggs
salt and pepper

1 Roll out or press the dough into a 25-cm/10-inch round on a lightly floured work surface (counter). Place on a large greased baking tray (cookie sheet) or pizza pan and push up the edge slightly to form a rim. Cover and leave to rise slightly for 10 minutes in a warm place.

2 Brown the sausages in a frying pan (skillet) with 1 tablespoon of the oil.

3 Mix the tomato sauce with the baked beans and spread over the base almost to the edge. Arrange the sausages on top.

4 Cut the bacon into strips and arrange on the pizza with the mushrooms and tomato. Sprinkle over the cheese and season.

5 Bake in a preheated oven at 200°C/400°F/Gas Mark 6, for 18–20 minutes,

or until the edge is crisp and golden brown and the topping is cooked.

6 Add the remaining oil to the pan and fry the eggs. When the pizza is cooked, cut into four and top each portion with a fried egg. Transfer to serving plates and serve immediately.

COOK'S TIP

If preferred, you could use sliced frankfurters or even Italian spiced cooking sausages. The pizza portions could be topped with poached eggs, if wished.

Florentine Pizza

A pizza adaptation of Eggs Florentine – sliced hard-boiled (hard-cooked) eggs on freshly cooked spinach, with a crunchy almond topping.

Serves 2–4
2 tbsp freshly grated Parmesan cheese
Potato Base (see page 194)
Tomato Sauce (see page 190)
175 g/6 oz spinach
1 small red onion, thinly sliced
2 tbsp olive oil
1/4 tsp freshly grated nutmeg
2 hard-boiled (hard-cooked) eggs
15 g/1/2 oz/1/4 cup fresh white breadcrumbs
50 g/2 oz/1/2 cup grated Jarlsberg cheese (or Cheddar or Gruyère/Swiss cheese, if not available)
2 tbsp flaked (slivered) almonds
olive oil, for drizzling
salt and pepper

1 Mix the Parmesan cheese with the potato dough. Roll out or press the dough, into a 25-cm/10-inch round on a lightly floured work surface (counter). Place on a large greased baking tray (cookie sheet) or pizza pan and push up the edge slightly all around to make a rim. Spread the tomato sauce almost to the edge.

2 Remove the stalks from the spinach and wash the leaves thoroughly in plenty of cold water. Drain well and pat off the excess water with kitchen paper (paper towels).

3 Sauté the onion gently in the oil for 5 minutes, until softened. Add the spinach and continue to cook until just wilted. Drain off any excess liquid. Place on the pizza and sprinkle with the nutmeg.

4 Shell and slice the eggs. Arrange them on top of the spinach.

5 Mix together the breadcrumbs, cheese and almonds, and sprinkle the mixture over the topping. Drizzle with a little olive oil and season well.

6 Bake in a preheated oven at 200°C/ 400°F/Gas Mark 6, for 18–20 minutes, or until the edge is crisp and golden. Transfer to a warm serving plate and serve immediately.

Aubergine (Eggplant) & Lamb Pizza

An unusual, fragrant, spiced pizza topped with minced
(ground) lamb and aubergine (eggplant) on a bread base.

Serves 2–4
1 small aubergine (eggplant), diced
Bread Dough Base (see page 192)
1 small onion, thinly sliced
1 garlic clove, crushed
1 tsp cumin seeds
1 tbsp olive oil
175 g/6 oz minced (ground) lamb
25 g/1 oz canned pimiento, thinly sliced
2 tbsp chopped fresh coriander (cilantro)
Special Tomato Sauce (see page 191)
75 g/3 oz mozzarella cheese, thinly sliced
olive oil, for drizzling
salt and pepper

1 Put the diced aubergine (eggplant)
in a colander and sprinkle with salt.
Set aside to let the bitter juices drain
for about 20 minutes; then rinse. Pat
dry with kitchen paper (paper towels).

2 Roll out or press the dough into a
25-cm/10-inch round on a lightly
floured work surface (counter). Place
the dough round on a large greased
baking tray (cookie sheet) or pizza pan
and push up the edge slightly all
around to form a rim.

3 Cover and set aside to rise slightly
for 10 minutes in a warm place.

4 Sauté the onion, garlic and cumin
seeds gently in the oil for 3 minutes.
Increase the heat slightly and add the
lamb, aubergine (eggplant) and
pimiento. Fry for 5 minutes, stirring
occasionally. Add the coriander
(cilantro) and season well.

5 Spread the tomato sauce over the
dough base almost to the edge. Top
with the lamb mixture.

6 Arrange the mozzarella slices on
top. Drizzle with a little olive oil and
season to taste with salt and pepper.

7 Bake in a preheated oven at 200°C/
400°F/Gas Mark 6, for 18–20 minutes,
until the crust is crisp and golden and
the cheese is bubbling.

8 Transfer the pizza to a warm serving
plate and serve immediately.

Roast Vegetable & Goat's Cheese Pizza

Wonderfully colourful vegetables are roasted in olive oil with
thyme and garlic. The goat's cheese adds a nutty, piquant flavour.

Serves 2–4
2 baby courgettes (zucchini), halved lengthways
2 baby aubergines (eggplant), quartered lengthways
¹/₂ red (bell) pepper, seeded and cut into 4 strips
¹/₂ yellow (bell) pepper, seeded and cut into 4 strips
1 small red onion, cut into wedges
2 garlic cloves, unpeeled
4 tbsp olive oil
1 tbsp red wine vinegar
1 tbsp chopped fresh thyme
Bread Dough Base (see page 192)
Tomato Sauce (see page 190)
75 g/3 oz goat's cheese
salt and pepper
fresh basil leaves, to garnish

1 Place all the prepared vegetables and garlic in a large roasting tin (pan). Mix together the olive oil, vinegar, thyme and plenty of seasoning and pour over, turning the vegetables to coat.

2 Roast the vegetables in a preheated oven at 200°C/400°F/Gas Mark 6, turning halfway through, for 15–20 minutes, until the skins have started to char. Let rest for 5 minutes.

3 Carefully peel off the skins from the roast (bell) peppers and the garlic cloves. Slice the garlic.

4 Roll out or press the dough into a 25-cm/10-inch round on a lightly floured work surface (counter). Place on a large greased baking tray (cookie sheet) or pizza pan and push up the edge a little. Cover and leave for 10 minutes in a warm place to rise slightly. Spread with the tomato sauce almost to the edge.

5 Arrange the roasted vegetables on top and dot with the cheese. Drizzle the oil and juices from the roasting tin (pan) over the pizza and season.

6 Bake in a preheated oven at 200°C/400°F/Gas Mark 6, for 18–20 minutes, or until the edge is crisp and golden. Transfer to a serving plate, garnish with basil leaves and serve.

Tofu (Bean Curd), Corn & Peas Pizza

Chunks of tofu (bean curd) marinated in ginger and soy sauce impart something
of an oriental flavour to this pizza.

Serves 2-4
1 litre/1³/₄ pints/4 cups milk
1 tsp salt
250 g/8 oz/1¹/₃ cups semolina
1 tbsp soy sauce
1 tbsp dry sherry
¹/₂ tsp grated fresh ginger root
250 g/9 oz tofu (bean curd), cut into chunks
2 eggs
50 g/2 oz/²/₃ cup grated Parmesan cheese
Tomato Sauce (see page 190)
25 g/1 oz baby corn cobs, cut into 4
25 g/1 oz mangetout (snow peas), trimmed and cut into 4
4 spring onions (scallions), trimmed and cut into 2.5-cm/1-inch strips
50 g/2 oz mozzarella cheese, thinly sliced
2 tsp sesame oil
salt and pepper

1 Bring the milk to the boil with the salt. Sprinkle the semolina over the surface, stirring all the time. Cook for 10 minutes over a low heat, stirring occasionally, taking care not to let it burn. Remove from the heat and set aside to cool until tepid.

2 Mix the soy sauce, sherry and ginger together in a bowl, add the tofu (bean curd) and stir to coat. Marinate in a cool place for about 20 minutes.

3 Beat the eggs with a little pepper. Add the eggs and Parmesan cheese to the semolina and mix well. Place on a large greased baking tray (cookie sheet) or pizza pan and pat into a 25-cm/10-inch round, using the back of a metal spoon. Spread the tomato sauce almost to the edge.

4 Blanch the corn cobs and mangetout (snow peas) in boiling water for 1 minute, drain thoroughly and place on the pizza with the drained tofu (bean curd). Top with the spring onions (scallions) and slices of cheese. Drizzle with the sesame oil and season to taste.

5 Bake in a preheated oven at 200°C/400°F/Gas Mark 6, for 18–20 minutes, or until the edge is crisp and golden. Serve immediately.

Herbed Onion & Anchovy Pizza

This tasty onion pizza is topped with a lattice pattern
of anchovies and black olives. Cut the pizza into squares to serve.

Serves 2–3
4 tbsp olive oil
3 onions, thinly sliced
1 garlic clove, crushed
1 tsp light brown sugar
$1/2$ tsp crushed fresh rosemary
200 g/7 oz can chopped tomatoes
Bread Dough Base (see page 192)
2 tbsp freshly grated Parmesan cheese
50 g/2 oz can anchovies
12–14 black olives
salt and pepper

5 Bake in a preheated oven at 200°C/
400°F/Gas Mark 6, for 18–20 minutes,
or until the edges are crisp and
golden. Cut into squares and serve
at once.

COOK'S TIP

For even more flavour, you could
use marinated olives.

1 Heat 3 tablespoons of the oil in a
large saucepan and add the onions,
garlic, sugar and rosemary. Cover and
cook gently, stirring occasionally, for
10 minutes, until the onions are soft,
but not brown. Add the tomatoes, stir
and season well. Let cool slightly.

2 Roll out or press the dough on a
lightly floured surface to fit a 30 x
18 cm/12 × 7 inch greased Swiss (jelly)
roll tin (pan). Place in the tin (pan)
and push up the edges slightly.

3 Brush the remaining oil over the
dough and sprinkle with the cheese.
Cover and leave to rise slightly in a
warm place for about 10 minutes.

4 Spread the onion and tomato
topping over the base. Drain the
anchovies, reserving the oil. Split
each anchovy in half lengthways and
arrange on the pizza in a lattice
pattern. Place olives in between the
anchovies and drizzle with a little of
the reserved oil. Season to taste.

Marinara Pizza

This pizza is topped with frozen mixed seafood, such as prawns (shrimp), mussels, cockles and squid rings.

Serves 2–4
Potato Base (see page 194)
Special Tomato Sauce (see page 191)
200 g/7 oz frozen seafood cocktail, thawed
1 tbsp capers
1 small yellow (bell) pepper, seeded and chopped
1 tbsp chopped fresh marjoram
$^1/_2$ tsp dried oregano
50 g/2 oz/$^1/_2$ cup grated mozzarella cheese
2 tbsp grated Parmesan cheese
12 black olives
olive oil, for drizzling
salt and pepper
sprig of fresh marjoram or oregano, to garnish

1 Roll out or press out the potato dough into a 25-cm/10-inch round on a lightly floured work surface (counter). Carefully transfer the base to a large well-greased baking tray (cookie sheet) or pizza pan and push up the edge slightly with your fingers all around to form a rim.

2 Spread the tomato sauce evenly over the base almost to the edge.

3 Arrange the seafood cocktail, capers and chopped yellow (bell) pepper on top of the sauce.

4 Sprinkle the marjoram, oregano, mozarella cheese and Parmesan cheese evenly over the topping. Arrange the black olives on top. Drizzle with a little olive oil and season generously with salt and black or white pepper.

5 Bake in a preheated oven at 200°C/400°F/Gas Mark 6, for 18–20 minutes, until the edge of the pizza is crisp and golden brown.

6 Transfer to a warm serving plate, garnish with a sprig of marjoram or oregano and serve immediately.

Alaska Pizza

You can use either red or pink canned salmon to top this tasty pizza.
Red salmon has a better colour and flavour, but it can be expensive.

Serves 2–4
Scone (Biscuit) Base (see page 193)
Tomato Sauce (see page 190)
1 courgette (zucchini), grated
1 tomato, thinly sliced
100 g/3^1/$_2$ oz can red or pink salmon, drained
50 g/2 oz button mushrooms, wiped and sliced
1 tbsp chopped fresh dill
^{1}/$_2$ tsp dried oregano
40 g/1^1/$_2$ oz/^{1}/$_3$ cup grated mozzarella cheese
olive oil, for drizzling
salt and pepper
sprig of fresh dill, to garnish

1 Roll out or press the dough into a 25-cm/10-inch round on a lightly floured work surface (counter). Place on a large greased baking tray (cookie sheet) or pizza pan and push up the edge a little all around with your fingers to form a rim.

2 Spread the tomato sauce evenly over the pizza almost to the edge.

3 Sprinkle the tomato sauce with the grated courgette (zucchini), then lay the tomato slices on top.

4 Remove any bones and skin from the salmon and flake the flesh with a fork. Arrange it evenly on the pizza, together with the mushrooms. Sprinkle the dill, oregano and mozzarella cheese on top. Drizzle with a little olive oil and season to taste with salt and pepper.

5 Bake in a preheated oven at 200°C/ 400°F/Gas Mark 6, for 18–20 minutes, or until the edge is golden and crisp. Transfer to a warm serving plate and serve immediately, garnished with a sprig of dill.

COOK'S TIP

Make sure that the salmon is well drained, otherwise the pizza base could become soggy.

Four Seasons Pizza

This is a traditional pizza on which the toppings
are divided into four sections, each of which
is supposed to depict a season of the year.

Serves 2–4
Bread Dough Base (see page 192)
Special Tomato Sauce (see page 191)
25 g/1 oz chorizo sausage, thinly sliced
25 g/1 oz button mushrooms, wiped and thinly sliced
40 g/1^1/$_2$ oz artichoke hearts, thinly sliced
25 g/1 oz mozzarella cheese, thinly sliced
3 canned anchovies, halved lengthways
2 tsp capers
4 stoned (pitted) black olives, sliced
4 fresh basil leaves, shredded
olive oil, for drizzling
salt and pepper

1 Roll out or press the dough into a
25-cm/10-inch round on a lightly
floured surface. Place on a large
greased baking tray (cookie sheet) or
pizza pan and push up the edge a
little all around with your fingers.

2 Cover and set aside to rise slightly
for 10 minutes in a warm place.
Spread the base with tomato sauce
almost to the edge.

3 Put the sliced chorizo on to one
quarter of the pizza, the sliced
mushrooms on another, the artichoke
hearts on a third, and the mozzarella
and anchovies on the fourth.

4 Dot the top with the capers, olives
and basil leaves. Drizzle with a little
olive oil and season to taste. Do not
put any salt on the anchovy section,
as the fish are very salty.

5 Bake in a preheated oven at 200°C/
400°F/Gas Mark 6, for 18–20 minutes,
or until the crust is golden and crisp.

6 Transfer to serving plates and serve
immediately.

COOK'S VARIATION

If wished, you could put green
olives with mushrooms and black
olives with the anchovies.

Onion, Ham & Cheese Pizza

This pizza is a favourite in Rome. It is slightly unusual
because the topping is made without a tomato sauce base and with a succulent
layer of vegetables instead.

Serves 4
Bread Dough Base (see page 192)

TOPPING

2 tbsp olive oil
250 g/9 oz onions, thinly sliced and pushed out into rings
2 garlic cloves, crushed
1 red (bell) pepper, seeded and diced
115 g/4 oz Parma ham (prosciutto), cut into strips
115 g/4 oz mozzarella cheese, thinly sliced
2 tbsp rosemary, stalks removed and roughly chopped

1 Roll out or press the dough to form a square or rectangular shape, then place it on an oiled baking tray (cookie sheet), pushing out the edges until even. The dough should be no more than 6 mm/¼ inch thick because it will rise during cooking. Push up the edges slightly all around to form a rim.

2 To make the topping, heat the oil in a pan. Add the onions and garlic and sauté over a medium heat for 3 minutes.

3 Add the (bell) pepper and sauté for a further 2 minutes.

4 Lower the heat, cover the pan and cook the vegetables, stirring occasionally, for 10 minutes, until the onions are slightly caramelized. Set aside to cool slightly.

5 Spread the vegetable mixture evenly over the pizza base. Place strips of Parma ham (prosciutto), mozzarella and rosemary over the top.

6 Bake in a preheated oven at 200°C/400°F/Gas Mark 6 for 20–25 minutes, until the crust is golden and crisp and the cheese is bubbling. Transfer to a warm serving dish and serve immediately, cut into rectangles.

COOK'S VARIATION

If possible, use Italian white onions for this pizza, as they have an especially mild, sweet flavour. If they are unavailable, a Spanish onion could be used instead.

Smoky Bacon & Peperoni Pizza

This flavour-packed pizza is topped with peperoni,
smoked bacon and (bell) peppers covered in a smoked cheese.

Serves 2–4
Bread Dough Base (see page 192)
1 tbsp olive oil
1 tbsp freshly grated Parmesan cheese
Tomato Sauce (see page 190)
115 g/4 oz/$^{2}/_{3}$ cup diced lightly smoked bacon
$^{1}/_{2}$ green (bell) pepper, seeded and thinly sliced
$^{1}/_{2}$ yellow (bell) pepper, seeded and thinly sliced
50 g/2 oz peperoni or other spicy sausage, sliced
50 g/2 oz/$^{1}/_{2}$ cup grated smoked Bavarian cheese
$^{1}/_{2}$ tsp dried oregano
olive oil, for drizzling
salt and pepper

1 Roll out or press the dough into a 25-cm/10-inch round on a lightly floured work surface (counter). Place on a large greased baking tray (cookie sheet) or pizza pan and push up the edge a little all around with your fingers to form a rim.

2 Brush the base with a little olive oil and sprinkle it with the grated Parmesan cheese. Cover and set aside to rise slightly in a warm place for about 10 minutes.

3 Spread the tomato sauce over the base almost to the edge.

4 Scatter with the bacon and (bell) pepper slices. Arrange the peperoni slices on top and sprinkle with the smoked cheese.

5 Sprinkle over the oregano and drizzle with a little olive oil. Season to taste with salt and pepper.

6 Bake in a preheated oven at 200°C/ 400°F/Gas Mark 6 for 18–20 minutes, or until the crust is golden and crisp and the cheese is bubbling.

7 Transfer the pizza to a warm serving dish, cut into wedges and serve immediately.

Avocado & Ham Pizza

A smoked ham and avocado salad is served on a pizza
with a base enriched with chopped sun-dried tomatoes and black olives.

Serves 2–4
Bread Dough Base (see page 192)
4 sun-dried tomatoes, chopped
25 g/1 oz/¼ cup stoned (pitted) black olives, chopped
Special Tomato Sauce (see page 191)
4 small chicory (Belgian endive) leaves, shredded
4 small radicchio leaves, shredded
1 avocado, peeled, stoned (pitted) and sliced
50 g/2 oz wafer-thin smoked ham
50 g/2 oz blue cheese, cut into small pieces
olive oil, for drizzling
salt and pepper
chopped fresh chervil, to garnish

1 Knead the dough gently with the sun-dried tomatoes and olives until well mixed.

2 Roll out or press the dough into a 25-cm/10-inch round on a lightly floured work surface (counter). Place on a greased baking tray (cookie sheet) or pizza pan and push up the edge a little all around to form a rim.

3 Cover and set aside to rise slightly in a warm place for 10 minutes. Spread the base with tomato sauce almost to the edge.

4 Top the pizza with shredded chicory (Belgian endive) and radicchio leaves and avocado slices. Scrunch up the ham and add with the cheese. Drizzle with a little olive oil and season well.

5 Bake in a preheated oven at 200°C/ 400°F/Gas Mark 6, for 18–20 minutes, or until the edge is crisp and golden brown and the cheese is bubbling.

6 Transfer to a warm serving dish, sprinkle with chervil to garnish and serve immediately.

Giardiniera Pizza

As the name implies, this colourful pizza should be topped with fresh vegetables from the garden, especially in the summer months.

Serves 2–4
6 spinach leaves
Potato Base (see page 194)
Special Tomato Sauce (see page 191)
1 tomato, sliced
1 celery stick, thinly sliced
½ green (bell) pepper, seeded and thinly sliced
1 baby courgette (zucchini), sliced
25 g/1 oz asparagus tips
25 g/1 oz sweetcorn, thawed if frozen
25 g/1 oz peas, thawed if frozen
4 spring onions (scallions), trimmed and chopped
1 tbsp chopped fresh mixed herbs
50 g/2 oz/½ cup grated mozzarella, cheese
2 tbsp freshly grated Parmesan cheese
1 artichoke heart
olive oil, for drizzling
salt and pepper

1 Remove any tough stalks from the spinach and wash the leaves in plenty of cold water. Pat dry with kitchen paper (paper towels).

2 Roll out or press the potato base into a large 25-cm/10-inch round on a lightly floured work surface (counter). Place the round on a large greased baking tray (cookie sheet) or pizza pan and push up the edge a little all around. Spread the base with the tomato sauce.

3 Arrange the spinach leaves on the sauce, followed by the tomato slices.

Top with the remaining vegetables and sprinkle with the mixed herbs. Mix the cheeses and sprinkle them on top. Place the artichoke heart in the centre. Drizzle with olive oil and season.

4 Bake in a preheated oven at 200°C/400°F/Gas Mark 6, for 18–20 minutes, or until the edges are crisp and golden brown. Transfer to a warm serving dish and serve immediately.

Wild Mushroom & Walnut Pizza

Wild mushrooms make a delicious pizza topping when mixed
with walnuts and Roquefort cheese.

Serves 2–4
Scone (Biscuit) Base (see page 193)
Special Tomato Sauce (see page 191)
115 g/4 oz/¹/₂ cup soft cheese
1 tbsp chopped fresh mixed herbs, such as parsley, oregano and basil
225 g/8 oz wild mushrooms, such as oyster, shiitake or ceps, or 115 g/4 oz each wild and button mushrooms
2 tbsp olive oil
¹/₄ tsp fennel seeds
25 g/1 oz/¹/₄ cup roughly chopped walnuts
40 g/1¹/₂ oz/¹/₃ cup blue cheese
olive oil, for drizzling
salt and pepper
sprig of flat leaf parsley, to garnish

1 Roll out or press the scone (biscuit)
base into a 25-cm/10-inch round on a
lightly floured work surface (counter).
Place on a large greased baking tray
(cookie sheet) or pizza pan and push
up the edge a little all around with
your fingers to form a rim.

2 Spread with the tomato sauce
almost to the edge. Dot with the soft
cheese and herbs.

3 Wipe and slice the mushrooms.
Heat the oil in a large frying pan
(skillet) and stir-fry the mushrooms
and fennel seeds for 2–3 minutes.
Spread over the pizza base and add
the walnuts.

4 Crumble the cheese over the pizza,
drizzle with a little olive oil and
season to taste with salt and pepper.

5 Bake in a preheated oven at 200°C/
400°F/Gas Mark 6, for 18–20 minutes,
or until the edge is crisp and golden.

6 Transfer to a warm serving dish
and serve immediately, garnished
with a sprig of flat leaf parsley.

(Bell) Pepper & Red Onion Pizza

The vibrant colours of the (bell) peppers and onion make this
a delightful pizza. Served cut into fingers, it is ideal for a party or buffet.

Serves 6
Bread Dough Base (see page 192)
2 tbsp olive oil
1/2 each red, green and yellow (bell) pepper, seeded and thinly sliced
1 small red onion, thinly sliced
1 garlic clove, crushed
Tomato Sauce (see page 190)
3 tbsp raisins
25 g/1 oz/1/4 cup pine nuts
1 tbsp chopped fresh thyme
olive oil, for drizzling
salt and pepper

1 Roll out or press the dough on a lightly floured work surface (counter) to fit a 30 × 18 cm/12 × 7 inch greased Swiss (jelly) roll tin (pan). Place in the tin (pan) and push up the edges slightly all around with your fingers to form a rim.

2 Cover and leave to rise slightly in a warm place for about 10 minutes.

3 Heat the oil in a large frying pan (skillet). Add the (bell) peppers, onion and garlic, and sauté gently for 5 minutes, until they have softened, but not browned. Set aside to cool.

4 Spread the tomato sauce evenly over the base of the pizza almost to the edge.

5 Sprinkle the raisins over the base and top with the cooled (bell) pepper mixture. Add the pine nuts and chopped thyme. Drizzle with a little olive oil and season to taste with salt and pepper.

6 Bake in a preheated oven at 200°C/400°F/Gas Mark 6, for 18–20 minutes, or until the edges are crisp and golden brown.

7 Cut into fingers, transfer to a warm serving dish and serve immediately.

Ratatouille & Lentil Pizza

This is the ideal vegetarian pizza. Ratatouille and lentils on a wholemeal (whole-wheat) bread base are topped with vegetarian cheese and sunflower seeds.

Serves 2–4
50 g/2 oz/¼ cup green lentils
½ small aubergine (eggplant), diced
1 small onion, sliced
1 garlic clove, crushed
3 tbsp olive oil
½ courgette (zucchini), sliced
½ red (bell) pepper, seeded and sliced
½ green (bell) pepper, seeded and sliced
200 g/7 oz can chopped tomatoes
1 tbsp chopped fresh oregano or 1 tsp dried
Bread Dough Base made with wholemeal (whole-wheat) flour (see page 192)
50 g/2 oz vegetarian Cheddar, thinly sliced
1 tbsp sunflower seeds
olive oil, for drizzling
salt and pepper

1 Soak the lentils in hot water for 30 minutes. Drain and rinse; then cover with fresh water and simmer for 10 minutes.

2 Sprinkle the aubergine (eggplant) with a little salt in a colander and leave the bitter juices to drain for about 20 minutes. Rinse and pat dry with kitchen paper (paper towels).

3 Sauté the onion and garlic gently in the oil for 3 minutes. Add the courgette (zucchini), (bell) peppers and aubergine (eggplant). Cover and cook over a low heat for about 5 minutes.

4 Add the tomatoes, drained lentils, oregano, 2 tablespoons of water and seasoning. Cover and simmer for 15 minutes, stirring occasionally, adding more water if necessary.

5 Roll out or press the dough into a 25-cm/10-inch round on a lightly floured work surface (counter). Place on a large greased baking tray (cookie sheet) or pizza pan and push up the edge slightly all around. Cover and leave to rise slightly for 10 minutes in a warm place.

6 Spread the ratatouille over the dough base almost to the edge. Arrange the cheese slices on top and sprinkle the sunflower seeds over them. Drizzle with a little olive oil and season to taste with salt and pepper.

7 Bake in a preheated oven at 200°C/ 400°F/Gas Mark 6, for 18–20 minutes, or until the edge is crisp and golden brown. Serve immediately.

Green Easter Pie

This traditional Easter risotto pie is from Piedmont in northern Italy.
Serve it warm or chilled in slices.

Serves 4
75 g/3 oz rocket (arugula)
2 tbsp olive oil
1 onion, chopped
2 garlic cloves, chopped
200 g/7 oz/1 cup arborio (risotto) rice
750 ml/1¼ pint/3 cups hot chicken or vegetable stock
125 ml/4 fl oz/½ cup white wine
50 g/2 oz/⅔ cup Parmesan cheese, grated
115 g/4 oz/1 cup frozen peas, thawed
2 tomatoes, diced
4 eggs, beaten
3 tbsp fresh marjoram, chopped
50 g/2 oz/1 cup breadcrumbs
salt and pepper

1 Lightly grease and line the base of a 23-cm/9-inch deep cake tin (pan).

2 Using a sharp knife, roughly chop the rocket (arugula).

3 Heat the oil in a large frying pan (skillet) over a medium heat. Add the onion and garlic and sauté for 4–5 minutes, or until softened.

4 Add the rice to the mixture in the frying pan (skillet), mix well to combine, then begin adding the stock a ladleful at a time. Wait until all of the stock has been absorbed before adding another ladleful of liquid.

5 Continue to cook the mixture, adding the wine, until the rice is tender and all of the liquid has been absorbed. This will take at least 15 minutes.

6 Stir in the Parmesan cheese, peas, rocket (arugula), tomatoes, eggs and 2 tablespoons of the marjoram. Season to taste with salt and pepper.

7 Spoon the risotto into the prepared tin (pan) and level the surface by pressing down with the back of a wooden spoon.

8 Top with the breadcrumbs and the remaining marjoram.

9 Bake in a preheated oven at 180°C/350°F/Gas Mark 4, for 30 minutes, or until set.

10 Cut into slices, transfer to warm serving plates and serve immediately.

Spinach & Ricotta Pie

This puff pastry pie looks impressive and is actually
very easy to make. Serve it hot or cold.

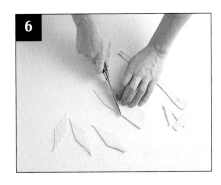

Serves 4
225 g/8 oz spinach
25 g/1 oz/¹/₄ cup pine nuts
115 g/4 oz/¹/₂ cup ricotta cheese
2 large eggs, beaten
50 g/2 oz/¹/₂ cup ground almonds
40 g/1¹/₂ oz/¹/₃ cup grated Parmesan cheese
250 g/9 oz puff pastry, thawed if frozen
1 small egg, beaten

1 Rinse the spinach, place in a large
saucepan and cook for 4–5 minutes,
until wilted. Drain thoroughly. When
the spinach is cool enough to handle,
squeeze out the excess liquid.

2 Place the pine nuts on a baking tray
(cookie sheet) and lightly toast under
a preheated grill (broiler) for 2–3
minutes, or until golden.

3 Place the ricotta cheese, spinach
and eggs in a bowl and mix together.
Add the pine nuts, beat well, then stir
in the ground almonds and grated
Parmesan cheese.

4 Roll out the puff pastry on a lightly
floured surface and make 2 × 20-cm/
8-inch squares. Trim the edges,
reserving the pastry trimmings.

5 Place 1 pastry square on a baking
tray (cookie sheet). Spoon the spinach
mixture on to it, keeping within 1
cm/¹/₂ inch of the edge. Brush the
edges with beaten egg and place the
second square over the top.

6 Using a round-bladed knife, press
the pastry edges together by tapping
along the sealed edge. Use the pastry
trimmings to make leaves to decorate
the pie.

7 Brush the pie with the beaten egg
and bake in a preheated oven at
220°C/425°F/Gas Mark 8, for 10
minutes. Reduce the oven temperature
to 190°C/375°F/Gas Mark 5 and bake

for a further 25–30 minutes. Transfer
to a warm serving dish and serve hot.

COOK'S TIP

Spinach is very nutritious as it is
full of iron – this is particularly
important for women and elderly
people who may lack it
in their diet.

French Bread Pizzas

Halved baguettes or ciabatta bread are a ready-made pizza base.
The colours of the tomatoes and cheese contrast beautifully on top.

Serves 4
2 baguettes
Tomato Sauce (see page 190)
4 plum tomatoes, thinly sliced lengthways
150 g/5 oz mozzarella cheese, thinly sliced
10 stoned (pitted) black olives, cut into rings
8 fresh basil leaves, shredded
olive oil, for drizzling
salt and pepper

1 Cut the baguettes in half lengthways and toast the cut side of the bread lightly. Spread the toasted baguettes with the tomato sauce.

2 Arrange the tomatoes and slices of mozzarella cheese alternately along the length.

3 Top with the olive rings and half of the basil. Drizzle a little olive oil over the pizzas and season to taste with salt and pepper.

4 Either place the pizzas under a preheated grill (broiler) and cook until the cheese has melted and is bubbling or bake in a preheated oven at 200°C/400°F/Gas Mark 6, for 15–20 minutes, until the cheese is bubbling.

5 Sprinkle the remaining basil over the pizzas, transfer to warm serving plates and serve immediately.

Olive Oil Bread with Cheese

This flat cheese bread is sometimes called *focaccia*. It is delicious served with *antipasto* or simply on its own.

Makes 1 loaf
15 g/$^1/_2$ oz dried yeast
1 tsp sugar
250 ml/8 fl oz/1 cup hand-hot water
350 g/12 oz/3 cups strong flour
1 tsp salt
3 tbsp olive oil
200 g/7 oz pecorino cheese, cut into cubes
$^1/_2$ tbsp fennel seeds, lightly crushed

1 Mix the yeast with the sugar and 8 tablespoons of the water. Set aside to ferment in a warm place for about 15 minutes.

2 Mix the flour with the salt. Add 1 tablespoon of the oil, the yeast mixture and the remaining water and mix to form a smooth dough. Turn out on to a lightly floured surface and knead the dough for 4 minutes, until smooth and elastic.

3 Divide the dough into 2 equal portions. Roll out each portion to form a round 6 mm/$^1/_4$ inch thick. Place 1 round on a baking tray (cookie sheet). Scatter the cheese and half the fennel seeds evenly over the round.

4 Place the second round on top and squeeze the edges together to seal so that the filling does not leak out during cooking.

5 Using a sharp knife, make a few slashes in the top of the dough and brush with the remaining olive oil.

6 Sprinkle the dough with the remaining fennel seeds and set aside in a warm place to rise for 20–30 minutes.

7 Bake in a preheated oven at 200°C/400°F/Gas Mark 6 for about 30 minutes, or until golden. Serve immediately.

COOK'S TIP

Pecorino is a hard, quite salty cheese, which is sold in most large supermarkets and Italian delicatessens. If you cannot obtain pecorino, use strong Cheddar or Parmesan cheese instead.

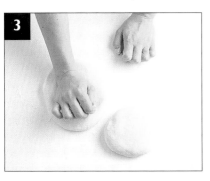

Calzone

A calzone is like a pizza in reverse – it resembles a large pasty
with the dough on the outside and the filling on the inside.

Serves 2–4
Bread Dough Base (see page 192)
1 egg, beaten
1 tomato, peeled and chopped
1 tbsp tomato purée (paste)
25 g/1 oz Italian salami, chopped
25 g/1 oz mortadella, chopped
25 g/1 oz ricotta cheese
2 spring onions (scallions), trimmed and chopped
¼ tsp dried oregano
salt and pepper

1 Roll out the dough into a 23-cm/
9-inch round on a lightly floured work
surface (counter). Brush the edge of
the dough with a little beaten egg.

2 Spread the tomato purée (paste)
over half the round nearest to you.
Scatter the salami, mortadella and
chopped tomato on top. Dot with the
ricotta and sprinkle with the spring
onions (scallions) and oregano.
Season to taste with salt and pepper.

3 Fold over the other half of the
dough to form a half moon. Press the
edges together well to prevent the
filling from coming out.

4 Place on a baking tray (cookie
sheet) and brush with beaten egg to
glaze. Make a hole in the top to allow
steam to escape.

5 Bake in a preheated oven at 200°C/
400°F/Gas Mark 6 for 20 minutes, or
until golden. Transfer to a warm
serving plate and serve immediately.

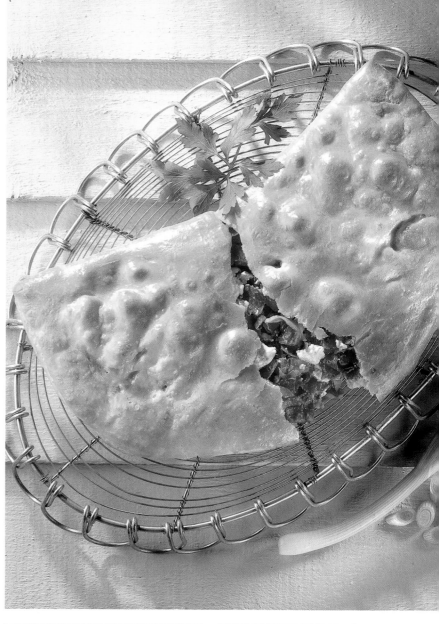

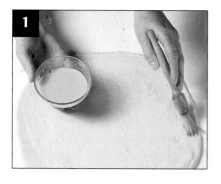

Roman Focaccia

Roman *focaccia* makes a delicious snack on its own or serve it
with cured meats and salad for a quick supper.

Makes 16 squares
7 g/¹/₄ oz dried yeast
1 tsp sugar
300 ml/¹/₂ pint/1¹/₄ cups hand-hot water
450 g/1 lb/4 cups strong white flour
2 tsp salt
3 tbsp rosemary, chopped
2 tbsp olive oil
450 g/1 lb mixed red and white onions, sliced and pushed out into rings
4 garlic cloves, sliced

1 Place the yeast and the sugar
in a small bowl and mix with
8 tablespoons of the water. Set aside
to ferment in a warm place for
15 minutes.

2 Mix the flour with the salt in a
large bowl. Add the yeast mixture,
half of the rosemary and the
remaining water and mix to form a
smooth dough. Turn out and knead
the dough for 4 minutes.

3 Cover the dough with oiled cling
film (plastic wrap) and set aside to
rise for 30 minutes, or until doubled
in size.

4 Meanwhile, heat the oil in a large
pan. Add the onions and garlic and
sauté for 5 minutes, or until softened.
Cover the pan and continue to cook
for a further 7–8 minutes, or until the
onions are lightly caramelized.

5 Remove the dough from the bowl
and knead it again for 1–2 minutes.

6 Roll out the dough on a lightly
floured work surface (counter) to
form a square. The dough should be
no more than 6 mm/¹/₄ inch thick
because it will rise during cooking.
Transfer the dough to a large baking
tray (cookie sheet), pushing out the
edges until even.

7 Spread the onions over the dough,
and sprinkle the top with the
remaining rosemary.

8 Bake in a preheated oven at 200°C/
400°F/Gas Mark 6 for 25–30 minutes,
or until golden. Cut into 16 squares
and serve immediately.

Sun-dried Tomato Loaf

This delicious tomato bread is great with cheese or
soup or for making an unusual sandwich.

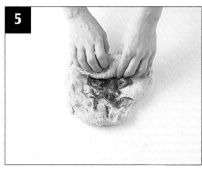

Makes 1 loaf
7 g/¹⁄₄ oz dried yeast
1 tsp sugar
300 ml/1¹⁄₄ cups hand-hot water
1 tsp salt
2 tsp dried basil
450 g/1 lb/4 cups strong white flour
2 tbsp sun-dried tomato paste
or tomato purée (paste)
12 sun-dried tomatoes, cut
into strips

1 Place the yeast and sugar in a bowl
and mix with 8 tablespoons of the
water. Set aside to ferment in a warm
place for 15 minutes.

2 Place the flour in a bowl and stir in
the salt. Make a well in the dry
ingredients and add the basil, the
yeast mixture, tomato paste and half
the remaining water. Using a wooden
spoon, draw the flour into the liquid
and mix to form a dough, adding the
rest of the water gradually.

3 Turn out the dough on to a lightly
floured surface and knead for
5 minutes, or until smooth and
elastic. Cover with oiled cling film
(plastic wrap) and set aside in a warm
place to rise for about 30 minutes, or
until doubled in size.

4 Lightly grease a 900-g/2-lb loaf
tin (pan).

5 Remove the dough from the bowl
and knead in the sun-dried tomatoes.
Knead again for 2–3 minutes.

6 Place the dough in the tin (pan) and
set aside to rise for 30–40 minutes.
Once it has doubled in size again, bake
in a preheated oven at 190°C/375°F/
Gas Mark 5 for 30–35 minutes, or
until golden and the base sounds
hollow when tapped. Cut into slices
to serve.

COOK'S TIP

You could make mini sun-dried
tomato loaves for children. Divide
the dough into 8 equal portions,
leave to rise and bake in mini-loaf
tins (pans) for 20 minutes.

Roasted (Bell) Pepper Bread

(Bell) peppers become sweet and mild when
they are roasted and make this bread delicious.

Serves 4
1 red (bell) pepper, halved and seeded
1 yellow (bell) pepper, halved and seeded
2 sprigs rosemary
1 tbsp olive oil
7 g/¹/₄ oz dried yeast
1 tsp sugar
300 ml/¹/₂ pint/1¹/₄ cups hand-hot water
450 g/1 lb/4 cups strong white flour
1 tsp salt

1 Grease a 23-cm/9-inch deep round cake tin (pan).

2 Place the (bell) peppers and rosemary in a shallow roasting tin (pan). Pour the oil over them and roast in a preheated oven, at 200°C/400°F/Gas Mark 6, for 20 minutes, or until slightly charred. Remove the skin from the (bell) peppers and cut the flesh into slices.

3 Place the yeast and sugar in a small bowl and mix with 8 tablespoons of hand-hot water. Set aside to ferment in a warm place for about 15 minutes.

4 Mix the flour and salt together in a large bowl. Stir in the yeast mixture and the remaining water and mix to form a smooth dough.

5 Turn out the dough and knead for about 5 minutes, until smooth. Cover with oiled cling film (plastic wrap) and set aside to rise for about 30 minutes, or until doubled in size.

6 Cut the dough into 3 equal portions. Roll the portions into rounds slightly larger than the cake tin (pan).

7 Place 1 round in the base of the prepared tin (pan) so that it reaches up the sides of the tin (pan) by about 2 cm/³/₄ inch. Top with half of the (bell) pepper mixture.

8 Place the second round of dough on top, followed by the remaining (bell) pepper mixture. Place the last round of dough on top, pushing the edges of the dough down the sides of the tin (pan) so that the loaf fits snugly.

9 Cover the dough with oiled cling film (plastic wrap) and set aside to rise for 30–40 minutes. Place in the preheated oven and bake for 45 minutes, until golden and the base sounds hollow when lightly tapped. Serve warm.

Desserts

Served only on special occasions, Italian desserts are worth a celebration of their own. Sicilians are said to have the sweetest tooth, but they are closely followed by many of their southern neighbours, who make full use of citrus fruits, honey and nuts. They create delicious confections in the north of Italy, too, often using seasonal fruits, such as plums and pears.

Desserts range from light-as-air Zabaglione and melt-in-the-mouth Tiramisu to the richly spiced Pear Tart and the once-eaten-never-forgotten Panforte di Siena.

Desserts may be kept for special occasions, but ice cream is frequently made at home. Italian ice cream is arguably the best in the world and is made in a vast range of flavours.

Italy has a long tradition of making sorbets and granitas, refreshing, palate-cleansing water ices. These are the perfect example of the Italian taste for pure basic flavours that complement each other superbly.

Orange & Grapefruit Salad

Sliced citrus fruits with a delicious walnut and honey dressing
make an unusual and refreshing dessert.

Serves 4
2 grapefruit, ruby or plain
4 oranges
pared rind and juice of 1 lime
4 tbsp clear honey
2 tbsp warm water
1 sprig mint, roughly chopped
50 g/2 oz/½ cup chopped walnuts

1 Using a sharp knife, slice the top and bottom from the grapefruit, then slice away the rest of the skin and cut away the pith.

2 Cut between each segment of the grapefruit to remove the fleshy part only. Discard the membranes.

3 Using a sharp knife, slice the top and bottom from the oranges, then slice away the rest of the skin and cut away the pith.

4 Cut between each segment of the oranges to remove the fleshy part. Add to the grapefruit.

5 Place the lime rind, 2 tablespoons of lime juice, the honey and the warm water in a small bowl. Beat with a fork to mix the dressing.

6 Pour the dressing over the segmented fruit, add the chopped mint and mix well. Chill in the refrigerator for 2 hours to allow the flavours to mingle.

7 Place the chopped walnuts on a baking tray (cookie sheet). Lightly

toast the walnuts under a preheated grill (broiler) for 2–3 minutes, or until browned.

8 Sprinkle the toasted walnuts over the fruit salad and serve immediately.

COOK'S VARIATION

Instead of the walnuts, you could sprinkle toasted almonds, cashew nuts, hazelnuts or pecans over the fruit, if you prefer.

Caramelized Oranges

The secret of these oranges is to allow them to marinate in the
syrup for at least 24 hours, so the flavours amalgamate.

Serves 4
6 large oranges
225 g/8 oz/1 cup sugar
250 ml/8 fl oz/1 cup water
6 cloves (optional)
2–4 tbsp orange-flavoured liqueur or brandy

5 Place over a low heat until the caramel has fully dissolved again, then remove from the heat and add the liqueur or brandy. Pour the mixture over the oranges.

6 Sprinkle the orange strips over the oranges, cover with cling film (plastic wrap) and set aside until cold. Chill in the refrigerator for at least 3 hours and preferably for 24–48 hours before serving. If time allows, spoon the syrup over the oranges several times while they are marinating. Carefully remove and discard the cocktail sticks (toothpicks) before serving.

1 Using a citrus zester or potato peeler, pare the rind from two of the oranges in narrow strips without any white pith attached. If using a potato peeler, cut the peel into very thin julienne strips.

2 Put the strips into a small saucepan and barely cover with water. Bring to the boil and simmer over a low heat for 5 minutes. Drain the strips and set aside. Reserve the water.

3 Cut away all the white pith and peel from the remaining oranges using a very sharp knife. Then cut horizontally into four slices. Reassemble the oranges and hold in place with wooden cocktail sticks (toothpicks). Arrange them in an ovenproof dish.

4 Put the sugar and water into a heavy-based saucepan with the cloves, if using. Bring to the boil and simmer gently until the sugar has dissolved, then boil hard without stirring until the syrup thickens and begins to colour. Continue to cook until a light golden brown, then quickly remove from the heat and carefully pour in the reserved orange rind liquid.

Sweet Mascarpone Mousse

A sweet cream cheese dessert that complements the
tartness of fresh summer fruits rather well.

Serves 4
450 g/1 lb/2 cups mascarpone cheese
115 g/4 oz/¹/₂ cup caster (superfine) sugar
4 egg yolks
400 g/14 oz/2¹/₂–3 cups frozen summer fruits, such as raspberries and redcurrants
redcurrants, to garnish
amaretti biscuits (cookies), to serve

COOK'S VARIATION

Try adding 3 tablespoons of your
favourite liqueur to the mascarpone
cheese mixture in step 1,
if you prefer.

COOK'S TIP

Mascarpone (sometimes spelled
mascherpone) is a soft, creamy
Italian cheese. It is becoming
increasingly available elsewhere.

1 Place the mascarpone cheese in a
large mixing bowl. Using a wooden
spoon, beat the cheese until smooth.

2 Stir the egg yolks and sugar into the
mascarpone cheese, mixing well. Chill
in the refrigerator for about 1 hour.

3 Spoon a layer of the mascarpone
mixture into the bottom of
4 individual serving dishes. Spoon a
layer of the summer fruits on top.
Repeat the layers in the same order,
reserving some of the mascarpone
mixture for the top.

4 Chill the mousses in the
refrigerator for about 20 minutes. The
fruits should still be slightly frozen.

5 Serve the mascarpone mousses
with amaretti biscuits (cookies).

Zabaglione

Serve this light dessert warm or chilled, accompanied by
sponge fingers (lady-fingers) or amaretti biscuits (cookies) and soft fruits.

Serves 4
6 egg yolks
6 tbsp caster (superfine) sugar
6 tbsp Marsala
amaretti biscuits (cookies) or sponge fingers (lady-fingers) (optional)
strawberries or raspberries (optional)

1 Put the egg yolks into a heatproof bowl and beat until a pale yellow colour, using a rotary, balloon or electric whisk.

2 Beat in the sugar, followed by the Marsala, continuing to beat all the time.

3 Stand the bowl over a saucepan of very gently simmering water, or transfer to the top of a double boiler, and continue to beat until the mixture thickens sufficiently to stand in soft peaks and leaves a trail when the whisk is lifted. On no account allow the water to boil or the zabaglione will overcook and turn into sweet scrambled eggs.

4 Scrape around the sides of the bowl from time to time while beating. As soon as the mixture is really thick and foamy, remove from the heat and continue to beat for a couple of minutes longer.

5 Pour into stemmed glasses and serve warm immediately or set aside until cold and chill in the refrigerator before serving.

6 Fruits such as strawberries or raspberries, or crumbled sponge fingers (lady-fingers) or amaretti biscuits (cookies) may be placed in the base of the glasses before adding the zabaglione.

COOK'S TIP

Marsala is a Sicilian wine that can vary in taste from dry and nutty to very sweet.

Pear Tart

Pears are a very popular fruit in Italy. In this recipe from Trentino
they are flavoured with almonds, cinnamon, raisins and apricot preserves.

Serves 4–6
275 g/10 oz/2½ cups plain (all-purpose) flour
pinch of salt
115 g/4 oz/½ cup caster (superfine) sugar
115 g/4 oz/½ cup butter, diced
1 egg
1 egg yolk
few drops of vanilla essence (extract)
2–3 tsp water
sifted icing (confectioners') sugar, for sprinkling

FILLING
4 tbsp apricot preserves
50 g/2 oz/1 cup crumbled amaretti or ratafia biscuits (cookies)
850–1 kg/1¾–2¼ lb pears, peeled and cored
1 tsp ground cinnamon
75 g/3 oz/½ cup raisins
50 g/2 oz/⅓ cup light brown or demerara (raw crystal) sugar

1 Sift the flour and salt, make a well in the centre and add the sugar, butter, egg, egg yolk, vanilla essence (extract) and most of the water.

2 Using your fingers gradually work the flour into the other ingredients to give a smooth, pliable dough, adding a little more water if necessary. Alternatively, put all the ingredients into a food processor and process until evenly blended, smooth and pliable. Wrap in cling film (plastic wrap) and chill in the refrigerator for 1 hour, or until firm.

3 Roll out about three-quarters of the dough and use to line a shallow 25-cm/10-inch cake tin (pan) or deep flan tin (pan). Spread the apricot preserves over the base and sprinkle with the crushed biscuits (cookies).

4 Thinly slice the pears. Arrange them in the pastry case (shell). Sprinkle first with cinnamon, then with raisins, and finally with the brown sugar.

5 Roll out a thin sausage shape using about one-third of the remaining

dough, and place around the edge of the pie. Roll the remainder into thin sausages and arrange in a lattice over the pie, 4 or 5 strips in each direction, attaching them to the strip around the edge.

6 Cook in a preheated oven at 200°C/400°F/Gas Mark 6, for about 50 minutes, until golden brown and cooked through. Remove from the oven and let cool. Serve warm or chilled, sprinkled with sifted icing (confectioners') sugar.

Pear & Ginger Cake

This deliciously buttery pear and ginger cake is ideal for serving with coffee or you can serve it with cream for a delicious dessert.

Serves 4–6

200 g/7 oz/14 tbsp unsalted (sweet) butter, softened

175 g/6 oz/³/₄ cup caster (superfine) sugar

175 g/6 oz/1¹/₂ cups self-raising flour, sifted

3 tsp ginger

3 eggs, beaten

450 g/1 lb eating pears, peeled, cored and thinly sliced

1 tbsp dark brown sugar

cream or ice cream, to serve (optional)

COOK'S TIP

To test whether the cake is cooked through, insert a fine metal skewer into the centre of the cake. If the skewer comes out clean the cake is cooked through.

COOK'S TIP

Dark brown sugar is often known as Barbados sugar. It is a darker form of light brown sugar. It is quite fine and soft textured and better for baking than raw sugar crystals.

1 Lightly grease and line the base of a deep 20-cm/8-inch cake tin (pan).

2 Using a whisk, combine 175 g/6 oz/12 tablespoons of the butter with the sugar, flour, ginger and eggs and mix to form a smooth consistency.

3 Spoon the cake mixture into the prepared tin (pan), gently levelling the surface.

4 Arrange the pear slices over the cake mixture. Sprinkle with the brown sugar and dot with the remaining butter.

5 Bake in a preheated oven at 180°C/350°F/Gas Mark 4, for 35–40 minutes, or until the cake is golden and feels springy to the touch.

6 Serve the pear and ginger cake warm, with ice cream or cream, if wished.

Tiramisu

A favourite Italian dessert flavoured with coffee and amaretto liqueur.
You could replace the amaretto with brandy or Marsala, if wished.

Serves 4–6

20–24 sponge fingers (lady-fingers), about 150 g/5 oz
2 tbsp cold black coffee
2 tbsp coffee essence (extract)
2 tbsp amaretto
4 egg yolks
75 g/3 oz/6 tbsp caster (superfine) sugar
few drops of vanilla essence (extract)
grated rind of $1/2$ lemon
350 g/12 oz/$1^1/_2$ cups mascarpone cheese
2 tsp lemon juice
250 ml/8 fl oz/1 cup double (heavy) cream
1 tbsp milk
25 g/1 oz/$^1/_2$ cup flaked (slivered) almonds, lightly toasted
2 tbsp cocoa powder (unsweetened cocoa)
1 tbsp icing (confectioners') sugar

1 Arrange almost half of the sponge fingers (lady-fingers) in the base of a glass bowl or serving dish.

2 Combine the black coffee, coffee essence (extract) and amaretto and sprinkle just over half of the mixture over the fingers.

3 Put the egg yolks into a heatproof bowl or the top of a double boiler, together with the sugar, vanilla essence (extract) and lemon rind. Stand over a saucepan of gently simmering water and beat until very thick and creamy and the whisk leaves a very heavy trail when lifted from the bowl.

4 Put the mascarpone cheese in a bowl with the lemon juice and beat until smooth.

5 Combine the egg and mascarpone cheese mixtures and when evenly blended, pour half over the sponge fingers (lady-fingers) and spread out evenly with a spatula.

6 Add another layer of fingers, sprinkle with the remaining coffee

and then cover with the rest of the cheese mixture. Chill in the refrigerator for at least 2 hours.

7 To serve, whip the cream and milk together until fairly stiff and spread or pipe over the dessert. Sprinkle with the almonds and then sift an even layer of cocoa powder (unsweetened cocoa) to cover the top. Finally, sift a light layer of icing (confectioners') sugar over the cocoa.

Rich Chocolate Loaf

A rich chocolate dessert, this loaf is very simple to make
and can be served as a coffee-time treat as well.

Makes 16 slices
150 g/5 oz dark chocolate
75 g/3 oz/6 tbsp unsalted (sweet) butter
210 g/7¼ oz can condensed milk
2 tsp cinnamon
75 g/3 oz/¾ cup almonds,
75 g/3 oz/1½ cups crushed amaretti biscuits (cookies)
50 g/2 oz/¼ cup no-need-to-soak dried apricots, roughly chopped

1 Line a 675-g/1½-lb loaf tin (pan) with a sheet of kitchen foil.

2 Using a sharp knife, roughly chop the almonds.

3 Place the chocolate, butter, milk and cinnamon in a heavy-based saucepan. Heat gently over a low heat for 3–4 minutes, stirring with a wooden spoon, until the chocolate has melted. Beat the mixture well.

4 Stir the almonds, biscuits (cookies) and apricots into the chocolate mixture, stirring with a wooden spoon, until thoroughly mixed.

5 Pour the mixture into the prepared tin (pan) and chill in the refrigerator for about 1 hour, or until set.

6 Cut the rich chocolate loaf into slices to serve.

COOK'S TIP

To melt chocolate, first break it into manageable pieces. The smaller the pieces, the quicker it will melt.

COOK'S TIP

For baking, butter has the finest flavour. If possible, it is best to use unsalted (sweet) butter.

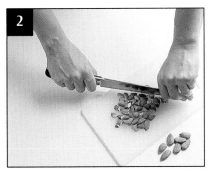

Panforte di Siena

This famous Tuscan honey and nut cake is a Christmas speciality.
In Italy it is sold in pretty boxes, and served in very thin slices.

Serves 12
115 g/4 oz/1 cup split almonds
115 g/4 oz/1 cup hazelnuts
75 g/3 oz/$\frac{1}{2}$ cup cut mixed (candied) peel
50 g/2 oz/$\frac{1}{4}$ cup no-need-to-soak dried apricots
50 g/2 oz/$\frac{1}{3}$ cup glacé or crystallized pineapple
grated rind of 1 large orange
50 g/2 oz/$\frac{1}{2}$ cup plain (all-purpose) flour
2 tbsp cocoa powder (unsweetened cocoa)
2 tsp ground cinnamon
115 g/4 oz/$\frac{1}{2}$ cup caster (superfine) sugar
175 g/6 oz/$\frac{1}{2}$ cup clear honey
icing (confectioners') sugar, for dredging

1 Toast the almonds under the grill (broiler) until lightly browned and place in a bowl. Toast the hazelnuts until the skins split. Place on a dry tea towel (dish cloth) and rub off the skins. Roughly chop the hazelnuts and add to the almonds, together with the mixed peel.

2 Chop the apricots and pineapple fairly finely, add to the nuts with the orange rind and mix well.

3 Sift the flour with the cocoa and cinnamon, add to the nut mixture and mix evenly.

4 Line a round 20-cm/8-inch cake tin (pan) or deep loose-based flan tin (pan) with baking parchment.

5 Put the sugar and honey into a saucepan and heat until the sugar dissolves, then boil gently for about 5 minutes, or until the mixture thickens and begins to turn a deeper shade of brown. Quickly add to the nut mixture and mix evenly. Turn into the prepared tin (pan) and level the top using the back of a damp spoon.

6 Cook in a preheated oven at 150°C/300°F/Gas Mark 2, for 1 hour. Remove from the oven and set aside in the tin (pan) until cold. Take the cake out of the tin (pan) and carefully peel off the baking parchment. Before serving, dredge the cake heavily with sifted icing (confectioners') sugar. Serve in very thin slices.

Lemon Mascarpone Cheesecake

Mouth-watering Italian cheesecakes are world famous. The mascarpone in this recipe gives this baked cheesecake a melt-in-the-mouth texture and the lemon gives a wonderfully tangy flavour.

Serves 8
50 g/2 oz/4 tbsp unsalted (sweet) butter
150 g/5 oz/1²/₃ cups ginger biscuits (cookies), crushed
2 tbsp chopped stem (preserved) ginger
500 g/1¹/₂ lb/3 cups mascarpone cheese
finely grated rind and juice of 2 lemons
115 g/4 oz/²/₃ cup caster (superfine) sugar
2 large eggs, separated
fruit coulis (see Cook's Tip), to serve

COOK'S TIP

Fruit coulis can be made by cooking 400 g/14 oz fruit, such as blueberries, for 5 minutes with 2 tablespoons of water. Strain the mixture, then stir in 1 tablespoon (or more to taste) of sifted icing (confectioners') sugar. Let cool before serving.

COOK'S VARIATION

Ricotta cheese can be used instead of the mascarpone to make an equally delicious cheesecake. However, it should be strained before use to remove any lumps.

1 Grease and line the base of a 25-cm/10-inch spring-form cake tin (pan) or loose-based tin (pan).

2 Melt the butter in a pan and stir in the crushed biscuits (cookies) and chopped ginger. Use the mixture to line the cake tin (pan), pressing it over the base and about 1 cm/¹/₂ inch up the sides.

3 Beat together the cheese, lemon rind and juice, sugar and egg yolks until smooth.

4 Beat the egg whites until they are stiff and fold into the cheese and lemon mixture.

5 Pour the mixture into the tin (pan) and bake in a preheated oven at at 180°C/350°F/Gas Mark 4, for about 35–45 minutes, until just set. Don't worry if it cracks or sinks – this is quite normal.

6 Leave the cheesecake in the tin (pan) to cool. Serve with a fruit coulis.

Cream Custards

Individual pan-cooked cream custards are flavoured with nutmeg
and topped with caramelized orange sticks.

Serves 4
475 ml/16 fl oz/2 cups single (light) cream
115 g/4 oz/¹/₂ cup caster (superfine) sugar
1 orange
2 tsp grated nutmeg
3 large eggs, beaten
1 tbsp clear honey
1 tsp cinnamon

1 Place the cream and sugar in a large non-stick saucepan and heat gently, stirring constantly, until the sugar has caramelizesd.

2 Finely grate the rind of half of the orange and add it to the pan along with the nutmeg.

3 Add the eggs to the mixture in the pan and cook over a very low heat, stirring constantly, for 10–15 minutes. The custard will eventually thicken, but do not allow it to boil.

4 Strain the custard through a fine strainer into 4 shallow serving dishes. Chill in the refrigerator for 2 hours.

5 Meanwhile, thinly pare the remaining orange rind and cut it into matchstick strips.

6 Place the honey and cinnamon in a pan with 2 tablespoons of water and heat gently. Add the orange rind to the pan and cook for 2–3 minutes, stirring constantly, until the mixture has caramelized.

7 Pour the mixture into a bowl and separate out the orange sticks. Leave to cool until set.

8 Once the custards have set, decorate them with the caramelized orange rind and serve.

COOK'S TIP

The cream custards will keep for 1–2 days in the refrigerator. Decorate with the caramelized orange rind just before serving.

Tuscan Pudding

These baked mini-ricotta puddings are delicious served warm
or chilled and will keep in the refrigerator for 3–4 days.

Serves 4
15 g/¹/₂ oz/1 tbsp butter
75 g/3 oz mixed dried fruit
225 g/8 oz/1 cup ricotta cheese
3 egg yolks
50 g/2 oz/¹/₄ cup caster (superfine) sugar
1 tsp cinnamon
finely grated rind of 1 orange, plus extra to decorate
crème fraîche or soured cream, to serve

1 Grease 4 small moulds (molds) or ramekin dishes with the butter.

2 Put the dried fruit in a bowl and cover with warm water. Set aside to soak for 10 minutes.

3 Beat the ricotta cheese with the egg yolks in a bowl. Stir in the caster (superfine) sugar, cinnamon and orange rind and mix to combine.

4 Drain the dried fruit thoroughly. Mix the dried fruit with the ricotta cheese mixture.

5 Spoon the mixture into the moulds (molds) or ramekin dishes.

6 Bake in a preheated oven at 180°C/350°F/Gas Mark 4, for 15 minutes. The tops should be firm to the touch, but do not allow them to brown.

7 Decorate the puddings with grated orange rind. Serve warm or chilled with a spoon of crème fraîche or soured cream.

COOK'S TIP

Crème fraîche has a slightly sour, nutty taste and is very thick. It is suitable for cooking, but remember that it has the same fat content as double (heavy) cream.

COOK'S VARIATION

Use the dried fruit of your choice for this delicious recipe.

Italian Bread Pudding

This wickedly rich pudding is cooked with cream
and apples and is delicately flavoured with orange.

Serves 4
15 g/¹/₂ oz/1 tbsp butter
2 small eating apples, peeled, cored and sliced into rings
75 g/3 oz/¹/₃ cup granulated sugar
2 tbsp white wine
115 g/4 oz bread, sliced with crusts removed (slightly stale French baguette is ideal)
300 ml/¹/₂ pint/1¹/₄ cups single (light) cream
2 eggs, beaten
pared rind of 1 orange, cut into matchsticks

1 Lightly grease a 1.2-litre/2-pint deep ovenproof dish with the butter.

2 Arrange the apple rings in the base of the dish. Sprinkle half of the sugar over the apples.

3 Pour the wine over the apple slices. Add the slices of bread, gently pushing them down with your hands to flatten them slightly.

4 Mix the cream with the eggs, the remaining sugar and the orange rind and pour the mixture over the bread. Set aside to soak for 30 minutes.

5 Bake the pudding in a preheated oven at 180°C/350°F/Gas Mark 4, for 25 minutes until golden and set. Serve warm.

COOK'S TIP

Single (light) cream is most commonly used for cooking, but it should never be allowed to boil, as it will curdle.

COOK'S VARIATION

For a variation, try adding dried fruit, such as apricots, cherries or dates, to the pudding, if you prefer.

Sicilian Orange & Almond Cake

This is a light and tangy citrus cake better eaten as a dessert than as a cake.
It is especially good served after a large meal.

Serves 8
4 eggs, separated
130 g/4^1/$_2$ oz/^{3}/$_4$ cup caster (superfine) sugar, plus 2 tsp for the cream
finely grated rind and juice of 2 oranges
finely grated rind and juice of 1 lemon
130 g/4^1/$_2$ oz/1 cup ground almonds
25 g/1 oz/^{1}/$_4$ cup self-raising flour
200 ml/7 fl oz/^{3}/$_4$ cup whipping (heavy) cream
1 tsp cinnamon
25 g/1 oz/^{1}/$_4$ flaked (slivered) almonds, toasted
icing (confectioners') sugar, to dust

1 Thoroughly grease and line the base of an 18-cm/7-inch round deep cake tin (pan).

2 Blend the egg yolks with the sugar until the mixture is thick and creamy. Beat half of the orange rind and all of the lemon rind into the egg yolks.

3 Mix the juice from both oranges and the lemon with the ground almonds and stir into the egg yolks. The mixture will become quite runny at this point. Fold in the flour.

4 Beat the egg whites until stiff and gently fold into the egg yolk mixture.

5 Pour the mixture into the tin (pan) and bake in a preheated oven at 180°C/350°F/Gas Mark 4, for 35–40 minutes, until golden and springy to the touch. Let cool in the tin (pan) for

about 10 minutes and then turn out to cool completely. The cake is likely to sink slightly at this stage.

6 Whip the cream to form soft peaks. Stir in the remaining orange rind, cinnamon and sugar.

7 Once the cake is cold, cover with the toasted almonds, dust with icing (confectioners') sugar and serve with the cream.

COOK'S VARIATION

You could serve this cake with an orange-flavoured syrup. Boil the juice and finely grated rind of 2 oranges, 75 g/3 oz/^{1}/$_2$ cup caster (superfine) sugar and 2 tablespoons of water for 5–6 minutes until slightly thickened. Stir in 1 tablespoon of orange liqueur just before serving.

Peaches in White Wine

A very simple but incredibly pleasing dessert, which is especially
good for a dinner party on a hot summer day.

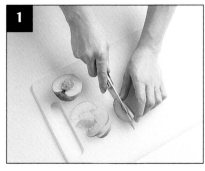

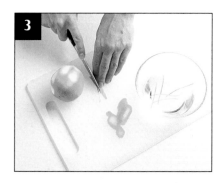

Serves 4
4 large ripe peaches
2 tbsp icing (confectioners') sugar, sifted
pared rind and juice of 1 orange
200 ml/7 fl oz/³/₄ cup medium or sweet white wine, chilled

COOK'S TIP

There is absolutely no need to use expensive wine in this recipe, so it can be quite economical to make.

COOK'S TIP

One of the best ways to pare the rind thinly from citrus fruits is to use a potato peeler.

1 Using a sharp knife, halve the peaches, remove and discard the stones (pits). Peel the peaches, if wished. Slice the peaches into thin wedges.

2 Place the peach wedges in a glass serving bowl and sprinkle the sugar over them.

3 Using a sharp knife, pare the rind from the orange. Cut the orange rind into matchsticks, place them in a bowl of cold water and set aside.

4 Squeeze the juice from the orange and pour it over the peaches, together with the wine.

5 Marinate the peaches in the refrigerator for at least 1 hour.

6 Remove the orange rind from the cold water and pat dry with kitchen paper (paper towels).

7 Garnish the peaches with the strips of orange rind and serve immediately.

Vanilla Ice Cream

Italy is synonymous with ice cream. This home-made version of real
vanilla ice cream is absolutely superb and so easy to make.

Serves 4-6

600 ml/1 pint/2½ cups double
(heavy) cream

1 vanilla pod (bean)

pared rind of 1 lemon

4 eggs, beaten

2 egg, yolks

175 g/6 oz/1 cup caster (superfine) sugar

1 Place the cream in a heavy-based saucepan and heat gently, beating well.

2 Add the vanilla pod (bean), lemon rind, eggs and egg yolks and heat until the mixture reaches just below boiling point.

3 Reduce the heat and cook for 8–10 minutes, beating the mixture continuously, until thickened.

4 Stir the sugar into the cream mixture, set aside and let cool.

5 Strain the cream mixture through a fine strainer.

6 Slit open the vanilla pod (bean), scoop out the tiny black seeds and stir them into the cream.

7 Pour the mixture into a shallow freezing container with a lid and freeze overnight until set. Soften in the refrigerator for 15–30 minutes before serving.

COOK'S TIP

Ice cream is one of the traditional dishes of Italy. Everyone eats it and there are numerous gelato stalls selling a wide variety of flavours, usually in a cone. It is also served in scoops and slices.

COOK'S TIP

To make tutti frutti ice cream, soak 115 g/4 oz/⅔ cup dried fruit, such as cherries, apricots and pineapple, in 2 tablespoons of Marsala or sweet sherry for 20 minutes. Omit the vanilla and add the fruit in step 5.

Ricotta Ice Cream

Ice cream is a traditional Italian dish, and the range of flavours available is astonishing – and constantly expanding. Nuts, candied fruits and liqueur are used here to create a special melt-in-the-mouth treat.

Serves 4-6
25 g/1 oz/$^1/_4$ cup pistachios
25 g/1 oz/$^1/_4$ cup walnuts or pecans
25 g/1 oz/$^1/_4$ cup toasted chopped hazelnuts
grated rind of 1 orange
grated rind of 1 lemon
25 g/1 oz/2 tbsp crystallized or stem (preserved) ginger
25 g/1 oz/2 tbsp glacé (candied) cherries
25 g/1 oz/$^1/_4$ cup dried apricots
25 g/1 oz/3 tbsp raisins
500 g/1$^1/_4$ lb/1$^1/_2$ cups ricotta cheese
2 tbsp maraschino, amaretto or brandy
1 tsp vanilla essence (extract)
4 egg yolks
115 g/4 oz/$^2/_3$ cup caster (superfine) sugar

TO DECORATE

whipped cream
a few glacé (candied) cherries, pistachios or mint leaves

1 Roughly chop the pistachios and walnuts and mix with the toasted hazelnuts, orange and lemon rind in a large bowl. Finely chop the ginger, cherries, apricots and raisins and add to the bowl.

2 Stir the ricotta evenly through the fruit mixture, then beat in the liqueur and vanilla essence (extract).

3 Put the egg yolks and sugar in a bowl and beat hard until very thick and creamy – they may be beaten over a pan of very gently simmering water to speed up the process. Set aside to cool if necessary.

4 Carefully fold the ricotta mixture evenly through the beaten eggs and sugar until smooth.

5 Line an 18 × 12 cm/7 × 5 inch loaf tin (pan) with a double layer of cling film (plastic wrap) or baking parchment. Pour in the ricotta mixture, level the top, cover with more cling film (plastic wrap) or baking parchment and chill in the freezer until firm, preferably overnight.

6 To serve, carefully remove the ice-cream from the tin (pan) and peel off the cling film (plastic wrap) or baking parchment. Place on a serving dish and decorate with whipped cream, glacé (candied) cherries, pistachios and/or mint leaves. Serve in slices.

Granita

A delightful end to a meal or a refreshing way to cleanse
the palate between courses, granitas are made from slushy ice rather than
frozen solid, so they need to be served very quickly.

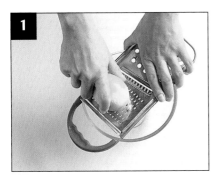

Serves 4
LEMON GRANITA
3 lemons
200 ml/7 fl oz/³/₄ cup lemon juice
115 g/4 oz caster (superfine) sugar
500 ml/18 fl oz/2¹/₂ cups cold water

COFFEE GRANITA
2 tbsp instant coffee
2 tbsp sugar
2 tbsp hot water
600 ml/1 pint/2¹/₂ cups cold water
2 tbsp rum or brandy

LEMON GRANITA

1 To make lemon granita, finely grate the lemon rind. Place the lemon rind, juice and caster (superfine) sugar in a pan. Bring the mixture to the boil and simmer for 5–6 minutes, or until thick and syrupy. Let cool.

2 Once cooled, stir in the cold water and pour into a shallow freezer container with a lid. Freeze the granita for 4–5 hours, stirring occasionally to break up the ice. Serve as a palate cleanser between dinner party courses.

COFFEE GRANITA

3 To make coffee granita, place the coffee and sugar in a bowl and pour in the hot water, stirring until completely dissolved.

4 Stir in the cold water and the rum or brandy.

5 Pour the mixture into a shallow freezer container with a lid. Freeze the granita for at least 6 hours, stirring every 1–2 hours in order to create a grainy texture. Serve with cream after dinner, if you wish.

COOK'S TIP

If you would prefer a non-alcoholic version of the coffee granita, simply omit the rum or brandy and add extra instant coffee instead.

Zuccotto

A layer of chocolate cream oozes between sponge fingers (lady-fingers) to give this rich dessert the traditional stripy markings of *Zuccotto*.

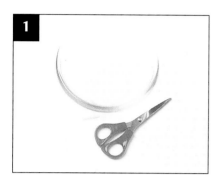

Serves 8
50 g/2 oz sponge fingers (lady-fingers)
2 tbsp brandy or rum
115 g/4 oz dark chocolate
300 ml/½ pint/1¼ cups whipping (heavy) cream
1 tbsp diced stem (preserved) ginger
25 g/1 oz/¼ cup desiccated (shredded) coconut, toasted

1 Line the base of a 1.2-litre/2-pint/ 5-cup steep sided pudding basin (heatproof bowl) with a circle of greaseproof (wax) paper.

2 Brush the sugared sides of the sponge fingers (lady-fingers) with the brandy or rum and use to line the sides of the basin, placing the sugar side facing outward. There should be a slight gap at the top between each biscuit. Brush the inside with the remaining brandy or rum.

3 Break the chocolate in pieces and melt in a heatproof bowl over a pan of gently simmering water.

4 Whip the cream until it is thick and stiff. Divide in 2, stirring the melted chocolate and ginger into 1 half. Use to line the inside of the pudding, spreading the mixture up the sides and pushing it between the fingers to create a striped effect on the outside.

5 Mix the toasted (desiccated (shredded) coconut with the remaining cream and fill the middle

of the pudding. Chill in the refrigerator for at least 2 hours.

6 To serve place a large plate over the top of the basin (bowl) and invert. If the zuccotto sticks, try running a flat-bladed knife around the rim or dipping in hot water.

COOK'S TIP

If you cannot buy toasted coconut, spread out the coconut and grill (broil) for 2–3 minutes, until golden brown. It toasts very quickly so watch it carefully.

Palermo Cake

This cake from Palermo in Sicily is a traditional Christmas treat,
but is good at any time of year.

Serves 8
250 g/8 oz/2 cups plain (all-purpose) flour
¹/₂ tsp baking powder
2 tsp mixed (apple pie) spice
130 g/4¹/₂ oz/9 tbsp butter, diced
40 g/1¹/₂ oz/4¹/₂ tsp caster (superfine) sugar
finely grated rind of 1 lemon
finely grated rind of 1 orange
2 eggs, beaten
50 g/2 oz/¹/₃ cup chopped dried dates
75 g/3 oz/¹/₂ cup mixed dried fruit
50 g/2 oz/¹/₂ cup chopped mixed nuts
1 tsp grated nutmeg
3 tbsp lemon curd
1 tsp cinnamon mixed with 2 tsp of icing (confectioners') sugar, for dusting

1 Sift the flour, baking powder and spice into a large bowl. Rub in the butter with the fingertips until the mixture resembles breadcrumbs.

2 Stir in the sugar and grated lemon and orange rinds.

3 Stir the eggs into the flour and lightly knead to form a dough.

4 Roll out the dough to form an oval shape, about 1 cm/³/₈ inch thick.

5 Mix the dates, mixed fruit, nuts, nutmeg and lemon curd together and spread over the dough. Starting at the long edge, roll up to form a Swiss (jelly) roll shape, squeezing the ends together to seal them.

Place on a greased baking tray (cookie sheet), seam side down, and cook in a preheated oven at 180°C/350°F/ Gas Mark 4 for 35–40 minutes, until golden. Transfer to a wire tray to cool. Dust with cinnamon and sugar and serve.

COOK'S TIP

Try varying the fruit combination; replace half of the dates with chopped figs or dried chopped apricots, if you wish.

Peach & Almond Shortbread

A deliciously rich butter shortbread cake which can be
served at any time of day or as a dessert with cream.

Serves 8-10

150 g/5 oz/10 tbsp unsalted
(sweet) butter

130 g/4$^1/_2$ oz/$^3/_4$ cup caster
(superfine) sugar

1 egg, beaten

200 g/7 oz/2 cups self-raising flour

2 tsp ground ginger

115 g/4 oz/1 cup ground almonds

400 g/14 oz canned peaches

sifted icing (confectioners') sugar,
for dusting

double (heavy) cream, to serve (optional)

1 Lightly grease and line a 20-cm/
8-inch loose-based cake tin (pan).

2 Cream the butter with the sugar
until soft and pale in colour. Add the
egg and beat thoroughly.

3 Sift in the flour, ginger and
ground almonds, mixing to form
a stiff dough.

4 Knead the dough lightly, then wrap
in cling film (plastic wrap) and chill in
the refrigerator for 30 minutes.

5 Drain the peaches and work in a
food processor or mash to a smooth
consistency with a potato masher.

6 Cut the dough in half and coarsely
grate 1 half into the base of the tin
(pan), ensuring there are no gaps.

7 Spread the peaches over the dough
then grate the remaining dough over
the top.

8 Bake in a preheated oven at
180°C/350°F/Gas Mark 4 for about
50 minutes–1 hour.

9 Transfer the shortbread to a wire
rack and let cool. Dust with icing
(confectioners') sugar and serve with
cream, if using.

COOK'S VARIATION

Try using apricots instead of
peaches. For a fruit sauce to serve
with the shortbread, purée another
can of peaches or apricots, adding
sugar to taste.

Moist Honey Cake

A spicy, sticky honey cake which keeps for up to 1 week in
an airtight container – if you can make it last that long!

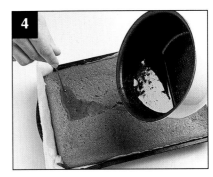

Makes 15 squares
175 g/6 oz/³/₄ cup butter
130 g/4¹/₂ oz/¹/₂ cup dark brown sugar
250 g/ 9 oz/1 cup clear honey
275 g/10 oz/2¹/₂ cups self raising flour
¹/₂ tsp bicarbonate of soda (baking soda)
2 tsp mixed (apple pie) spice
2 eggs, beaten
150 ml/ ¹/₄ pint/²/₃ cup milk
1 tsp cinnamon

COOK'S VARIATION

Try adding 2 tbsp of
marmalade to the mixture.

COOK'S TIP

For baking, it is always best to use
eggs at room temperature.

1 Line and lightly grease an 18 cm ×
28 cm/7 × 11 inch oblong cake tin
(pan). Melt the butter in a pan with
brown sugar and 175 g/6 oz/¾ cup of
the honey. Do not allow the mixture
to boil.

2 In a large bowl sift the flour,
bicarbonate of soda (baking soda) and
spice. Make a well in the centre and
pour in the melted butter and honey
mixture. Stir well.

3 Beat the eggs and milk together and
beat into the mixture.

4 Pour the batter into the prepared
tin (pan) and bake in a preheated
oven at 180°C/350°F/Gas Mark 4 for
50 minutes–1 hour, or until a skewer
inserted in the middle of the cake
comes out clean.

5 Warm the remaining honey with
the cinnamon and pour over the cake.
Make small skewer holes all over the
cake to allow the honey to seep in.
Leave in the tin (pan) to cool, then cut
into squares and serve.

Index